*Everyman, I will go with thee,
and be thy guide*

THE EVERYMAN LIBRARY

The Everyman Library was founded by J. M. Dent in 1906. He chose the name Everyman because he wanted to make available the best books ever written in every field to the greatest number of people at the cheapest possible price. He began with Boswell's 'Life of Johnson'; his one-thousandth title was Aristotle's 'Metaphysics', by which time sales exceeded forty million.

Today Everyman paperbacks remain true to J. M. Dent's aims and high standards, with a wide range of titles at affordable prices in editions which address the needs of today's readers. Each new text is reset to give a clear, elegant page and to incorporate the latest thinking and scholarship. Each book carries the pilgrim logo, the character in 'Everyman', a medieval mystery play, a proud link between Everyman past and present.

THREE ARTHURIAN ROMANCES: POEMS FROM MEDIEVAL FRANCE

CARADOC
THE KNIGHT WITH THE SWORD
THE PERILOUS GRAVEYARD

*Translated with an
introduction and notes by*
ROSS G. ARTHUR

EVERYMAN
J. M. DENT · LONDON
CHARLES E. TUTTLE
VERMONT

Introduction, translations, notes and other critical apparatus
© J. M. Dent 1996

This edition first published in 1996
All rights reserved

J. M. Dent
Orion Publishing Group
Orion House, 5 Upper St Martin's Lane,
London WC2H 9EA
and
Charles E. Tuttle Co., Inc.
28 South Main Street,
Rutland, Vermont 05701, USA

Typeset in Sabon by CentraCet Ltd, Cambridge
Printed in Great Britain by
The Guernsey Press Co. Ltd, Guernsey, C. I.

This book if bound as a paperback is subject to the
condition that it may not be issued on loan or otherwise
except in its original binding.

British Library Cataloguing-in-Publication Data
is available upon request.

ISBN 0 460 87577 9

CONTENTS

Note on the Translator vii
Introduction ix
Note on the Translations xvii

THREE ARTHURIAN ROMANCES:
POEMS FROM MEDIEVAL FRANCE

Caradoc 3
The Knight with the Sword 85
The Perilous Graveyard 107

Notes 209
Suggestions for Further Reading 215

NOTE ON THE TRANSLATOR

ROSS G. ARTHUR is Professor of Humanities at York University in Toronto, Canada. He has published critical studies of Middle English narrative and visionary poetry, Old French and Provençal *lais* and romances, Modern French and Catalan lexicography and morphology, and scholarly traditions in the editing of medieval texts. He is the translator of a number of Old French and Provençal romances.

From *Fabliaux ou contes, fables et romans du XIIe et XIIIe siècle*, ed. Le Grand d'Aussy (Paris, 1829).

INTRODUCTION

For most modern readers, the words 'Round Table' and 'Arthurian Romance' conjure up images of an enchanted kingdom peopled with virtuous knights and beautiful damsels whose lives consist of a series of noble adventures and passionate love affairs which test and reward their virtues or, all too often, result in tragic and lamentable death. Some medieval texts do indeed offer such a picture, but they are decidedly in the minority. Stories of the illicit affair of Lancelot and Guenevere, the tragic passion of Tristan and Isolde, and the mystic Quest for the Holy Grail represent only a small portion of the surviving material from twelfth-, thirteenth- and fourteenth-century Europe; while such poems aroused a great deal of interest in the nineteenth century, when modern notions of what constitutes the 'spirit of the Middle Ages' were created, medieval audiences spent a great deal more time listening to tales of a quite different nature.

The didactic texts of the period – the sermons, theological treatises, the manuals of good conduct – provide a normative perspective on medieval thought with Christian, other-worldly values as their reference point, but their views are insufficiently shaped by lived social experience. The adventure romances may be grounded in comparable norms, but they are more closely tied to the lives of their intended audience, less tightly controlled, and less determined by explicit intellectual projects. They are therefore surer guides to the concerns of a larger group of people, and better evidence of their understanding of their own lives, with all the attendant aspirations, contradictions and failures. The genre had its origin in large-scale epic and historical narratives of events which transformed the world – the fall of Troy, the founding of Rome, the history of Britain from the beginning to the conquest by the Saxons – but the interest in the everyday lives of the members of the audience, already evident in the vernacular adaptations of Virgil, Statius, and Geoffrey of

Monmouth, very quickly replaced such elevated matters. The great majority of surviving adventure romances, whether in French, Provençal, English, German or Icelandic, focus on a few crucial days in the life of a single young knight. Such heroes show their ability to deal with the competing demands of a variety of personal and social imperatives by making correct choices when they are confronted by particular situations analogous to those experienced by the young men listening to the stories. The priest in church told them explicitly how to purify their souls so as to be worthy of salvation; the poet in the hall displayed indirectly how to act in order to face challenges in an honourable manner or, more optimistically, in order to acquire a wife, a castle and all the trappings of earthly prosperity. The poets generally set the action of their poems in the distant past, and often in a world liberally provided with giants, fairies, magicians, enchanted swords and exotic castles 'from which no man ever returned alive': yet for all their fantasy they never failed to address and respond to the problems of the culture in which they lived.

The amount of surviving material is immense, and to do justice to any one of the possible subdivisions would require a lifetime of effort. What is more, concentration on any one area is next to impossible, since one of the defining features of the genre is its propensity to extend across the boundaries between individual texts, languages and eras. The scholar who decides to focus on one poem soon makes assertions about the poet's originality which are easily falsified when it is discovered that analogous scenes (or effects, or turns of phrase) are present in five or six other works. A conscientious study of one hero's story – Yvain, for example – requires mastery of Old French, Middle Welsh, Middle High German, Middle English and Old Norse, reading a century and a half of scholarly bibliography on each version of the tale, and becoming embroiled in controversies about origin, genetic relationships and meaning which go in and out of fashion but are never definitively resolved.

When it comes to making these poems available again to a wider audience, scholars have been selective, questionably discriminating and limited by the requirements of their own profession. Each modern nation has declared some portion of its medieval inheritance to be 'major' and 'important', relegating the rest to the margins, suitable for mention only in footnotes. English professors may build a career writing about Malory or *Sir Gawain and the Green Knight,* and a German professor may specialize in Gottfried von Strassburg or Wolfram von Eschenbach, but *Ywain and Gawain* and *Gauriel von Muntabel* should at most be only a small component of the writings of an ambitious scholar. The consequence is that, although there may be a considerable amount of intelligent scholarship about the 'minor' poems, it is scattered here and there, and read only by specialists – just as the poems in question are readily available only to the very few people who have mastered the relevant language.

In the Old French segment of the field, the privileged position belongs unquestionably to Chrétien de Troyes and to the story of Tristan and Iseult, as may easily be seen either from an examination of the year's output of scholarly articles or the publishers' lists of in-print translations. There is a good medieval justification for each of these choices. Most later Old French romance poets borrow lines from Chrétien, fashion episodes similar to his, refer to the characters he used and the events he described and, not infrequently, name him as a model to be emulated. Many of them make some reference to Tristan and Iseult, not as characters in a particular poem but as people whose story is generally known; the function of such references is usually to contrast their tragic, adulterous love caused by drinking a potion with the pure love – caused by natural emotion and consummated by marriage – which inspires the hero and heroine of the later poet's own composition.

The extension of this respect into veneration and the assumption that these exceptional medieval texts were normative – tendencies which have fortunately been losing strength in recent years – have had deleterious consequences both for the field as a whole and for specific studies of the canonical texts. Rather than faulting the heroes of the 'minor' poems for being more brutal or more refined than Chrétien's or rebuking the poets for being too original or too derivative, we need to see their works as important alternative witnesses to the tastes and attitudes of the age. They are, in addition, useful for establishing by contrast what Chrétien and the various *Tristan*-poets were trying to accomplish: insightful scholars frequently come, after long analysis of a difficult aspect of one of Chrétien's poems, to conclusions which would have instantly leaped out from a comparison with an analogous set of scenes in a lesser-known romance.

There is nothing particularly daring or innovative in offering the three poems in this volume to an English-speaking audience. Although each of them has features which will surprise and even shock readers of the more familiar texts, they all lie close to the centre of the Old French – indeed, the entire medieval – collection of romances. They are late enough – c. 1200–1250 AD – that their proponents have felt obliged to defend them against the charge of 'decadence', but not so late as to make that task require a great deal of special pleading. Each in its own way is representative of a larger group of romances, and each, in addition to its own inherent value, will be of interest to readers of other medieval works. *Caradoc* is classed as one of the 'biographical' romances, telling the story of the whole life of a particular knight, or at least of that portion of his life which culminates in his marriage and entry into the establishment, while *The Knight with the Sword* and *The Perilous Graveyard* are 'episodic' romances, focusing on only a portion of such a chivalric career. Each poet has his own particular style, but it is comprised of elements – the use or avoidance of line-fillers, a tendency to long, periodic sentences or sentences no longer than the octosyllabic line, a delight in or aversion to a highly varied vocabulary – shared with many other texts. Readers of medieval English literature will find that *Caradoc* and *The Knight with the Sword* make use of motifs later employed by the author of *Sir Gawain and the Green Knight*. King Arthur's court is here, but the depiction of its internal tensions at the end of *Caradoc* may cause some readers some consternation; there are good knights here, and renegade knights, although the poets' ideas of knightly virtue may not correspond to the modern reader's, just as their praise of virtuous women and their depictions of 'strong' women prove to be as disquieting as their condemnations of the unworthy or their representations of helpless damsels in distress.

Chrétien de Troyes's *Perceval* (*The Story of the Grail*), left incomplete at his death, provided subsequent poets with a variety of opportunities for further creative work. In the first place, there was the Grail itself, which became a central element in a large number of works dealing with its history before the events described in *Perceval* and with the quests of the knights of the Round Table to find it. Other poets – at least four of them – took up the story of *Perceval* itself and produced *Continuations*, carrying on the action of the poem for thousands and thousands of lines, often paying precious little attention either to the Grail or to Perceval. The story of Caradoc is found in *The First Continuation*, a work which survives in a number of manuscripts and in three distinct versions (known as the Short, the Long and the Mixed) which differ considerably in verbal style and occasionally in incident. As the lineation of the translation shows, the story begins some way into the poem, but a reading of the preceding or the following lines provides no more information about its events or characters and little that would assist in their interpretation: as a story, it is an independent, detachable unit.

Like Chrétien's *Erec and Enide*, *Caradoc* argues that a young man must display the qualities and endure the experiences of a complete knight before he is fit to be a king. He must show that he possesses great military skill; he must control his own (and in this case, other people's) sexuality; and he must undergo and survive a period of total loss of power. The poet (or his lost and unknowable source) has created a fascinating set of events for exploring the questions of sexuality and the loss of power and a truly astonishing way of demonstrating the need for the assistance of a loyal companion and a faithful woman to escape the trials imposed by the older generation: it would spoil the story to say more about them here. The demonstration of his hero's martial prowess is unfortunately rather less imaginative. Modern readers may well suffer a loss of interest in the lengthy tournament scene, begin to skim, and need to be reminded that the original audience found such passages as interesting in themselves as some people now find detailed descriptions of football matches; in addition, the brutality of the combat is a useful corrective to idealized views of medieval jousting, and the lack of 'fair play' should provoke a reconsideration of what constitutes masculine virtue for the poet.

The translation follows *The Continuations of the Old French Perceval of Chrétien de Troyes: The First Continuation, Redaction of Mss E M Q U*, edited by William Roach and Robert H.

Ivy (Philadelphia, 1950), with the exception of a few minor places where I have followed a manuscript other than the one chosen by the editors as their base text.

Le Chevalier à l'Épée (The Knight with the Sword) is a short romance, surviving in only one manuscript, which tells a story about Gawain, the Round Table's 'ladies' man', in a way which justifies the genitive plural. The romance *corpus* recounts a great many of Gawain's love affairs, some of which even result in offspring, but somehow he never manages to 'settle down'. While other works suggest that this situation is a result of magic or bad luck or even Gawain's generosity in passing on the woman he has won to another knight who really loves her, this poem blames the woman herself, as an embodiment of a generalized female inconstancy. Until recently, most critics have rather surprisingly taken the poet's (and the hero's) moral judgements at face value rather than considering the value systems of an author and readers who could accept such evaluations of what is really a rather sordid set of circumstances. The remedy for such credulity is really quite simple: we need only to imagine, on the basis of information given in the poem, what the heroine's life was like before she met Gawain, and what happened to her after they parted, what sort of man her father must have been, and what would have happened to Gawain if it were not for the help she gives him. Such a 'thought-experiment' makes it clear that the poet has been highly selective in his project of reinforcing a very pointed set of opinions about the relationships between males and females, between sexuality and power.

The translation follows the text in *Two Old French Gauvain Romances*, edited by R. C. Johnston and D. D. R. Owen (Edinburgh, 1972); in a few minor cases I have followed a different punctuation of the text and in three small but significant instances I have followed the manuscript rather than the editors' emended version.

L'Atre Périlleux (The Perilous Graveyard or perhaps *The Dangerous Crypt)* is not the title that modern editors would have given to our third poem without manuscript support (see line 6670), for it is strictly appropriate only to one episode in the poem. 'Episodic' is indeed the operative word for this poem. It survives in three relatively complete manuscripts, but the best of the three, chosen by the editor as his base text, simply omits two passages, one of which is rather lengthy and contains an apparently detachable episode which turns out to be necessary for the full understanding of a later passage in the poem: hence the lines marked with a ⁌, which denotes sections taken from the other two manuscripts. The hero (Gawain again) is led away from King Arthur's court to face a series of separate adventures with no apparent causal connection, and it is a very attentive reader indeed who does not need to stop and think for a moment to recollect earlier events when a character from the early part of the poem reappears later on, or to remember that Gawain's current closest companion is the knight who a few thousand lines earlier was cruelly abusing an innocent woman and then doing his utmost to kill the hero.

Taken separately, each of the poem's episodes reveals in Gawain qualities which were of value in the young knights of the time. He is, of course, the best warrior: he is victorious in every battle – against opponents several of whom are said to be the fiercest that any knight ever fought – until a final combat which, in order to end the poem on a note of harmony, is 'called' on account of friendship. In addition, if Knight A, who is a friend of Gawain's, defeats Knight B before Gawain can get to him, then Knight C must defeat Knight A and Gawain must then defeat Knight C, as if the poet had in mind an elaborate series of quarter-finals, semi-finals and finals so that there is absolutely no doubt about Gawain's pre-eminence. The women in the poem are neither as virtuous as Guinier in *Caradoc* nor as 'faithless' as the young lady in *The Knight with the Sword*: they are, for the most part, presented as poor weak creatures in need of Gawain's assistance, which he provides on cue. The one episode in which there are stubborn women suggests that it is up to the knight to choose whether to submit to their whims or to overrule them, but whichever path he follows, everything ultimately turns out as the knight would want. Unlike *The Knight with the Sword*, where Gawain's loss of power is signalled only by the temporary loss of his honorific title 'messire', in this poem he loses his name and is widely believed to be dead – a motif also found in other near-contemporary romances. His need to recover his name becomes the overriding motif of the poem, and when this task is accomplished, what it means to be 'Gawain' becomes clearer: the wandering knight at the mercy of the elements and beset by challenges of all sorts becomes the controller, transforming erstwhile enemies into boon companions, pairing off his friends with the available maidens, often without any concern for their own wishes, and managing to have his own views and judgements accepted without question by his king.

The Old French text may be found in *L'Atre Périlleux: Roman de la Table Ronde*, edited by Brian Woledge (Paris, 1936).

ROSS G. ARTHUR

NOTE ON THE TRANSLATIONS

Translating medieval romances requires choices between alternatives which are often equally unsatisfactory. Presenting a prose version of a poem entails some loss of tone and often wit, since the poets frequently played with the words they put in rhyme-position; but Modern English rhymed octosyllables sound sing-songy, and there is always the danger that words a translator includes for the sake of a rhyme will influence a reader's interpretation. Old French poets frequently wrote in the 'historical present', and it has been argued that they said 'Gawain sees ...' rather than 'Gawain saw a strange knight coming out of the woods' in order to create a mood of immediacy; but these poets frequently shift back and forth between present and past tense verbs in a way which seems more conditioned by syllable-count than artistic impact, and following them in English has quite different effects. Similarly, the loose, paratactic word-order of the originals does not work as well in a version meant to be read as it did when the poems were heard. It is desirable to maintain consistency in the translation of particular words, to avoid archaism, and to preserve the original's symmetry when there are masculine and feminine forms of the same noun; I have therefore used 'maiden' for *pucele*, chosen 'young lady' rather than 'damsel' in order to preserve the idea of noble birth and to make a pair with 'young lord', and used 'adventure' even when the context seems to suggest nothing more than 'accident' or 'interesting event'. But *pucele* sometimes means 'a virgin' and sometimes does not, and in a list of people present at a feast, 'lords, young lords, ladies and young ladies' seems awkward. Young men and young women call each other *amie* and *ami*: is there an appropriate, gender-neutral word in English less old-fashioned than 'sweetheart'? A *roi* is obviously a 'king', but when it is part of a direct address or a greeting 'King ...' sounds less respectful than 'Your Majesty'.

Names are a problem in every romance. Where there are obvious, well-known English equivalents, such as Arthur and Gawain, I have of course used them, and have chosen a standardized French form for the others from among the often numerous different manuscript spellings. Poets frequently keep the antagonist's name a secret until he has been defeated by the hero, and so a major player in the action is known only as 'the knight' throughout a large number of lines. Some names have translatable meanings, but while 'the Rich Mercenary' and 'the Handsome Coward' work, 'the Bold Ugly' and 'the Proud Fairy' do not. Throughout a considerable section of *The Perilous Graveyard*, Gawain is known as *cil sans nom*, 'the masculine one without a name', which creates complications when he is fighting with another knight whose name we do not yet know. In that same poem, not one of the women has a name – nor, for that matter, does a noble 'lad' whose assistance is absolutely essential to Gawain's progress – and we are left with 'the feminine one whom Gawain brought'.

Figurative use of legal terminology, technical terms for pieces of armour, culture-specific everyday activities – when people about to eat ask for water, it is for washing not for drinking, though they rarely say so – line fillers such as 'in my opinion', and phrases used only for the sake of rhyme – maidens watching battles often sit under 'elm trees' (or, to be more botanically precise, 'hornbeams') only because *charmes* rhymes with *armes* – all these things complicate the task of transferring these texts across the boundaries of time. The result, I hope, is a book which will be read with interest and enjoyment, which will not disappoint the many excellent scholars who have mastered the original poems, and which will encourage others to look more deeply into the romances and the world which produced them.

THREE ARTHURIAN ROMANCES:
POEMS FROM
MEDIEVAL FRANCE

CARADOC

Around this same time that I've been telling you about, when King Arthur was in Quinilli, there came to the court a tall and well-built knight, strong and bold. His name was Caradoc of Vannes and he was king and lord of that realm. He was a young man and well established, except that he had no wife, and he had come to the King to ask for one. He firmly believed it would be to his advantage if it was the King who gave him a wife, saying that even if he had to stay unmarried for fourteen years or more, no one but the sovereign of kings would ever give him a wife: it was from him that he wished to receive this gift. It wasn't very long before the King gave him his niece, the beautiful Ysave of Carahés, a most courtly and prudent woman. (6690)

On the day set for the wedding, the King summoned all his lords and everyone who could serve him well and be worthy of his great gifts. Ladies and maidens came there, damsels from the chambers, kings, dukes, princes, governors, lords, castellans and vavasours. So many people gathered there that all the city trembled, and there was so much rejoicing that God's thunder could not be heard! It would take a great deal of talking for me to tell you about everyone who was present at the wedding or to list everything they ate and drank, so I will pass over it briefly, without even making the attempt. (6708)

It was a Tuesday morning when God in His providence brought about such great joy. The beautiful Ysave had been made ready; concerning her beauty, I tell you that she couldn't have been more beautiful in her face or body. She was exquisite both in appearance and in demeanour, and her garments suited her extremely well. The good King took her by the hand and then, with no more ado, they all went to the church where the marriage was celebrated, much to everyone's delight. The service began, and when the offering was completed and the mass had been sung, the King left the church with all his knights and escorted the newly married Queen to her rooms. (6730)

Sir Kay had the trumpet sound for distributing the water, and after the King had been given the water, he sat down at high table.* I do not want to tell you about all the dishes, but they had plenty to eat. When they had finished drinking and eating, they went into the fields and began the jousting – but I do not want to spend time on that, for I must recount something else* which grieves my heart greatly. I would truly be willing to go to prison if I could do away with this scandal, if it never had happened, for then I would have accomplished a great thing: ladies, who are often unjustly reproached, would have much less blame! (6748)

A knight had come to the court who was the most accomplished enchanter you could ever see. His name was Eliavrés, and he gazed constantly at the beautiful Ysave and the splendid finery she wore. He gave her all his love, and couldn't be cured unless he had her. He pursued her everywhere, and enchanted and bewitched her and tricked her so well by his magic, ruses and incantations that she dishonoured her lord. When Caradoc thought that he was sleeping with her, he could not keep watch well enough to avoid lying with a greyhound that first night. The enchanter deceived him, so that he did not notice at all; he thought that his wife was sleeping with him and that she was a virgin. I believe the enchanter lay with the wife that night. On the next night – and this brings me great pain – he caused Caradoc to lie with a sow, and all that night the enchanter held the lady pleasurably in his arms. And on the next night – it's the truth! – he made him lie with a mare, and all night long the enchanter took his pleasure with the lady. It was on that night, I believe, that the lady became pregnant, but the deception was not discovered. (6784)

When the splendid court broke up, many beautiful gifts were passed out. King Caradoc and his wife returned to his kingdom, and the enchanter went his way: but you will not learn from me what happened to him until I come to the proper place. When Caradoc realized that the lady had conceived – no matter who the child's father was – he cherished the mother even more. When she came to the time for giving birth, she was delivered of a very beautiful son. There was great joy in all the country, and no one could describe the joy which his lord Caradoc showed. He had the child baptized solemnly; because he held him so dear, he had him given his own name, and called him Caradoc. (6806)

The child had many nurses, and when he was five years old he had a teacher to develop his valour and intelligence. Within four years he had learned so much that he surpassed his master. He was far from clumsy in his speech. When he was ten years old, he went to his lord the King and said that – with his permission – he would gladly go to join the good knights who resided with his uncle. The Queen and the King equipped him properly, and when they had done so, he did not delay for long. He took his leave of his lord and set out on his way at once, taking plenty of gold and silver, and bringing his master and a fine company of noble men and lads with him. King Caradoc sent many handsome, well-born men with him. Because of affection, the King did not go along with him, and she who ought to love him the most, his mother the Queen, accompanied him as far as the sea, shedding many bitter tears, kissing him and weeping. The boy did not wait any longer. 'My lady,' he said, 'give me your leave to go.' (6837)

'Dear son, I commend you to God! May He preserve you from all shame.' With that they separated. (6840)

They pushed out from the shore and a good wind carried them off. They sailed joyfully and pleasantly until they reached port at Southampton. I will not speak about the lady, who did not move a step away from the shore; unwilling to turn away, she accompanied them with her gaze. When she lost sight of the ship, she left the harbour, accompanied by many followers. I tell you truly that they travelled by roads and paths until the lady was brought back to Nantes, a prosperous city which belonged to her and to her lord. He had been in residence there for a long time, without going away, and he remained there for a long time afterwards, never leaving Nantes, and the Queen stayed with him. Both of them missed the lad, who had arrived at Southampton. (6863)

He travelled across England with his companions and found the court at Cardueil. I do not want to linger over a description of the joy that greeted them at the court: King Arthur rushed to meet him. Everyone showed great joy for Caradoc, but I couldn't describe it if I had all day, so I don't wish to delay over it. The King was in residence at Cardueil, a strong city of his realm, well situated on the border between England and Wales, surrounded by forests and rivers. He was with his closest followers, and he often went out to shoot in the woods and amuse himself along the riverbanks almost every day of the week. He took Caradoc with him, to instruct him and to teach him how to catch game. Later he showed him very skilfully how to handle a hunting bird and to release it at the proper moment. Then he taught him that he must be courteous and sensible, and proficient at playing chess and checkers and all the other games a nobleman should know. (6894)

Let him respect ladies and damsels and be the defender of maidens; when they need his aid, let him take care not to fail them. As for the poor but valiant knight, he ought to be loved and cherished. Let him never consort with traitors or flatterers; let him always be amiable with good people and keep aloof from evil people, for one will never enjoy any lasting advantage from bad company. When he becomes a knight, let him not be boastful about his own deeds; let him be the best in time of need, but the most reticent about it in the hall. If a man trumpets his own valour, his own boasting cuts him down and strangles him. In this way the good King taught him how to take valour for his ensign. Let him have good sense and moderation for his banner, and he will be much more worthy: insolence and excess have nothing in common with honour or chivalry. Let him rather be courteous and well bred, and so he will earn honour and esteem. He will win esteem and honour and be loved by all, great and small. (6922)

Caradoc was most diligent, and I tell you that even when he was still a very young man he was so eager to prove his worth that before he was fifteen years old he had gained more glory than anyone else at King Arthur's court. Sir Gawain loved him greatly, you may be sure, and Sir Yvain also. The King loved and cherished him, as did all the other knights, and with good reason. (6935)

Now I speak about King Arthur again. For several years after the siege of Branlant he had not worn his crown, held a noteworthy court or put on arms of war: instead, he amused himself on his lands with his closest companions, the most well-bred knights in the world. He had gone out hunting one day, to pursue and track game. His companions went with him and captured a great quantity of game. When they had taken their game, they set out for Cardueil where the good King was in residence: he hardly ever left there because he enjoyed frequenting its river and forests. It was on the border of his lands, between Wales and England. As they were travelling, you may be sure that they were very excited and far from quiet: you could have heard a great noise of hunting horns. The King fell into a reverie: his companions paid no attention and didn't notice, but rushed along the road at full speed, cantering, galloping and trotting, and soon they had left the King far behind, following them slowly. I tell you that Sir Gawain noticed it suddenly, when he saw the knights going so quickly. He looked back and saw the King coming in the distance, all alone and riding very slowly and pensively, with his head lowered. Sir Gawain stopped: you may be sure that he was very surprised to see the King so lost in thought, and so he brought his companions to a halt. When the King saw that they had stopped to wait for him, he quickened his pace a little, put his horse at a fast walk and rejoined them. (6983)

'You have travelled alone long enough, my lord,' said Sir Gawain, 'and we have been most discourteous! Please forgive us, and grant us a gift: tell us why you are so pensive, when you have your friends and devoted followers with you. You have no enemy left anywhere in the world, for you have struck them all down, destroyed, checked and confounded them. And so I tell you that we are not happy to see your sad and pensive expression: we would like you to be so joyful that all the world can hear it.' (7000)

The King smiled, rested his hand on Sir Gawain's head, and said: 'I will tell all my thoughts. I have been thinking that I have gone many winters and summers without holding full court. Now a desire has come upon me to wear my crown at Pentecost. I want to hold the noblest court from here to Constantinople, so renowned throughout the entire world that there will be no talk of any court that I have ever held nor of any gift I have made, in comparison with the court I will hold now. And I will tell you more: I wish to make my dear nephew Caradoc a knight.' (7020)

'Truly,' said Sir Gawain, 'this is not the thought of a base or stingy man, but of a valiant and powerful king!' (7024)

They passed the night in great joy. On the next day, the King sent messengers throughout all the land: fool or wise man, let no one fail to come to the court at Cardueil! Everyone hastened there: it really was quite marvellous! I won't mention each one by his name, for there would be too many names if I wished to count them all. A man is a fool to take on the task of listing something he can't even count! (7036)

It was in May, in the summer season when God – for nothing costs Him anything – provided that beautiful day they call Pentecost, and the King wanted to hear mass. You should have seen the joy of the King's nephew Caradoc! There were fifty lads with him, and for love of him King Arthur wanted to make them all knights that day: sons of counts and lords, sturdy, tall young men, courteous, valiant and well bred. They were washed and bathed. Guenevere, the noble Queen, certainly wasn't stingy: she brought the most beautifully embroidered linen shirts to Caradoc and his companions, the best that could be found. Even a great duke would have been resplendent in their outer robes, for everyone wore cloth of silk with gold embroidery, woven in the land of Gris. Their mantles were trimmed with fur and bordered with sable, and their surcoats were fringed with ermine and richly sprinkled with gold. These lads were certainly richly dressed! Caradoc's clothes were far from shabby: his mantle was so fine that if Charles Martel had worn it on the day he was crowned it would have brought him great honour. His tunic suited him very well, and he was incredibly handsome. He had strong arms and shoulders, and a thin, well-formed body. Nature had designed him so perfectly that there was nothing in his body or his face that needed refashioning. I do not know what more to tell you about it. (7080)

Caradoc kept vigil all night long, never sleeping or slumbering, accompanied by many sons of dukes and barons, and there was plenty of merriment and song. Sir Gawain fastened on Caradoc's right spur, I tell you, and Sir Yvain fastened on his left spur; the King girded on his sword and then gave him the accolade. 'Dear nephew,' he said to him, 'may God by His grace make you a brave man!' A hundred of the finest knights fastened on all the other men's spurs, with great affection. Then, I believe, they girded swords on all of them and gave them the accolade: and so they were made knights! (7099)

And so my story continues. They went to the church to hear the divine service. The Archbishop of Canterbury began to celebrate the mass of the Holy Spirit for them. The service was glorious and marvellous and there were many people in attendance. The King wore his crown that day, and he looked magnificent. When the service was complete, they returned to the hall, and the servants prepared the cloths and spread the tables with bread, wine, precious knives, and gold and silver cups and chalices. I couldn't describe all the wealth of plate even if someone threatened to cut off my nose! The tables were elegantly spread indeed. The brave knights passed the time agreeably with the King, and every one of them honoured him. Sir Kay, wearing no mantle, came out of a room and crossed the hall towards the King, holding a small baton in his hand. 'My lord,' he said, 'when it pleases you, it will be time for you to take the water.' (7128)

'Kay,' replied the King, 'don't be in such a hurry! By all God's saints, you know very well that as long as I have been holding royal court I have never eaten, and water will never be distributed before some cause for wonder has been seen.* I do not want to begin now!' (7136)

Even as they spoke, a knight on a grey horse came through the door. His horse was carrying him quickly and he rode along singing a little song. He was wearing a hat because of the great heat and an ermine robe, and over it he had girded on a sword with a fine silk strap, which soon would have cut off his head! He rode right up to the King and said: 'May God protect you, Your Majesty, the best and the greatest king on earth! I have come to ask you for a gift, if it pleases you to give it to me.' (7153)

'Welcome, my friend,' said the King, 'I greet you in return. When I have heard what gift you want to ask of me, you may be sure it won't be refused.' (7158)

'I do not want to deceive you, Your Majesty. The gift that I ask for is to receive a blow to the neck in exchange for another.' (7161)

'What? You'll have to explain that to me.' (7162)

'I will tell you, Your Majesty: here in your presence, I will give this sword to a knight. If he can cut off my head with a single stroke, let him strike away. If I can recover from this blow, let him accept one from me in turn, a year from now, here in your presence.'* (7170)

'By Saint John,' said Kay, 'I wouldn't do that for all the wealth in Normandy! Sir Knight, a man would be a fool to strike you on those terms!' (7174)

The knight dismounted. 'Your Majesty,' he said, 'I seek the gift from you. If you refuse it to me, it will be reported throughout the world. I will surely know how to reveal that at your court I failed to find a little gift I was seeking – and I have come a long way to obtain it from you.' (7182)

He drew his sword from the scabbard. The King looked pensive, and everyone, great and small, was amazed. They wondered in their hearts what honour they could win by striking him. Caradoc, who had just become a knight, could bear it no more; he threw off his mantle at once, rushed towards the knight, and took the steel blade in his hand. The other man asked him one of his questions: 'Have you been chosen as the best knight?' (7194)

'Certainly not, just the biggest fool!' (7195)

The knight placed his head on a table and stretched out his neck. You may be sure that the King and all the nobles of the court were very disturbed. Sir Yvain almost ran up to grab the sword from his hands: but nothing came from that, he won't take it from him! Caradoc raised the sword and delivered such a blow that the sword plunged into the table. The knight's head flew off, no small distance, but the body followed it so closely that before anyone was aware of it, the body had retrieved its head and placed it back in its proper place. The knight leaped up in their midst in front of the King, perfectly safe and sound. 'Your Majesty,' he said, 'do not be false now! Since I have received a neck-blow, another must be received in turn from me, at your court a year from today.' (7217)

The King did not delay: he ordered all his lords from all over the kingdom to be present again at his court the next year, in that same place and on exactly the same day. 'Caradoc,' said the knight, 'you have given a hard blow to my neck in the presence of the King: one year from today, you will receive mine in return.' (7227)

Then the knight set out on his way and departed from the court, and the King remained in sad and troubled thought. No one could describe the sorrow of the ladies and the knights: they hardly laughed at all during their meal and all the court was dumbfounded. Caradoc was not upset, but said: 'Give up your sorrow, uncle; it now depends entirely on God.' (7238)

Many eyes shed tears for Caradoc. The court was announced for Cardueil the next year, at Pentecost. Caradoc the King of Vannes and his wife Lady Ysave heard this painful news, and felt such great sorrow for their beloved child that no one could recount or describe the despair and torment they suffered all that year. Caradoc stayed at the court of his uncle the King, caring little for his life, but going out in search of adventures. Never in all your life have you heard of any one knight performing as many acts of prowess as he did during that one year. He was spoken about in many places; everyone who saw him mourned and wept for him. The end of the year did not delay, and they had to reassemble at the court. Everyone who had heard about it came there by land and sea to witness these marvels, but many maidens and ladies, and even King Caradoc and his wife, were so sorrowful that they didn't dare come. You may be sure, however, that they were far from idle: on that day they performed many acts of charity and good deeds on Caradoc's behalf so that God, who surpasses all good things, would preserve him from all shame that day. (7272)

It was the day of Pentecost, and Caradoc was very troubled and disturbed by the adventure which was threatening his life. The whole court was assembled and the processions were completed; the masses had been sung in the churches and the water was distributed for the meal. The knight arrived on a horse, with his sword at his side; his face was not fresh-coloured, but red with the heat. 'Your Majesty,' he said, 'may God protect you.' (7284)

'My friend, may God bless you as well.' (7285)

'Caradoc, I can't see you: come forward, and you'll get your reward! Present your head to me at once. Just as I offered you mine before, now it's proper for people to see how I can strike with my sword, and so you will receive your neck-blow!' (7292)

Caradoc understood that his task was awaiting him. He removed his mantle, leapt forward, and offered his head to the knight at once, saying, 'Dear lord, now you have me; do the best you can.' (7298)

'Sir Knight,' said the King, 'do not be so uncourtly as to refuse to take ransom for him.' (7301)

'Ransom? Name the gift to me.' (7302)

'I will do so gladly. I will give you a large ransom. Without a lie, I will give you all the plate to be found in my court, no matter who brought it, and a knight's full equipment, because he is my nephew and I hold him very dear.' (7310)

'I will certainly not accept that! I will take his head at once, and nothing else will happen.' (7313)

'I will say more to you. I will give you all the treasures, whether precious stones, silver or gold, to be found in my land, in Brittany or England or in all my kingdom!' (7319)

'I will certainly not accept that. Rather I will cut off his head. You may think me cruel, but I will take his head at once; he cannot escape me. Nothing else will happen!' (7325)

'And yet I will add something more still . . .' (7326)

The knight raised his hand and prepared to strike. The King saw this and fainted with sorrow. Caradoc shouted angrily, 'Why do you not strike, dear lord? You are making me die twice, by taking so long to strike. Now I believe that you are a great coward!' (7333)

For her part, the Queen came out of her room with a hundred ladies and maidens of great beauty to entreat the knight. 'Sir Knight,' she said, 'do not touch him. It would be a sin and a great pity if he were killed. In God's name, have mercy on him! If you spare his life for me, you will be well rewarded. Take my advice and you will profit from it! Will you do something for me? Grant me this much: release the King's nephew Caradoc from this neck-blow. A large ransom will be paid for it! You see here many young ladies with pleasing bodies and many beautiful maidens: you can have them all! Let him go, and you'll be acting wisely.' (7354)

'My lady,' the knight replied, 'I will not take all the ladies in the world or any other payment but his life! If you do not dare to watch, go back and stay in your room.' (7359)

The Queen covered her head and began her lamentations again. She went back to her room with the ladies of the country. They all felt such extreme sorrow that they almost died. Neither the King nor any of his knights knew what to do, but displayed such grief that no mortal man could describe it. (7371)

Caradoc approached a table and laid his head on top of it; the knight raised his sword, and struck him with the flat of it without doing him the least harm! 'Caradoc,' he said, 'get up now. It would be a great pity and an outrage if I killed you. Come and talk with me alone; I want to have a few words with you.' (7380)

He spoke to him privately: 'Do you know why I didn't kill you? You are my son and I am your father.' (7383)

'I will certainly defend my mother,' said Caradoc. 'She is not and never has been your lover and she never did anything she shouldn't!' (7387)

The knight told him to be quiet. He recounted all the story to him just as it happened, about how he lay with Ysave for three nights. It would be too tiresome to tell it to you all over again. Caradoc wanted to fight with him, for the words he heard caused him uncommon sorrow. 'Knight,' he said, 'you are boasting about a lie: you never deceived my father, you never lay with my mother, and you never did anything to her so that she bore me or anyone else! If you dare to say it again, I will make you regret it!' The knight paid no attention to him; he mounted his horse at once, took his leave, and went on his way. (7408)

The court was left in great joy. The trumpet was sounded, the King asked for water, and it was given to him. The ladies and the knights washed and then took their places to eat. King Arthur sat down at the dais. I do not want to describe all the dishes to you, for even when I was wearied by it myself, I would not have said enough! When the court broke up, many presents of great value and inestimable beauty were given out: gold, silver, horses, and birds. No matter how poor they were, everyone who came to that court went home rich. Each one returned to his own country, but the King preferred to stay there with his closest companions. (7425)

Caradoc returned to Brittany, where he had not been for a long time. He proceeded to Nantes, where he found his lord the King and his mother, who was staying with him. When the King learned that he had come, his heart was overjoyed. He went to meet him, embraced and kissed him, and spoke sweetly:

'Welcome, my dear son. Now that I see you, I am sure and certain that God loves me.' (7437)

'Alas, dear lord, why have you welcomed me so joyfully when I am not your son!' (7440)

'You are not my son?' (7440)

'No, not at all. Would you like to know the truth?' (7442)

'I certainly would!' (7442)

'I will tell you, and I won't lie to you.' They moved off to the side and Caradoc told him the whole story, just as it had happened: how his mother had been bewitched by the wicked enchanter, and how on the day he married her, the enchanter had placed a greyhound in bed with him, and how the enchanter was without question the first to enjoy his wife, just as he himself had said. 'Do not believe that I am deceiving you, my lord,' he said; 'he made you sleep with a sow the next night, and you lay with a mare the third night, without being aware of it. The enchanter did what he wanted with my mother. That night, I believe, she became pregnant with me. That is why I do not consider you my father even though she is my mother. Nevertheless, I am not saying this because there is any man in the world that I love as much as you!' (7471)

When the King heard this his heart was so saddened that he almost went mad. When she heard, the Queen rushed to her son as quickly as she could and embraced him, kissing his eyes and his face. 'My lady,' he said, 'I must leave you at once. I know that you are my mother, but I do not cherish or love you at all. Do you know why? You have acted badly towards the King, your good lord and mine. You know very well how that came about.' (7487)

The King could no longer restrain himself. 'My lady,' he said, 'you are very bold to come into my sight when you have done such a thing to me! Get out at once, for my anger might make me treat you so harshly you will have to be carried away!' The Queen went away, very sad and upset. You may be sure that she was not slow to leave his palace. I will tell you no more about her sorrow, but I will speak to you about the King, who was most distraught. The story will turn out very badly for the Queen. (7503)

Without delay, the King asked Caradoc for advice: 'My dear sweet friend,' he said, 'tell me, what is to be done with your mother? Nothing that you say will be contradicted: I will want whatever you want.' (7510)

'My lord,' replied Caradoc, 'not for anything in the world would I want to see my lady suffer any harm: after all, she is my mother. But so that the enchanter may not be with her again, I advise you to build a very tall and narrow tower. Let my mother be closed up inside it so that the enchanter's heir* cannot boast that he had what belonged to you. For I tell you truly, he should certainly not have it.' The King spent so much of his wealth that the tower was finished and the Queen was closed inside it: no one could enter it except himself and those he permitted. The Queen had no one but women as her companions, and that is the end of it. (7532)

Once the Queen had been enclosed in the stone tower at Nantes, Caradoc did not stay there any longer, but went to the honoured court of his uncle, good King Arthur: there was no better king in all the world after God. The man who was endowed with all virtues and beauties – Caradoc, I mean – said that he had no desire for rest but wanted to perform deeds of arms, for it is not proper for a knight to remain inactive if he wishes to be praised: a knight cannot win fame by resting! Such was his desire and intention. Bolder than a lion, Caradoc crossed again into England. (7551)

King Arthur had summoned his court to Caerlion in May, when the rose is in bloom: all those men and women who held lands from him and owed him homage should assemble at Pentecost. Let them come by road or ship, from both sides of the sea, to grace his court: every maiden should come there. (7561)

Cador, a young lord of great valour, came from Cornwall. He brought his sister with him, the beautiful and virtuous Guinier, who did not primp or fuss over herself or care to add to what God had given her. She was such a beautiful creature that if Nature had spent seven years making her, she could not have given her any more beauty. As beautiful as she was, she was even more loyal. She is the one who never betrayed or failed true love. I do not wish to make a long story of it for you, but everything that is pleasing in a maiden – head, eyes, face, body – she had it all without exception. Her brother Cador was a handsome and valiant knight. Their father, who had been King of Cornwall, had died that summer. They came to King Arthur's court because they held their land from the King.* The two of them travelled alone; in those days, maidens travelled with smaller retinues* than they do now! (7590)

As they were travelling, a well-armed knight came towards them out of a valley. Cador was not completely disarmed, but he had taken off his helmet and had thrown it back on his shoulders because it was very hot and he had no reason to expect an attack. The other man spurred his horse until he came close to them, and when he saw the maiden he realized that she was the one who had refused his love. I haven't told you how that happened yet, I believe, but I can't say everything all at once! It's best to say one thing after another, and so things work out in the end. The knight you've been hearing about was called Aalardin du Lac in his country. He loved the maiden very much, and had asked for her from her father – before he died – and from her brother, because he wanted to take her as his wife and make her the lady of his country. But she said that she did not want to be his wife or his sweetheart. She couldn't find it in her heart to marry him under any circumstances, even though he was more handsome and had more prowess than any other knight in the region. He was so smitten with her that before her father died, he did everything he possibly could to win her, with requests and many other methods, but he had no success at all. (7629)

When he saw her, this is how he acted: he spurred the horse he was riding and said to her brother Cador: 'Knight, by your faith, give your sister to me! You are not in a position to take her any farther now. If you don't want to give her to me, you'll see me attack you. I advise you to put on your helmet, or by Saint Paul I will strike you right where you are tallest!' (7641)

Cador was no less brave, and replied to him at once: 'You're in a great hurry! Do you know who I am? My name is Cador. Not for your weight in gold would I lower myself so much as to give my sister to you: my love for her would be wasted!' (7649)

With these words, Cador covered his head and the two knights separated at once; they charged each other, struck with their lances and broke and shattered them to pieces. The horses were carrying them so swiftly that they were both thrown to the ground: horses and knights fell, all tangled in one mass. By bad luck, Cador's horse fell on top of him, with him stretched out below. He broke his leg, as the saddle struck him in such a way – and in such a place – that he couldn't be blamed for fainting. Such great pain struck his heart that he didn't move, any more than a stump. (7668)

When Aalardin saw that, he spoke to him cruelly: 'Sir Cador, your sister is going to belong to me and my companions, against your will: she will be handed over to them!* You were very foolish when you refused her to me. If you had given her to me, I would have offered her all my love, taken her as my wife, and made her my lady. Now, I am in a much better position than I could ever have imagined!' (7683)

He jumped on his horse without a second thought, and then grabbed the maiden. I do not know what more to say to you: he carried her off by force. (7687)

The maiden gave out the greatest cries of sorrow that have ever been heard. Cador lay stretched out in the middle of the road, completely stunned and despising his life and himself. You can well imagine how great his sorrow was: his sister had been under his protection and she was being carried off, right in front of him, and he couldn't be any help to her or to himself. Anyone who heard him wishing for death would have been very cruel indeed not to have pity on him! For her part, the girl struck and beat and tore at herself, often fainting and crying out over and over: 'Ah, my God! Dear Virgin Mary! What will my sweet mother say when she hears this news? When she hears this news, she will be filled with sorrow! Death has taken my father from her, and now this devil has deprived her of my brother and me. But, truly, a man who takes a woman by force is no knight, but commits an act of pure wickedness!' (7714)

While she was crying out like this, Caradoc arrived at a gallop, on the way to his uncle's court. Completely armed, he rode his horse down a small hill and he looked down in the valley where he heard the maiden's loud cries. He spotted her close by and knew that she needed help. He spurred his horse and approached as fast as he could. As soon as she saw him, she began to beg him for mercy, saying, 'Alas, noble, valiant knight, in God's name, help me against this devil, this monster! He has wrongly wounded my brother right in front of me and now he is carrying me off! I would rather be dead – burned, drowned, or tortured – than have him be able to make me do what he wants! The man who could take me from him would surely have won me. Sir Knight, by your nobility, have pity on me, for the love of God! Help me, so that he does not take me any farther!' (7743)

Caradoc leapt in front of him and said: 'My friend, let me have that maiden, by your faith!' (7746)

'Let you have her? Are you mad? Damn me if I ever give her to you! Don't think you'll get off so easily! Why do you care about her? Go mind your own business!' (7752)

Sir Caradoc replied: 'I wouldn't abandon her to you for anything in the world, or lower myself so much as to allow you to carry her away, since she has appealed to me for help!' (7758)

Then he seized her horse by the reins; he was holding his lance in his hand. Aalardin struck him with his sword and almost cut off his hand where he held his lance: he struck him so hard with his sword that he cut the lance near his fist. Then Caradoc struck him back on the head with the rest of his lance, so hard that Aalardin couldn't stay in the saddle; he fell off his horse head first. The battle had begun! (7770)

'Sir Knight,' said Caradoc, 'shame on you, for turning your back on us now!' (7773)

He dismounted from his horse at once; Aalardin, full of shame, jumped up again. They attacked one another fiercely with their sharp steel swords, striking each other without warning. Anyone who saw them dealing out blows would not have had any desire to leave! There you could have seen many a bold stroke of violent sword-play: they struck shields with swords, now advancing, now retreating. They cut the shields into pieces and completely unravelled their hauberks. The more each one could strike, the more he struck! The more valiant pressed hard against the other. They battered and buffeted, thrust and pushed, for each found the other fearsome. And so they hammered and pounded away at each other. (7791)

The battle was extremely violent and the combat lasted for a long time. Each one raised his sword so often before the first skirmish came to an end and they battered each other's shields so much that they were completely destroyed and not worth two straws! Even though the mail was solid, the hauberks they were wearing were completely unravelled, and the men had drawn blood before they retired from the first skirmish. (7805)

Aalardin leapt back and Caradoc did not pursue him further, since he too was harassed by the great hardship and pain he had endured. When the two knights had their breath back, they seized their swords and began striking at each other's head and neck and everywhere that they could reach: they stained the earth with great streams of blood! The grass was completely red with it. Their hauberks were split and the iron was stained by the blood bubbling out between the rings. (7821)

Caradoc struck a blow that – if Aalardin had not dodged it – would have been the end of him. He followed through with a victory blow. If the sword had not turned in his hand, and if Aalardin had been slow to avoid it, it would have cut him down to the teeth! Although Aalardin had retreated, Caradoc still managed to cut off the whole right half of his helmet. Aalardin was losing; his head was protected only by the coiffe, but I assure you that if it had not been for the blow which had weakened him, he would not have been the lesser man. He had certainly put up a good show during the battle, and without that misadventure he would not have been close to being vanquished. Aalardin was furious; the combat was turning out badly for him. He tried hard to avenge himself, striking at Caradoc's hand. But often a man plans to avenge his misfortune and only makes it irremediably worse! Aalardin tried in vain: his sword slipped between Caradoc's hand and the sword-hilt, and didn't hit his hand at all. Then Aalardin's sorrow grew even greater: his sword broke in two! One sword broke on the other, and so it turned out that Aalardin had to surrender to Caradoc. He handed over his sword, hilt first, realizing that it would be pointless to defend himself. (7860)

'My lord,' he said, 'I surrender to you and throw myself on your mercy, because you are the best knight who ever mounted a charger! I am your prisoner. Now, since you have broken my bones, tell me your name!' (7867)

'My lord, my name is Caradoc and I am King Arthur's nephew. Now tell your name.' (7870)

'My lord, my name will never be hidden: I am called Aalardin du Lac in my country. I met this maiden who spurned my love and I wanted to make her the lady of my property and my land.

Since I was powerful, I waged constant war against her father to win her, and I have just now taken her from her brother. I would certainly have taken her away from you if you had not beaten me so badly. But you are so valiant that you have defeated me, and we have fought so much, my lord, that I surrender to you.' (7886)

'My friend,' Caradoc said to him, 'go at once and surrender to the maiden.' (7889)

'My lord, since you command it, I will surrender to her willingly.' (7891)

'Ha, Caradoc, my dear sweet friend,' replied the noble maiden, 'that will not happen, not for all the world! I cannot find it in my heart to pardon his wickedness in taking my brother from me, unless he gives him back to me safe and sound. Even then, I would rather hang myself than take him as my lord!' (7900)

'Maiden,' said Aalardin, 'I will return him to you safe and sound, and that's the end of it. You see I am ready to do it, at least, I mean, if he is alive.' (7904)

All three of them mounted their horses again and rode until they found Cador, very near the place where he had made his fight. He lay there, so gravely wounded that he would never have been able to get up again, for he was breathing very feebly. The knights, weakened by the loss of blood and the effort of their fight, succeeded in lifting him from the ground and putting him on a horse. Then they set out on a road which led through a valley. Caradoc carried Cador with him, both on one horse, for Cador could not have held himself on it without someone else's help. Caradoc took him along him very gently. The maiden showed wondrous grief! (7925)

Finally they arrived at a pavilion pitched by a riverbank. It was magnificent, with so much gold and silver that people wouldn't believe me if I wanted to describe it. All around, the meadow was flourishing and the banks were charming and agreeable. That place delighted Caradoc because it was pleasant, and the great joy of the birds he heard singing in the woods eased all his sorrows. (7938)

'Ah, God, glorious celestial King,' he said, 'how beautiful this place is, and how beloved of God is the man who is its master!' (7942)

He had just finished saying this when he heard a carol, beautifully sung by some maidens who were complaining about their lovers. Then he heard another marvel which made him joyful again and attracted his attention even more: at the entrance of the pavilion there were two magical statues of gold and silver. One closed the door of the pavilion and the other opened it: there was no other porter. They also served another function: one statue was adept at playing the harp, and the statue on the other side held a javelin in its hand. It never saw a churl enter without striking him at once with a heavy blow. The other statue, which held the harp, had as its custom that no self-styled virgin could hide it if she had lost her virginity. As soon as she came to the entrance, the harp played out of tune, and one of its strings would break.* The pavilion was strewn with fresh herbs and rushes and with flowers of aromatic plants, in order to perfume the air for their lord. It was so beautiful that no mortal man could describe it. (7976)

Caradoc heard the great merriment of all the men and women in the pavilion. Ladies and knights were singing, and lads and many beautiful maidens were amusing themselves in the meadow. Caradoc asked Aalardin if he knew who owned this beautiful pavilion. (7986)

'My lord,' Aalardin replied, 'I am the nearest neighbour to the lord of this pavilion, for it has no lord but me! You may therefore know truly that I am taking you to my own dwelling. The people who are singing are all my men and my vassals. When you enter the pavilion, you will see my great wealth; and you will see my sister – may God give her joy and honour – whom I love as much as myself.' (7999)

Out of the pavilion came all the men and women, great and small, to do honour to their lord. The maiden held his stirrup. All the others came to help the wounded knight to dismount, and carried him very gently into the pavilion. Now he was comforted, for as soon as he heard the melody of the harp – don't think it's a lie – his spirits revived as if he had awakened from a dream. They were all astonished at that. He found such joy in the sweet music that he forgot his pain. Then Aalardin summoned his beautiful sister, the Maiden of the Pavilion – I never heard any other name for her. 'Dear sister,' he said, 'I pray you, care for these knights as if for myself; and please, dear sister, look after this maiden. Devote all your efforts to healing these knights, for the good of your brother; and as for myself – for I am grievously wounded – help me!' (8030)

That is what he asked his sister, and she performed her duty well, because she made such an effort to heal them that in a week she made them healthy again. But I do not wish to lengthen my story or delay by telling you how the lords were healed. The Maiden of the Pavilion honoured and cherished the beautiful Guinier so much that I would be worn out before I had said enough about it. They passed that week in great joy, and you have often heard less pleasant visits described. Caradoc, Aalardin and Cador pledged their faith that they would be companions all the days of their lives, and that is the end of it. Aalardin made amends to the beautiful Guinier for having done violence to her. (8052)

Then they decided, I believe, that they would go together on the next day without delay to the court of good King Arthur. When they were all ready, they all set out on the road, taking the straightest route. Caradoc rode beside his sweetheart, the gracious Guinier. As for the Maiden of the Pavilion, she kept company with Cador. (8063)

They spoke about adventures as they rode. Caradoc was very valiant. Because of the heat, he had taken off his mantle: he was very handsome and attractive. The beautiful Guinier burned with love for him: she did not dare throw a glance at him. She loved him more than herself, but did not dare to show it: it is not seemly for the maiden to dare be first to tell the man that she loves him in that way. Now I will leave them there, as they rode along at great speed. (8078)

The King was holding his court at Caerlion and many people had come from faraway lands, from Normandy and from England. Alexander never assembled so many knights and ladies in all his life! Before leaving, King Cadoalant and King Ris wanted to organize a magnificent tournament. Cadoalant was King of Ireland and Ris was King of Valen, a land near Caerlion surrounded by woods. Aalardin, Caradoc and Cador came there for that reason; they arrived at the proper time, because the tournament was just beginning. There were elm trees in those woods, under which they put down their armour. They spread them out on beautiful carpets and began to arm themselves.

They put on their iron greaves, laced on hauberks and coiffes, girded on steel swords, laced on helmets, picked up sturdy shields and covered their horses with iron. One was chestnut, the second bay, and the third was dappled. The lords mounted them, each one holding a lance and a standard. The lance-tips were sharp! (8109)

Now I will tell you about the shields they wore on their necks. Caradoc had a shield of gold with a precious sparkling border. He lit up the whole country with it, and there were three beautiful small rampant lions of sinople on it. Aalardin had a shield of red gules with a white ermine eagle, apparently in flight. Cador had a shield of sinople, all bordered with gold. Armed in this way, they rode until they reached the place where the tournament was being held. The maidens, I believe, moved off to one side, where a beautiful bower had been made for them. (8128)

The men parted from the maidens, leaving two knights and a great number of Aalardin's followers and vassals with them. The three men mounted their horses at once, spurred them vigorously, and rushed until they saw the castle keep. Then they decided, by God, that Aalardin would go to the tournament yard to joust first. He left them and proceeded towards the place where he could display his abilities most openly and skilfully, until he arrived beside the tower. A very beautiful maiden had come to a window on its most beautiful side, and she beautified the tower more than any other ornament. She glanced down and saw the knight stop there on his horse. She was not content simply to grant him a glance, but gave him everything. She spoke to him politely: 'May God protect you, Sir Knight!' (8159)

Aalardin looked up and replied courteously to her: 'May He who does not fail and does not lie grant you a good life, maiden. Do not be apprehensive about seeing me here.' (8165)

'My lord, when I know what your name is – do not be upset, for if you have to hide it I will keep it hidden for you – I will feel more secure. And tell me if you can, why you have stayed here so long.' (8172)

'Maiden, I will tell you everything and will not lie to you, for if it pleases God, being acquainted with you will never cause me any trouble. My name is Aalardin du Lac, and I have come here only because I want to take part in the tournament; I won't deny that I will go there without being recognized if I can.' (8182)

'Will you go there alone?' (8183)

'Yes, certainly, do not doubt it. But tell me truly, maiden – may God be your guide! – do you know if Sir Yvain and Sir Gawain are there?' (8188)

'Yes, they will certainly be there; they are the best knights in the world and I have heard them say that they will not fail to take part in the tournament and strike hard blows there.' (8194)

Aalardin was very pleased at what she told him about those valiant knights. He reared back on his horse, greatly pleasing the maiden. Her heart leaped in her breast. She turned pale and perspired, and her colour often changed because of the knight she saw. She gave every bit of her heart to him, and didn't keep even a little piece for herself: she was left without a heart! Since she wanted him to love her, she gave him a courtly love-token, her embroidered sleeve made of precious cisclaton, and he made it his standard. Calling him by name, she said to him: 'My lord, truly it will never be concealed from you – may God wish me well and give me honour in this world – that of all the men I know you are the one I would most like to know much better, for you are from this land. King Ris is infatuated with me, and so is King Cadoalant, but it hasn't yet come to the point where I would accept either of them, not for anything! That is why I tell you that I love you and I protest to you about those two. Dear friend, I want it to be known that I have seen you, for it is because of pride that they want me when I do not want to have either of them. It is this pride, this arrogance, which has made them undertake this combat today in front of the King and myself, so that I will decide for the better of the two of them. If their pride were brought down, that would ease the anger in my heart.' (8239)

Aalardin saw that the knights were in place. 'Maiden,' he said, 'please tell me your name, if it is possible.' (8244)

'My lord, my name ends in "or": I am called Guigenor and I am King Arthur's grandniece. My mother was his niece, the sister of Sir Gawain. My father is named Guiromelant and my mother is called Clarissant. The battle between my father and my uncle, during which they wounded each other so cruelly, was brought to an end through her. I have spoken to you a great deal about myself, and I pray God who caused me to be born that He may allow me to see the day when you will speak to me at greater leisure.' (8258)

'Maiden,' said Aalardin, 'I am entirely yours, and that is the end of it.' (8260)

With these words, he left her. He saw on one side a powerful man of high birth who seemed ready to engage in the first joust of the combat. He was accompanied by many knights, and was wearing rich and beautiful armour. He came to joust first, most arrogantly, in front of the maiden. Do you know what happened then? King Ris had established himself with all his men in the precinct of the tower. On the other side of the field King Cadoalant of Ireland had his camp, and I'll tell you how things were arranged. The field was surrounded by a big ditch, wide and deep, which could be crossed by a passage. Now I wish to come back to the two kings I've been telling you about, who had organized the tournament. King Ris advanced to the gate of the castle in full armour, wanting to be the first to joust. Aalardin spurred his horse and rushed forward, carrying the sleeve which the girl had given him on his lance. They hurled themselves at each other violently. Spurring their chargers impetuously, they stood on the stirrups: each one thrust with a sharp point, each one struck the other when they met. King Ris hit Aalardin so violently that he put an end to his lance. Aalardin struck back such a blow that King Ris couldn't avoid being knocked down in a heap with white Lionceau – that was the name of his horse. King Ris was a valiant knight. Aalardin rushed against him, and now it would be clear which of the two was slower! But King Ris had more companions who thought they could defeat Aalardin easily. They were trying to put the King back in his saddle when Aalardin returned. He held his drawn sword in his hand and struck a powerful blow on the King's helmet; not for all his kingdom could he avoid falling to the ground! Twenty knights rushed headlong between them: they put the King back on his horse and turned upon Aalardin. It was a very unequal battle, one single knight against twenty! Nevertheless, it turned out well for him, for no matter how strong they were or how hard they tried, they couldn't have managed to put the King back in the saddle if it weren't for the great help of the men in the castle. (8328)

But before you hear me say anything more, I want to tell you about the most famous knights in the entire world, the knights of the Round Table, and to tell you how, according to the story, they were divided into two camps. On King Cadoalant's side there were the two most valiant, Sir Gawain and Sir Yvain, as well as Sir Kay, the Seneschal, who was an excellent knight, Lucan the Bottler and several thousand other knights, whom I won't take the trouble to name or to count. In the other camp, King Ris of Wales had with him the King of Estregales, the Rich Mercenary, Le Bel Hardi, the son of Nut and a hundred other knights – hundreds or maybe thousands, I don't know. When Aalardin arrived by good fortune – they didn't recognize him – they came to his aid with all their power. There were some dead and some wounded; from then on the combat centred on Aalardin. You may be sure that it was a good day for him and he won much praise. They were attacking him from all sides and he was dealing out strong strokes in return, when he saw his companion Cador coming towards the tower. Let the one who meets Cador first be on his guard! (8365)

It was the Rich Mercenary who came seeking to joust with him. They clashed so violently that the Rich Mercenary's lance bent until it broke. Cador struck back so hard that horse and rider fell in a heap. Cador told him to surrender, but he had no desire to yield and was ready to defend his life dearly! Each of them drew his sword and was ready to strike the other when Sagremor the Impetuous, richly equipped and accompanied by a large following, rushed at Cador with his lance lowered. Blows rained down on him thick and fast from all sides. Everyone attacked him together, but they could not budge him from his horse. Oh, if you could have seen how he fought! Sword in hand, he struck out all around him, more ferocious than a tiger or a leopard! You could have heard the sound of the blows pounding down on him and the clash of arms, and you could have seen him defend himself vigorously, cutting and rending everything, leaving one man one-handed and another lame. With his steel blade, he split the crowd and saddened the boldest man! Nevertheless they managed to assist the Rich Mercenary and put him back in his saddle by force. Cador noticed Aalardin, whom Cadoalant was being slow to help. He did not want to delay going to his aid. When the companions met, all the others trembled before them, for they gave them a good fight! (8407)

Even the maidens in the tower wondered what could be happening, except for the one in the window, to whom Aalardin had spoken. She was not surprised, for she had already seen him, though she had not known that he was so valiant. If she was delighted to have seen him before, what she saw of him now pleased her even more! She had found him handsome, now he was valiant. She did not give him any more of herself – except her eyes to look at him, her beautiful mouth to speak to him, her heart to think of him, and her body which she would grant to no one else! (8423)

For his part, Aalardin gave her many glances that day while dealing out a great many blows. He took up a position where she could see him, for the noble knight thought in his heart that Lord God in His goodness ought to take as much care in protecting him as he did in looking at her. There was a noble and beautiful maiden who was attracted to Cador; she spent her time looking at him, but she didn't yet know anything about him, not even who he was or what country he came from, or who his father and mother were. She was very sad and upset at not knowing him. She made a great effort to find out who he was, for she saw him dealing out blows, attacking and defending himself splendidly. No man could have done better, and nothing that he did had to be done again. She gave him her heart and her thoughts, and swore to herself that she would never be satisfied until she knew his name. This maiden I am telling you about was the sister of the valiant Cahadis, and Caradoc's cousin. She was born in Brittany and was a cousin of Sir Yvain. She was called the beautiful Ydain. (8454)

She went to the beautiful Guigenor to ask her about Cador. 'Ah, young lady, do you see those two marvellous knights striking so vigorously in the midst of those others and displaying their bravery? Have you ever seen two others like them? Could there ever be sorrow as great as would be shown for those two if they die? See how handsome he is, the one with the shield bordered with gold, riding on the chestnut horse. Look at how bravely he acts! He is the one who holds my heart.' (8468)

'He certainly is brave,' replied the other girl, 'but the one who has the ermine eagle on the shield with the red gules is doing splendidly also. He is the one who will do the best and will rout the others.' (8474)

So each one praised her own; but they did not dare to give their opinions or reveal their thoughts, neither to tell everything nor to conceal everything. While they were speaking, Cadoalant came up with Sir Kay, and, I tell you truly, with him came a good knight, the valiant Perceval the Welshman, along with the best company of knights ever brought to a tournament by a king. Many a noble man was in that tournament! When it began, you could have seen the ground trembling, lances breaking, shields being pierced, terrible blows delivered by cutting blades, one man falling and another rising, weak and strong being wounded, knights stretched out on the ground, and horses running free! Anyone who saw it could have said that it would have been better not to be part of it! The man who could not defend himself would soon be thrown down, unable to keep his stirrups. It was to their misfortune that bad knights came there, and I assure you that cowards did not dare to approach the place. (8504)

King Cadoalant of Ireland did not act timidly; you may be sure that the first man he met had a hard time of it: he struck him down in the joust. It was the good King Yder. Sir Kay the Seneschal acted like a good knight, for in his first charge, I tell you truly, he faced off against a most quarrelsome man, Agravain the Proud. No better match could be found: one was puffed up with vanity and the other even more so! They were both equally quarrelsome, always disagreeable and full of mockery. They rushed furiously at each other, pushing their horses as hard as possible, so that both of them were thrown from their fearsome grey horses. I won't bother about how they got up. Only a fool would come between them! (8526)

Good Perceval the Welshman knocked down three opponents in a single attack: first Cligés, and then the son of Arés; and do you know who was the third? It was Yder the son of Nut once again. Each of his companions, for his part, had fared very well, but I would be completely exhausted before having told you about all the victors and the vanquished. (8537)

The two companions, Cador and Aalardin, were still in good form although they had been fighting for a long time with scarcely any rest. They won more praise than anyone, and they deserved it, for they attacked King Ris and dealt with him in such a way that they forced him to retreat. Neither the Rich Mercenary, nor Sagremor, nor Bedevere, nor any other knight could manage to return his charger to him, the white Lionceau. The King himself, despite his people, would have been captured and held prisoner if the Fair Good Knight* had not come to his aid with many of his followers. They showed such honour to the King that they mounted him on another horse. (8559)

No one could describe to you the anguish and pain of Aalardin and Cador, or their bravery and prowess. They knocked Sagremor to the ground, but Bleheris got him up again. Then King Ris rushed at the two loyal companions. Sir Perceval, arriving at that moment, struck the Fair Good Knight, to the great sorrow of his followers; he could not endure the blow and fell to the ground. When Perceval had knocked him to the ground, he then faced Bleheris – who did not find it funny – and did the same to him. They were all afraid of his attack, for every man he struck was done for! Perceval saw that Aalardin was faring very well with the good horse he had captured by his prowess. Aalardin entrusted it at once to his dear companion Cador for the maiden Guigenor. Before he left the tournament, Cador struck many blows. He went under the window and said to Guigenor: 'Maiden, may He who caused you to be born protect and bless you, both you and your beautiful companions! I greet you on behalf of your knight, whom you see riding down there, with the shield of red gules; he has accomplished great exploits in the tournament! You saw him here just now and gave your beautiful and elegant sleeve to him as a standard. Through me, he offers you this horse which he has won today from your enemy, King Ris. It is his prize, certainly, the first of the tournament!' (8602)

'My lord,' replied the maiden, 'may God who grants all knowledge and who formed every creature grant him good fortune! Of all the knights I know, he is the one who most inclines my heart to love. I have certainly noticed today that I was not misled concerning his good qualities. My heart is very joyful about that, for I see even more bravery in him than I was told. He is surely worthy of having a sweetheart, and he will not lack one, for he has one already! Thank him for his present, and tell him from me that I am his to command, and I will be so all my life. But do not judge me impolite if I ask you your name and whether you and he are companions, because you are very brave and seem to be of noble birth.' (8626)

'Maiden, I tell you without fail that my name is Cador of Cornwall. He and I are companions. Now with your permission, I will depart, for I am eager to be back there.' The beautiful Ydain, deeply moved by the love she felt for him, gave him a lance with a silk pennon and said to him: 'My lord, take this lance and bring me the knight I see in the valley, galloping straight towards the tournament. He is a very bold man, called Guingambresil, and he is one of your enemies.' (8642)

Cador did not want to delay any longer. In order to show his courage, he rushed against Guingambresil with such speed that when they met he knocked him from his horse. He carried out the maiden's orders quickly, for through such force, like it or not, Guingambresil was sent to her as a prisoner. But Cador, far from turning back, rushed into the fray, holding in his hand the lance which the beautiful Ydain had given to him. He hurled the first man that he met to the ground. He used his sword so well that he sent him after Guingambresil to surrender; he sent seven or eight others, much to the delight of the beautiful Ydain. On that day, she said many a time that the lance she gave to Cador had been well used. She often boasted to Guigenor that her sweetheart was not forgetting her. He accomplished so many chivalrous deeds for her that not half of them – nor a third of them nor even a quarter – could be told today! (8668)

The King of Estregales arrived with his troops. Aalardin held a strong, solid, powerful lance, and he threw himself at the King with such speed that the King was forced to abandon his horse. His followers rushed to his assistance and worked bravely until they put him back on his horse. But now there arrived three brave men: Sir Girflet the son of Do, Lucan, and Sir Mado. Perceval the Welshman was with them, as well as Cador and King Cadoalant. They bore their attack so well that they pushed them back in the fray. They struck such blows with their swords that their foes could not stand it! Each of the newly arrived knights struck so often and so well with their cutting swords that they took the place from them. Aalardin did not want to let King Ris escape, even though they both were tired because they had fought so much. The King's men rushed to aid their lord, but Perceval came to help Aalardin and drove away the crowd. Aalardin, looking up at his sweetheart, rushed at the King and told him that he would never survive if he didn't surrender. The King thought he could defend himself and escape despite Aalardin; but his companions were already too far away, pursued by Perceval the Welshman, Cadoalant and Cador, who were skewering them and their horses. When Aalardin saw the King separated from his people, he struck him such a blow to the head that he fainted and fell to the ground without a word. When he came to, he threw himself on Aalardin's mercy, without any argument. Aalardin put him back in the saddle, on condition that he surrender to his sweetheart Guigenor at the tower window. Then Aalardin left the battlefield with his prisoner. (8722)

Then up came the Fair Good Knight, along with the Rich Mercenary: he expected to earn his pay and make merry at another's expense. They thought that they could attack Aalardin scot-free, but they themselves were caught as they attacked him: in their own hands they picked up the very rod that would beat them! King Ris rode straight to the window where the maiden was, greeted her courteously and surrendered to her nobly, and she received him willingly. Aalardin stayed among people who were far from friendly to him and would gladly have taken vengeance on him for the pain he had caused them that day. As they rushed angrily against him, swords drawn, they began to strike him fiercely in every way they could. One pushed him and another pulled, and they would have been happy to kill him if they could. But his helmet was sound, his strength still great, and his sword still cut well: he could still see his sweetheart, and that increased his valour, you may be sure. He defended himself so ferociously that he split the Rich Mercenary's helmet and cut his coiffe. He did not strike in vain, for the blade didn't stop until it cut his skull and reached almost to his brains: he fell over backwards. Now the Fair Good Knight was left all alone, with no help from his companions, since he could not expect anything from the Mercenary, who was wounded and in a bad way. He and Aalardin began a harsh combat. What can I tell you? At the end of it all, Aalardin had defeated the two knights who had attacked him and sent them to surrender to his sweetheart, to the beautiful courteous maiden. She received them nobly. (8773)

The tournament was going badly for King Ris, for all his knights had been put to flight. King Cadoalant of Ireland had almost driven them from the field, and they were fleeing before him. Then Caradoc threw himself into their midst at full speed, but without recognizing any friends or knowing where to find them. He was eager to win honour. As fast as his horse could carry him, he went to comfort the prisoners, for he thought he would win more honour if he aided those who were in the worst condition. For their part, they helped out a great deal, for to tell the truth in the first line he struck Cadoalant, then Sir Mado, and then Girflet the son of Do. He struck those three down in a single attack. (8795)

Sir Kay wanted to fight against him, and Caradoc recognized him: I will tell you what happened. Sir Kay was very bold, but he was full of harsh words. His rash boldness often turned out very badly for him. He did not fare well in the fight with Caradoc, for he fell and rolled on the ground in such a way that he sprained his hand. Caradoc came up to him and struck him until he was exhausted. (8808)

'Kay,' he said, 'by my neck, now you are the fool, more than I was three years ago in front of my uncle at Cardueil. I still resent you for it: you wickedly treated me as a fool and picked a quarrel with me. You said whatever you felt like then, but you would have done better to keep silent. What folly for you to joust with me today! You are dead, I think, unless you surrender on the spot!' (8222)

'My lord, I surrender willingly!' (8223)

Caradoc took his word after setting his conditions: without delay, and with no protest or grumbling, Kay would go to surrender to Caradoc's sweetheart, the beautiful Guinier, in the bower in the woods. Sir Kay made his way to the maiden at once and surrendered to her on her sweetheart Caradoc's behalf, according to his promise. She received him graciously, and when she recognized him she was delighted, for she knew that Kay was a haughty man. (8838)

The tournament was very violent. Caradoc fought on all sides and was very pleased with how he performed. But since Sir Bran de Lis came up with many companions, it's no surprise that the battle then became much harsher. Caradoc was nevertheless very strong, and braver than any of the others in the tournament. I assure you that he weakened them so much with the strong blows he delivered and he fought so well that he put the powerful King Cadoalant and all those on his side to flight – except for Aalardin and Cador, whom I wish to exclude, along with the good Perceval the Welshman: these three were the noblest knights who fought against King Ris. Sir Perceval took Cligés prisoner by force; for his part, the noble young man Aalardin captured Tor the son of Arés. As for Cador, he forced Sagremor the Impetuous to go, like it or not, to surrender to the maiden. As I have told you, each of these three took his opponent prisoner. Aalardin took his prisoner back to Guigenor, and Cador, to tell the truth, turned his own over to his sweetheart Ydain. But good Perceval had no sweetheart at the time, so I will tell you how nobly he acted. You have heard how Kay surrendered to a maiden, the beautiful, courteous Guinier, to whom her sweetheart Caradoc had entrusted him. When she had nobly accepted his surrender, she asked him for news of the battle: which knight was winning the greatest praise? (8888)

'Maiden,' said Sir Kay, 'I tell you truly, the one who sent me here to you a prisoner has the greatest honour. He is very valiant, since he defeated me, and no one has ever defeated me in combat before King Arthur.' (8896)

When the maiden heard Kay say this, she was delighted and thrilled to hear of her sweetheart's prowess. She wanted to watch the tournament, so she set out at once, taking no friend or companion except the Maiden of the Pavilion, who was so prudent, elegant, beautiful, courteous and gracious. You may be sure that both of them asked Kay if the tournament yard was far away. (8909)

'By my faith,' he said, 'if you need to go there, you may go quickly: it is very near here.' (8912)

They left Sir Kay in their lodgings and proceeded until they had a clear view of the field, the magnificent array of knights and the tower. They sat down in a comfortable patch of shade and watched what the valiant knights were doing, at their ease. (8919)

But I want to tell you here about Sir Perceval: he had seen the maidens and came straight to them. He spurred his horse and went towards them, bringing his prisoner. First he spoke to the Maiden of the Pavilion: 'May God protect you, maiden, you and your beautiful companions!' (8928)

'Dear lord, may God bless you and your companions!' (8932)

'Maiden,' said Perceval, 'what chance has brought you to these woods and this valley?' (8935)

'Dear sweet lord, it is for the great pleasure of seeing the tournament that we have come to sit here.' (8938)

While they were speaking, the courteous Lucan arrived at full speed. He knelt before the beautiful Guinier and surrendered to her. 'Maiden,' he said, 'I greet you loyally on behalf of a friend of yours who has sent me here to you. He is a valiant knight with the three rampant lions on his shield of gold, but I do not yet know his name. On his behalf, without fail, I make myself your prisoner, ready to do whatever you wish.' (8953)

The maiden received him politely, and said to him: 'Sit down here, my lord. On behalf of the man who captured you – may God grant him honour and praise – I will keep you here willingly.' (8959)

Meanwhile, Perceval had become friendly with the Maiden of the Pavilion; out of affection, he had his prisoner surrender to her. Cligés now had someone to talk to, since he had Lucan as his companion. Both of them admired the beauty of the two maidens greatly. Perceval stayed there, enjoying himself with them until he saw the two other valiant knights who had sent their prisoners to their maidens coming directly towards them. They did not yet know who these two maidens were, with whom the knights were staying. When they reached them, they were completely astonished to find their sisters. But when they learned of the capture of Sir Kay and Lucan, they recovered from their astonishment and wanted to return to the tournament. (8987)

I wish to speak to you about Perceval, to whom the Maiden of the Pavilion had granted her love: that day he sent to her ten knights he had captured during the fray. Do not blame me if I don't name all the prisoners Caradoc captured that day: that would be too wicked on my part. But in truth and without a lie, I tell you that he captured twenty or thirty of them, and because of love he sent them to surrender to his sweetheart. Let us leave the maidens, for the three knights had departed from them.

Aalardin, Perceval and Cador spurred their horses and hurled themselves into the battle, but they found their companions in a completely different situation from when they left. The strongest were wounding the weakest, and King Ris's men were pursuing King Cadoalant's at will. He got no praise from it, for it all was the work of Caradoc and Sir Bran de Lis who were thoroughly enjoying themselves. It was easy for them to bait their foes like bears, and no one could reproach them for not being successful that day. (9017)

One man, who was neither foolish nor uncourtly, had stayed inactive for too long: you must know that I mean Sir Gawain. When he saw his companion flee, he began to burn with rage and could not stand it any longer. Now he was in the battle, and Sir Yvain was with him. Both of them were very valiant: they knocked the first knights they met off their horses and down to the ground. The knights who came with them conducted themselves marvellously: each one knocked down at least one foe, until Caradoc threw himself in their midst and knocked down Sir Yvain right in front of Sir Gawain. Then he struck a good blow to the shield of Le Laid Hardi so that he was almost done for: he fell from his horse in a faint. Caradoc then attacked Perceval, who took it from him and didn't fail to pay him back. Caradoc made him retreat, and he made Caradoc retreat in turn. I tell you without a doubt that they could not avoid falling to the ground, horses and knights together. But they remounted at once, it seems to me, one aided by Sir Bran de Lis, an excellent knight, the other by Sir Gawain. Perceval was furious at Caradoc for knocking him down. He pursued him here and there until they jousted again and knocked each other and their horses in a heap. But they had soon remounted, for they were both very valiant. Their swords were well sharpened, and they would have come to blows then, if the others had not separated them. (9062)

Nevertheless Caradoc didn't have any desire at all to rest: he went to attack the bravest man. All day long he raised problems that had no solution: he prosecuted the strongest so well that he could not defend his cause! He dealt with them all in such a way that he drove them to flight. King Cadoalant was greatly troubled by it: his bravest men had fled. Sir Bran de Lis pursued them and won great praise there by striking Cador and knocking him off his chestnut horse. If Perceval had not helped him,

Cador would have been captured. Sir Bran de Lis was furious with Perceval, who was quite pleased because he had rescued Cador from his hands. When he realized that he was losing, Bran de Lis struck Sir Perceval and hurled him from his horse, and Sir Perceval did the same to him. The two of them found themselves on the ground. They would have split each other's skulls if Caradoc and many other knights hadn't come and returned their horses to them. Perceval was enraged at having been knocked down so often. He will avenge himself personally on Caradoc, if he has the power! (9097)

He took up his lance and went straight to where Caradoc was fighting furiously. When Caradoc saw him coming, he got ready to face him. He prepared for him well and welcomed him fiercely, for in the joust it was impossible to say which was better or worse. If they were looking for each other, they could find each other on the ground, for they didn't use the stirrups to dismount! Perceval was furious; he drew his sword from the scabbard, believing that he could avenge himself without pain or risk. But Caradoc did not fear him at all. He pushed him back and drew his own sword. The combat began, harsh and violent, as the knights did each other grievous damage: their shields were in pieces, their hauberks unravelled, their helmets broken. The stronger of them was exhausted. One of the two was going to be shamed – it would have been a great misfortune and a pity – when Aalardin and Cador arrived, with visors lowered. When Caradoc saw them, he was afraid that Perceval might do something to cause him shame. He was delighted when he accomplished nothing, for before they departed, Aalardin and Cador had separated the two opponents. But Caradoc did not stop responding and provoking, attacking and defending, defying and being defied. (9140)

Now I don't know what more I can tell you or how to make a longer story by describing his prowess, but I tell you that Caradoc made King Cadoalant retreat with all his men. Without a lie, he sent his sweetheart the beautiful Guinier many prisoners whose names I cannot say. There was Kay the Seneschal, Girflet, Gales the Bald, the courteous Lucan and at least thirty-three others whom I do not want to mention by name, for a man who was named would then become less famous; so I prefer to leave them out of the story rather than cause them shame by naming them. But if the story isn't faulty, they were some of the most valiant men of King Arthur's household. Caradoc showed great prowess: on that day, he won great praise because of the knights he captured and the King he put to flight. (9167)

Sir Gawain felt upset at this and declared that he had endured seeing his companions being conquered for too long without helping them. Full of anger, he rushed at Caradoc; all day long he had been observing him in the tournament. The great acts of prowess which Caradoc had accomplished in the combat displeased him. They jousted with each other three or four times, but neither of them could knock the other down, for they were both extremely strong. King Cadoalant struck vigorously: he and his men did so well that they recovered the advantage, and I am going to tell you how it happened. Perceval attacked Caradoc, as did Sir Yvain, and Sir Gawain attacked him from another side. Each one wished to be the first to fight with him: seeing him so valiant, each one wanted to defeat him. They did not think at all about his interests! They assailed him from three sides and succeeded in knocking him to the ground; in that part of the battle, Cadoalant recovered the advantage over King Ris. But Caradoc quickly rose again from the ground and attacked Perceval. Realizing that he had lost his horse, he killed Perceval's horse as he defended himself in vain. Nevertheless Perceval came very near Caradoc, and so did Sir Gawain, you may be sure, and Sir Yvain! Each one cried out to him to surrender and not to resist them any more, for they knew that he was so full of valour that they wouldn't have wanted to wound him for anything! Sir Gawain called on him nobly to surrender, for he had not yet recognized him. But Caradoc answered him at once that rather than surrender, he would defend himself with all his might. He was bold indeed to face three such knights who had no equals in all the world! (9218)

He defended himself for a long time, putting up a stiff resistance. He fought so well against them that he gave them all a hard battle. He struck blows so fast that they could not get the best of him or seize him from any side. But what's the use? He could not have avoided being killed or captured if the fair Cahadis had not seen him. And you may be sure that with him was the valiant Yder the son of Nut and Le Laid Hardi. Le Beau Couard, I believe, was the fourth. The fifth was Sir Bran de Lis, an excellent knight. As soon as they saw Caradoc, they helped him generously. I tell you that you could have seen a hundred of King Ris's knights rushing to help him. They did not take the matter lightly, you may be sure, because they said they would lose their honour if they let him be taken: 'It would be better for us to give up everything for him than to let him be captured without us. If we have him on our side, we have all that we need, and without him we can do nothing!' (9246)

That is what they said, and I tell you the truth about it, they rushed to his rescue. Each one had his sharp steel sword in his hand. Lord Bran de Lis came straight at Sir Gawain, his drawn sword in his hand. 'My lord,' he said, 'I have come here to challenge you for this prisoner. Don't be so foolish as to try to take him any farther.' (9258)

'He will certainly not be yielded to you, but will be vigorously defended!' (9260)

Then you could have seen knights assembling, ground trembling, lances broken, swords striking, hands and fists cut, shields and hauberks pierced! Iron tips passed through, steel helmets were broken and split, knights were stretched on the ground, some injured and others dead. Even the strongest man was exhausted! It was for Caradoc that they had undertaken this combat; they would not finish such a battle without great sorrow. No matter who was the victor, I can tell you that Cadoalant was the loser, for Caradoc was snatched from him in the battle. Sir Gawain, who was trying to take him prisoner by force, was very upset by this. They surrounded him on all sides and struck many blows, and they saved Caradoc. But you may be sure that Caradoc defended himself especially well and did not feel any fear, thanks to the help that he had received. He attacked his foes so well with his sword that he terrified them all and was able to escape from them. Sir Gawain was very sad at this, as was the courteous Yvain. Perceval was enraged that Caradoc, with the help of his excellent companion Sir Bran de Lis, had escaped them again after killing all three of their horses and throwing them to the ground. (9298)

Cador and Aalardin knew nothing about all this: they were fighting splendidly elsewhere. Cador separated from Aalardin: in the place where they had been, they had won honour, renown and glory, capturing many knights and sending them to the maidens. They separated, for they both wished to arrive first where they could see the blows raining down on Caradoc. When they saw him escape, they were extremely upset, but thought they could catch him again, and tried very hard to hold him back. They did not recognize him, for he had lost his shield and now had a different one, and he no longer had his own horse: now he was riding a very good Hungarian horse, which he had won to replace his own. In his hand he held a solid lance. Cador threw himself at Caradoc first with his lance lowered, and Caradoc brandished his own lance. I tell you, they rushed against each other and struck each other with their lances so hard when they met that Cador's horse could have been taken without him noticing: he fell head first, legs in the air. Even if someone gave him the whole world, he couldn't have said who he was! (9335)

Aalardin was furious: he could not endure seeing his companion Cador rolling in the dust. He won't value his courage if he does not avenge him at once! Firmly seated on his galloping charger, he held the shaft of his lance. Caradoc noticed and recognized him perfectly, but still he would not fail to attack him because of that! It is a custom of tournaments not to show favour or hold off from attacking anyone because of kinship or friendship. The two men rushed against each other fiercely, as they both could do very well. They met violently, struck each other's chests, and knocked each other off their horses. They leaped up and started to strike with their cutting swords: blood flowed, flesh and bone were stripped! Caradoc was prevailing and Aalardin was in a bad way, when Sir Gawain attacked Caradoc angrily. He thought he had caught him this time, but he won't get him yet, I believe, for Caradoc's bravery was extraordinary and he defended himself bravely. Sir Gawain attacked him and believed that he had conquered him: he struck him on the helmet with his sword and stunned him completely. Aalardin pressed against him from the other side and struck him in turn. He almost fell, after taking such a beating, and if they had been able to return to the charge, I believe that they would have knocked him down. (9378)

Sir Bran de Lis arrived at the best possible time to help Caradoc. He came ready for action: he met Aalardin and struck a cutting sword-blow to his helmet: steel resounded on steel! He struck two more blows which almost threw him to the ground. The third blow was so strong that it split the helmet and reached Aalardin's head. The fourth blow would have felled him, if he had been able to give it and if Caradoc, who knew him well, had not turned the blow away and made the sword veer aside. As he did so, he happened to turn his back to Sir Gawain. Lord Gawain saw him turn, and struck him: Caradoc could hardly keep from falling to the ground! Caradoc jumped up and struck Sir Gawain back as he deserved: he gave him such wages on his helmet that he could consider himself well paid for his efforts! (9408)

Then they began a battle which could not be stopped until they had exchanged many blows. Even the strongest man was quite exhausted: they weren't just playing then, but struck their foes everywhere they could reach them! They battled and skirmished, hitting each other hard, sometimes pushing and sometimes pulling, full of respect for the strength of each other's arms. They dealt out marvellous blows and shed much blood! They completely unravelled their hauberks, shattered their shields, split their helmets; everyone was depleted and exhausted. Never in any of the trials he had encountered in all his life had Sir Gawain been so drained. But he was very curious to know where this knight came from who resisted him for so long – not only resisted but also harmed him grievously. He wanted to know what his name was, for he had never been so harshly treated, so troubled and harassed, by just one man. He couldn't count on any of his companions, for they all had their hands full: everyone had to defend himself, to die or to beg for mercy. (9440)

King Ris's troops had the greatest success; but Caradoc especially carried off the prize of the tournament. None of the others accomplished so much or won as much honour as Caradoc did that day. Then there could be no more fighting, for night made them separate. The knights distributed blows of sword and fist most generously as they parted, but those who were in the worst position and were the least valiant were King Cadoalant's troops. Sir Gawain realized that Caradoc had no fear and that his own companions had clearly been defeated. He spoke to Caradoc: 'Sir Knight,' he said, 'tell me, by your faith, where you come from and what your name is.' Caradoc gave him no answer, for he did not want him to recognize him yet. Sir Gawain urged him and begged him quite amiably: 'Sir, noble knight, I pray you most politely to tell me your name; for if you conceal it from me, you'll be thought impolite.' (9469)

'Dear lord, my name is Caradoc, you may be sure, and I am from Brittany. But do not believe that it stops there, not at all: I want to know in return what your name is.' (9475)

'I don't want to hide it from you, dear friend. I am called Gawain. My name has never been concealed.' (9478)

'Gawain, I knew it!' said Caradoc; 'but I wanted very much to try your courage and test your famous valour.' (9483)

Gawain was delighted and considered Caradoc to be an accomplished man. 'My friend,' said he, 'are you related to the beautiful Ysave, the niece of King Arthur? Do you know her?' (9488)

'Yes, I know her well indeed: I tell you that she is my mother.' (9490)

'Ah, Caradoc! Is it really you? Now I recognize you. You are a brave knight, and my cousin.' (9493)

With these words, they both threw their shields and cutting blades to the ground and unlaced their helmets. You could have seen them taking off their coiffes and embracing with joy! They cried and laughed at the same time: cried because they were wounded and laughed because they had found each other. In that way, the two men who had caused each other so much trouble that day recognized each other: the joy they felt was greater than the sorrow they had caused each other. Each one rejoiced because the other was so brave. Everyone else felt great joy when they recognized Caradoc. Aalardin especially, but also Cador his companion, showed great joy at finding Caradoc again, and it was proper to do so. They were both surprised that they had not recognized him during the day. He had completely confused them that day by changing his clothes and putting on different arms several times. He did not want anyone to recognize him and so hesitate to give him the proof of his force, especially if it was greater than his own, just because he had recognized him. But now they considered him the best; they all thought he was the most valiant knight at the tournament, and they couldn't keep it secret. (9529)

You should have seen all those knights gathered there in

twenties, hundreds and thousands! They were drawn by the great joy which Sir Gawain was showing for Caradoc and because they wanted to know who this knight was, who had made them suffer so much, wounding some grievously, helping the others so much. Cadoalant came from his side and Ris from his; because of their great joy, they put an end to the tournament. I tell you that when they had stopped the tournament, King Arthur gave his niece Lady Guigenor to the courteous Aalardin and the beautiful Ydain to Cador. They were the maidens of the window, who had been up in the tower. As for the Maiden of the Pavilion, the King was pleased to make a gift of her, to Aalardin's satisfaction, to a fine young man, the valiant Perceval the Welshman. Those three were well placed, and Caradoc was not left out: the beautiful Guinier was his sweetheart. (9558)

I have told you enough about the engagements but I am not able and I could not find it in my heart to tell you the place, the time or the day of the marriages. I won't take the time, for I have many other things to do. Each one returned to his home. The tournament was over and Aalardin, Cador and their companion Caradoc shared their prizes. They found each other as I have told you, and they promised and swore that they would always be friends. When they had kissed each other, they asked King Arthur for leave to go; but he saw such virtue in them that he would not give them his leave for anything in the world. He made them stay with him for a long time without sending them back. They stayed with him in great joy and happiness, I believe, for a year. For a long time the King lived this life of ease. (9583)

I can no longer ignore the King's niece, Lady Ysave, the mother of the valiant Caradoc. I can no longer delay the moment when I must recount something which displeases me greatly, for only an uncourtly man could enjoy this story, recount it with pleasure, or speak evil of a noble lady. Yet if one lady commits an act of folly, it is nevertheless not proper to say that all women are the same, for they are not at all alike. For every one who acts badly, seven act well. But what I must say about one of them pains me more than anything. Would to God that I could abandon my source here, without damaging my story! But this reassures me: if the beginning of the story puts a little blame on women, the end of it is good and profitable for them. One single woman thrusts away the blame and tramples on it: the valiant, beautiful Guinier. I do not wish to speak of her now, but I will speak of her later, when I find the time and opportunity. (9612)

I want to return to my story and take up my subject where I left off earlier. I think that I told you about Lady Ysave and why she was locked up in the high tower at Nantes. But the enchanter Eliavrés, who was Caradoc's father, kept hanging around her, knowing that she had been locked up because of him. He didn't care about causing disorder, even if it displeased King Caradoc and everyone in the country. If he found his way in, it was partly because he was in love and partly because his great knowledge of sorcery helped him enter. No other lovestruck man, no matter how bold he was, would have dared to undertake it, but the enchanter tried because he knew all the science of magic. It would have been surprising if he hadn't tried to do something which would earn his sweetheart's praise. And that is what he did: he didn't take long in getting into the tower. But he did one thing which turned out badly for him: by his magic he brought harpists into the tower to play the harp, minstrels to play the viol, dancers to dance, and acrobats to tumble. That is the sort of life he led there whenever he came to the tower. (9650)

King Caradoc felt inclined to travel around his other towns to amuse himself in his lands, thinking that no one could harm him or do anything against him. While the King was about his business, the enchanter came to see the Queen and they led the kind of life of distractions and enjoyments that you have heard me describe. So they lived for a long time, so much so that the neighbours were kept awake every night by the noise of their revelry when the King's back was turned. The people sent messengers to tell the King about it secretly, and when he heard about it he was sad and angry, and sighed from the bottom of his heart. He had the tower watched for a long time, but he couldn't accomplish anything; he couldn't find any way to catch Eliavrés there. Because of the noisy enjoyment and entertainment and jokes they heard in the tower, it was called 'Bofois', and it is still called 'Bofois' in that region. The King heard the enchanter's strange diversions with his own ears, and you may be sure that he was very displeased. He sent for his son Caradoc. (9685)

The messenger took to the road at once and arrived in England by the shortest route. He soon found King Arthur's honoured court and asked for Caradoc until he found him at the court. He gave him his father's greetings, and informed him at once about the great need besetting the King. Caradoc went to take his leave of King Arthur, and told him the whole story from beginning to end, explaining what he had to do. The King gave him leave, on condition that as soon as he had accomplished his task he would return and let no other obligation restrain him. Along with him, and this is the end of it, Aalardin took his leave of the King, as did his companion Cador. The King had his treasuries thrown open for them, and gave them as much as they wanted to take and more. They did not wish to delay any longer, and took leave of their companions and set out on the road at once. Sir Gawain and Sir Yvain accompanied them for a long way, until they reached the road where Caradoc had found Aalardin carrying off the beautiful, gracious maiden Guinier. It was there that each one found the best road to return to his own country. When they separated, each of them began to cry. They dismounted from their horses and, without delaying any longer, they took leave from each other, kissed each other and remounted their horses. The knight filled with virtues – I mean Sir Gawain – and his companion Yvain escorted Caradoc as far as the sea, where they put him on a fine, sturdy boat. They were very upset for him, and the departure of their friends plunged them into deep thoughts. They returned to the court and remained with the King. (9738)

Cador went to Cornwall, along with the beautiful Ydain and his sister the beautiful Guinier: Caradoc did not want to take her to Brittany on any condition, but preferred her to stay with her brother who loved her so tenderly. He was afraid that if she came with him she would learn tidings about his mother which weren't very pretty. I tell you, no matter where he went, his heart and all his thoughts remained with her in Cornwall. What did it matter if he crossed the sea? I can tell you truthfully that they will feel many heartfelt sorrows before they see each other again. (9755)

Once he had left the sea, Caradoc rode at full speed. Elegantly dressed in gold-embroidered silk, he went straight to Nantes. In Nantes, he found his lord the King in great distress. The King saw him and felt great joy and pleasure and welcomed him magnificently. After they had finished eating and drinking, he told him all the story just as it had happened. Caradoc began to keep watch, so well that he surprised his father the enchanter with his mother one night in the tower. I tell you that he caused him plenty of shame and dishonour. In order to avenge himself, the King forced him to lie carnally with a hound, then with a sow, and then to avenge himself further, he made him cover a mare. When he lay with the bitch, the enchanter engendered a large greyhound which was called Guinaloc and was Caradoc's brother, and with the sow, a huge boar which they called Tortain, and with the mare a great war horse, the powerful, spirited Loriagort.* I tell you they were Caradoc's brothers and his father's sons. Afterwards, he would have hanged him and flayed him alive if he hadn't let him off out of pity. After all, he was his father, and he was very worried about that: he was afraid of offending God by mistreating his father when he had him in his power. The King took vengeance on him as you have heard me tell, and then they let him go away. (9800)

Eliavrés was very sad, and I tell you that he was not far from inactive; he didn't stop until he came back to the Queen, who was in the tower. He complained bitterly about his son, his tormentor, and she lamented and wept over the great sufferings he had endured. 'If you do not find a way to avenge yourself, my dear sweet friend,' she said, 'it is because you have lost all your sense.' (9813)

'My lady, it would be a great sin and a horrible cruelty if I killed my child!' (9817)

'If you kill him? A fool's errand! Do you pity him now? He had no pity on you! Are you worried on my account? Are you so weak that you will not take vengeance on him? I can see it now: we have lost all our pleasures forever! We can't stop him from taking away everything from us! But you may be sure of this, without any doubt: you will be failing me if you do not think up a plan to harm the one who has harmed us. You are truly a failure if you have pity on him!' (9833)

'But I am his father,' he replied, 'and I cannot find it in my heart to kill him, not on any account. But just to please you, I will make him live without any power, if you will take part in it with me.' (9839)

'I'm quite ready to put all my energy and effort into it, without hesitation. Prepare, therefore, to avenging yourself quickly!' (9838)

The enchanter left her at once and brought her back an enchanted snake, tamed by his sorcery. Then he explained to her what to do with the serpent. He arranged everything by magic and put it in a wardrobe. After he had closed the snake up, he revealed all his plan to the Queen: 'My lady, by this snake we will be avenged.' (9853)

'How, my lord?' (9854)

'How? I will explain it to you. In God's name, I beg you not to touch that wardrobe or even approach it, for anyone who touches it will do so to his sorrow. When your son comes here to you to relax and rest, begin to undo your hair, and ask him to bring your comb to you from that wardrobe. When he has opened the wardrobe, you will see the evil snake throw itself on him furiously and wrap itself around him. Even his best friend will not be able to remove the snake from him, for two and a half years; after that, he will have to taste death.' (9874)

'My lord,' she said, 'thank you! That is good vengeance! Languishing like that will be much worse for him than dying a quick death. Although I am his mother, I will be no less cruel to him. I will do all that you have told me, and prepare his death for him!' (9882)

With that, the wicked enchanter left the lady. It wasn't very long before Caradoc felt a desire to go and see his lady. Alas! He did not yet know truly what cruelty and marvels his mother was preparing for him and was completely off his guard. He climbed slowly up the tower and approached his lady. 'My lady, may the Creator of the world, who purifies all evil from what is good, save you, guard you, and bless you.' (9896)

The Queen's reply was very different from what she felt in her heart: 'Dear son, may the Lord God protect you. I was not expecting you to come here now, since I have not seen you for a long time! You have come here unexpectedly, and you have found me all in disarray, because I had a headache and I wanted to comb my hair a little bit with a comb which was brought to me from Cesarea. It is there in that wardrobe: go there and bring it to me. Spend the whole day with me up here. I want to visit with you so much, and I've been so bored up here all alone!' (9914)

When he heard his lady's request, Caradoc rose to his feet at once and went to the wardrobe. When he had opened it, he put his arm into it. The snake which was inside thrust forth its teeth, caught his arm, and curled around it. Caradoc jumped backwards: he thought he could easily defend himself from the snake's attack. He started shaking his arm, believing he could shake it loose. But the snake attached itself there ever more firmly and squeezed more tightly. Caradoc began to change colour, to grow pale, to tremble and sweat because of the pain, and didn't know what to do. His mother – his enemy! – jumped up as if she didn't know the truth of the matter. She cried out, uttered feigned moans, struck herself, wrung her hands and often begged for death: 'Poor, wretched me!' she said, 'I find death too slow, to leave me alive! This snake, this viper, put here by devils, why has it attacked my son and left me alone? It should have thrown itself on me, this wicked snake! I had no desire to live! Dear, sweet son, make your confession, and free yourself from the heavy burden that you have from your father and from me, your mother. It is for your sin, it is for your misdeeds towards us both that the Lord God is taking vengeance on you. Endure it patiently, and cry out to God for mercy, so that He may take this demon away.' (9960)

So his mother preached to him, and Caradoc didn't say a word. In his heart he sighed, and thought that everything she said was for his own good. No human mouth could describe the terrible suffering he felt! When the King heard this news, he felt great sorrow and anger. No one could tell you how much anger was in his heart! He went there as soon as he could, and could scarcely be restrained from killing the Queen. They took her into another room so he wouldn't kill her in his fury, right in their midst. Caradoc felt great anguish as the snake ravaged and broke his arm. The King saw it and fainted for sorrow; he despised and blamed his life, uttered deep, heartfelt sighs, and tore his hair and beard. (9982)

He ordered that Caradoc be brought away from that place. The King swore that now the enchanter was done for: spells and magic won't preserve him! If he catches him, he'll put all his power into inflicting every harsh punishment on him that he can. Nothing can save him from dying in misery! (9992)

As many as fourteen knights took Caradoc in their arms and carried him out of the tower. They carefully prepared a splendid bed for him, took him to a room magnificently decorated with silk and diverse ornaments and put him on the bed. But he did not rest at all there, for he could not find a comfortable position: the snake wrapped itself ever more tightly on his arm and squeezed more and more painfully, so much so that the King sent for doctors throughout all his kingdom, to see if anyone knew how to remove the serpent from him. When they had all tried, no one could find any way to remove it and they did not dare try any more. The King began to fall into despair: he did not know what to do for Caradoc or how to free his arm from the serpent which was torturing him. He sent messengers to England, to France, to the entire world! He asked and begged all those who had any knowledge of medicine, stones, herbs, roots, magic or spells to come to him at once: if anyone could free Caradoc from the snake, the King would grant him a great reward. From his wealth he would give him everything he might want to have. Plenty of doctors came, but neither the best nor the worst knew how to apply any remedy which could make the wicked snake detach itself. (10034)

In her chamber, the Queen rejoiced as she thought back on the pain and the torment which her son had inflicted upon her. 'You wretch, may God take clear vengeance on you for all the pains you have caused your father and your mother! You will do your penance now. You will consume your life in suffering and then you will go to your death, without ever knowing any ease!' That is how the lady rejoiced every day of the week. Many people heard her, but it would not have been good or courteous for them to trouble the King with this and increase his anger, for one can easily double a man's anger. If anyone had told the King about it, he would have become so enraged with his wife the Queen that he would have chased her from his kingdom. He was so strong that if it had not been for King Arthur, whose niece she was, he would have chased her out of his kingdom or killed her. (10062)

The report quickly spread far and wide, and King Arthur learned of Caradoc's situation and of the serpent which was clamped so tightly around his arm that no remedy or spell could detach it from him. The King was under an elm tree in his woods when he heard the news. He felt such anguish that he fainted. Such great sorrow struck his heart that he let himself slide in a faint by a pallet on the ground. When he revived, he blamed himself and began to reproach himself for letting his dear nephew Caradoc leave him. 'It would have been better for my soul to leave my body,' he said, 'the day that I let him leave, without accompanying him or sending Gawain or Yvain to bring him back! I tell you truly that if God gives me health, I will not sleep in any town more than one night until I have reached my nephew Caradoc.' (10089)

That is the vow which the King made. He rose quickly and set out on his voyage at once. I tell you that he crossed the sea with a sorrowful heart, so anxious about Caradoc that his body and soul grew weak. There was a storm on the sea which delayed him greatly: chased and beaten by a contrary wind, they did not come to Brittany but landed in Normandy instead. The ship arrived in a port called Outreport. The King and his captains left there on horseback and rode along the road without stopping until they came to Brittany. I will leave them there and speak to you about Cador. (10110)

The news about Caradoc came to Cador – who certainly didn't hate him – and to his beautiful sweetheart Guinier in Cornwall. When the girl learned the news, she fell over backwards to the ground. Such anguish struck her heart that she did not know what was happening to her, no more than if she had been killed. Pale and drenched with perspiration, she lay in a faint a good long time before getting up. When she revived from her faint, senseless and irrational, she began to babble and change colour: her heart almost broke. Finally she burst out weeping pitifully and began to curse her father's engendering of her: 'Dear Lord God,' she said, 'You have been cruel to me if You are taking my sweetheart from me. Damn me if I don't resent You for it! Sweet Lord God, if I had seen him just one more time before he died, my faith in You would be twice as great, but now it is very feeble and troubled! Wretch that I am! Vile, infamous Death! Such a fine man you are taking! Why do you wish to take possession of him so soon? You give no pleasure at all, taking my sweetheart from me!' (10145)

She seized her hair with both hands, pulled it and tore at it, then fell fainting to the ground again. Her heart was breaking in her breast. When she came to, she wrung her hands. 'Death,' she said, 'you are wrong to take good people and let the wicked live! Death, Death, you do not love the good: you want to take them when they are at the height of their glory! Why do you wish to take my sweetheart? If you want to take him from me, in God's name, take away my life of torture too! If he dies, may I not escape! That would be just and proper, for never in all my days could I find any comfort after my sweetheart's death. It would be a very good thing, it seems to me, for us to die together. A woman who outlives her sweetheart lives out her life in sorrow, but those who have served true love deserve a reward: to repay us for our pain, God should make us die together!' (10174)

With these words she fainted. When she revived, she behaved as if she were accustomed to tormenting her body with her own hands, as if she wished to pluck out her eyes and to tear out all her hair: it was astonishing how deranged she was! 'Ah God! By Your Holy Name, my Lord, I implore You! Sweet Lord, I plead with You about this diabolical snake, this viper, which is taking my sweetheart's life away. Alas, alas, hideous viper, detach yourself from Caradoc's arm, unlace yourself from my sweetheart's arm, and come attach yourself to me! Alas, my dear sweet brother Cador, take me to Caradoc now, to find out if I can see him before he dies, and die with him, with pleasure!' (10197)

She felt such sorrow and sadness for her sweetheart as I have described to you, and more, I think, than I could describe in a day and a half. Cador felt such great sorrow that his lords and vassals did not know what to do. He had a boat prepared to go to see the man he loved so much, and they took to the sea. He took his sister with him, and they journeyed together until they arrived in Brittany; they travelled over hill and dale until they arrived in Nantes. (10214)

Rumour, which is quick to spread, brought Caradoc the news that King Arthur of Britain was coming with a great company to see him and that Cador and the beautiful Guinier, who loved him more than she could say, were coming from Cornwall to visit him and comfort him in his malady. When he heard this news it made his condition worse. In his great sorrow, he did not know what in the world he could do, but he had those who were around him retire, so that no one was left in that room but himself; he felt so desperate that no one could describe it. (10235)

He spoke to himself bitterly: 'Sweet Lord God,' he said, 'how she will despise me now, the one I cherish most in all the world, when she sees my face and my blackened flesh, and this snake fastened on me! She will be right to do so, for to tell the truth, I'm not worthy of having her as my sweetheart. I never have been. I never will be! Lord God, sweet God, what will I do? How can I survive? How can I bear to have the most beautiful, innocent creature Nature ever made see my great misfortune? Alas! I am tortured horribly, for I do not want what I want! I would be delighted to see my sweetheart in joy and health, but I know that as soon as she sees me she will hold me in disdain. That is why I can not endure it or allow her to see me. I know what I will do: God help me, I will flee! Flee? What have I said? True love forbids me to commit such a base action as to flee from my sweetheart. For if she sees me in a miserable condition and if she feels any true love for me at all, she will never despise me. There is a proverb which says: "One who loves truly is slow to forget." Yet I am afraid, for in the *Dit au Vilain* it says: "You are worth as much as you have and that's how much I love you." Alas, I possess nothing, and so I am worth nothing. That is my lot!' (10280)

Caradoc lay for the whole day with his face turned to the wall. He wished to deceive anyone who wanted to visit him by pretending to sleep. When evening came, King Caradoc came to see him with a courteous messenger, sent to him by Cador the night before. When Caradoc saw the messenger, he hid his thoughts prudently. One should keep plans hidden until the proper time for revealing them, and a man with a mad plan should not make it known: so Caradoc kept quiet. The lad came directly up to him: 'My lord,' he said, 'your companion Cador has set out on the sea with his sister the beautiful Guinier, who loves you more than her own heart. I tell you, she sends you her greetings. Tomorrow, before noon – or at noon at the latest, if she is not mistaken – you will see your sweetheart Guinier here, and your companion Cador. He would give you his weight in gold – all that he possesses! – so that your good health might again be a subject for rejoicing and songs. And so it will be, you may be sure of it!' (10313)

'Dear friend, my sweetheart and my companion are most welcome! Alas, how wretched I am that I cannot come to meet them!' (10317)

With that he fell silent. Thinking about his disease made him grow pale; when he thought about his sweetheart, all his limbs trembled with anguish. When he remembered his love, such sorrow came to his heart that it was obvious from his appearance. Death almost took away his heart, failing to do so only out of fear of being blamed. Nevertheless Caradoc fainted. What great blame Death would have if Caradoc died for love! Love was so bitter to him and caused him such suffering! Love made him desire to see his sweetheart, and his fear also came from love, for he was afraid to display his love for her openly. It often happens that a man fears what he loves: that is what happened to Caradoc, who wanted to see the beautiful Guinier, and along with this desire was terrified at the very idea of seeing her. He was afraid that if she saw him in such a wretched condition, she would recoil at the sight. That fear bothered him so much that he decided, wisely or foolishly, to flee. He thought that there was nothing to gain by waiting for his sweetheart in the state he was in. (10350)

He turned back to the messenger: 'My friend,' he said, 'you have brought me comforting news, telling me I can be sure that the maiden will not despise me when she sees the wicked snake lying beside me: but I do not know how that could be possible. Truly, I detest my own state. In this combat with death, I would certainly rather be dead than alive. My lord, in the name of God,' he said to the King, 'see to this messenger's needs and comfort. Leave me one servant, for it is neither good nor proper that I should be with any more people. Let me rest alone and take counsel with myself. In my sickness I have no desire for a crowd, and these people pressing around me are killing me.' Before the King there stood a page who had come from England with Caradoc. 'I pray you,' he said, 'let this lad stay here with me, and you go off and eat.' (10378)

'You must eat also! (10378)

'I will not. Leave now, and I will rest.' (10380)

The King went away to eat, taking the messenger with him. When they had eaten at their leisure, they went to bed, I tell you, for they did not want to tire Caradoc any more or keep him awake. Leaving the page with him, all the men and women went to bed; but whether they slept or not, I tell you truly that Caradoc did not sleep, but called to his page: 'My friend, do not be upset or astonished if I make you my counsellor and put so much faith in you. I'm far from confident in my own health now, for I have none, and so I wish to entrust myself to you. Keep my plans secret once they have been revealed to you. There is a chapel nearby where a hermit leads a holy life praying to God. I am eager to go to see him. Dear friend, do not be upset, but I want to go there this very night, for I believe that when he has prayed for me this cruel snake cannot stay attached to my body, but will be forced to depart. It is this holy man's custom never to leave his bed, no matter what the need might be. Take with you all the wealth that you brought from England: do not look for any more.' (10416)

'My lord, I am just the one to do everything you please: I am ready to follow your orders.' (10420)

When they were ready, they opened a door to an enclosed garden with high walls. They searched all around, but could not find a gate, so they spent the night digging a hole and went out. When they were outside, I tell you that Caradoc was soon able to find all the back roads and hidden paths of the country. He was very sad and pensive, and I tell you that because of his shame he would not have turned back for a thousand pieces of gold: if he stayed there, his sweetheart would come to visit him. He followed the road until he arrived at the house of the virtuous hermit in a deep forest. In front of them as far as the hermitage, there was nothing but forest. I do not know the name of the hermit or of the hermitage. You could have seen so many wild beasts, great and small, assembled there that if someone gave you a truthful description you would consider it a lie. (10447)

Caradoc went straight there and entered the chapel. The hermit called him amiably and greeted him, and Caradoc returned his greeting politely. Then he made a short prayer, because the serpent was causing him dreadful pain. When he had prayed, they sat down at once. Caradoc was exhausted by his voyage: the soles of his feet caused him great pain because he had come all the way from Nantes and was not accustomed to walking. The holy man spoke to him and asked him his name, then where he was born and what he was seeking. Caradoc told the hermit his name, recounted the whole story, and made his confession to him. Then he showed him the great burden of the serpent and explained the whole situation to him, how the serpent had caught him by surprise, through the trick of his father and mother. He humbled himself before the hermit, accused himself and blamed himself, declaring that he was guilty towards his father and that he had greatly sinned towards his mother. He said that he deserved to suffer even more, and that was why he had fled: he did not ever want to have any joy or pleasure until he was certain that he had done penance for the pain he had caused them. He was weeping and sighing from the bottom of his heart. 'Certainly,' he said, 'I am the worst man who ever walked the earth!' (10487)

His sorrow was so great that he fell to the ground. The good man saw his remorse, imposed a penance on him, and gave him absolution because of his true compunction.* Then Caradoc asked him in God's Holy Name not to answer anyone who came to look for him and not to reveal that he had ever seen him. I tell you that Caradoc spent a long time staying in those woods with the holy man in the hermitage. This holy life pleased him and he did penance. The hermit generously shared what food he had with him and procured other food for him from dwellings he knew in the neighbourhood: Caradoc could not have lived as poor a life as the holy man, since he had not learned how. Because he lived apart from all people, the good man had a servant who used to follow all his orders discreetly. And Caradoc had his own servant, who did whatever he knew his master wanted, without contradicting him in anything. This is the kind of life Caradoc led: as penance, he ate moderately and would fast three days each week. So they lived for a long time without being discovered. The hermit was clever: the hermitage was by ten or twelve leagues from Nantes, separated from it by a forest with narrow paths, and the nearest habitation was at least four leagues away. (10534)

That is enough about Caradoc now, who was enclosed with the hermit and enduring a harsh and austere life with him. The story returns to King Arthur who had crossed the sea with a great number of his people to see Caradoc, for he was most disturbed by his torments. When King Caradoc learned that he was coming, he was joyful about it. Arthur's messenger had ridden all night, for he had gone astray, turning this way and that, after leaving King Arthur at Mont Saint Michel the previous morning. He had in his hand a letter which Arthur sent to the King of Vannes, saying that he was coming to his country to see his dear friend Caradoc because he had heard about the snake hanging on his right arm and was very troubled about it. (10559)

The messenger arrived in Nantes at daybreak, quite exhausted. The King had risen early, full of sorrow and anxiety. The messenger appeared before the King, greeted him and gave him the letter. The King began to read the letter, and when he had read it he ordered his horse to be saddled, saying that he wanted to go to meet King Arthur. Then he went straight to the room where he thought Caradoc was sleeping and resting, for he wanted to tell him the news. He came to the door and called Caradoc. When he realized that no one said anything to him, he did nothing more because he loved Caradoc and thought that he was sleeping. He went to his horse and mounted it, accompanied by more noble and important people than I can say. They went to welcome their lord joyously: for King Arthur was lord over them and all the empire. On both sides of the sea, no one would have dared claim lordship of a land if he had not received it from Arthur and had not served him as he should. Everyone went to meet him, and after having gone down a hill and climbed up a mountain, they found Arthur of Britain. (10592)

As soon as they were near, they rushed towards each other, laughing and crying at the same time. They laughed in their customary joy and cried in great sadness. This often happens when friends see each other in times of sorrow and trial: sadness and affliction increase. That is what happened here, for when they saw each other they began to cry before they could speak to each other – but if they had known more about it, they would have wept even more. If they had known what awaited them, there would have been no joy or merriment. But no one knew anything, not even Caradoc's beautiful sweetheart Guinier or her brother Cador, who were coming to see Caradoc. (10612)

They arrived in Nantes early in the morning to a sad situation. They were welcomed with great honour. Alas, how they were deceived! They were not to find what they were seeking. They asked immediately how Caradoc was and where he was resting. They were taken to his room, but the door was tightly closed; when they left the room, Caradoc and his page had closed it from the inside. The beautiful Guinier approached first and called at the door: 'My friend,' she said, 'open your door. Since I do not find you outside, open it, and your sweetheart will come in and see you. It is not courtly to hide yourself when you hear your sweetheart calling you. Open, open, dear, sweet friend! You have made me mad with worry. Since I learned of your misfortune, I have not felt any joy or pleasure.' (10636)

When she saw that he would not open it and that she would not see her sweetheart – who could nevertheless trust her completely – she began to call out more loudly: 'Dear, sweet friend, what wrong have I done to deserve this torment? Should you hide from me? I will have it opened with the King's key, so help me God, the King of Heaven! I do not know what can be happening: I am sure that if he were alive and not in paradise, and he heard me knocking at his door – how happy that would make me! – nothing would stop him from coming to see me. I am afraid that he is dead! Dear brother, is this door so solid that no one can do anything about it?' (10655)

She kept trying until she found a way to open the door, and they saw clearly that Caradoc was not there. They soon discovered the door opening into the garden and began to search it from top to bottom and examine the wall surrounding the house, spurred on by their anguish. But 'if you find nothing you catch nothing', and no matter what they did they couldn't find anything but the hole Caradoc had gone through. In vain they lamented that he had escaped them forever. If they want to find him, they will have to look farther away! They were all distraught at not finding him. Every one of them was shocked and distressed because of Caradoc. (10675)

'Alas, alas, my sweetheart, alas!' said the beautiful Guinier, 'How could you imagine that you would deceive me? How could you dream of fleeing without me? No, it is not possible! I believe you fled because you plan to die without me. Fleeing will not accomplish anything, certainly, for I know full well that I will not survive you on this earth for even a day. You should not have fled from me! As soon as the snake had seized you, you should have sent a messenger asking me to come: then I would have shared in your misfortune. For I know truly that a burden is lighter for two people than for one alone.' (10695)

Her lamentations broke out again: 'Alas, poor me, why was I born? My sweetheart turns his back on me and flees from me! I should surely be burned and consumed alive in fire, for now I am positive that he fled only because he could not bear to hear me weeping and lamenting in front of him. That is why he did not dare to stay. Wretched me! He is going away now, taking my heart! If he dies, then I am dead, for I could not live without my heart, and if he dies, I will die too! So God will have shown us His favour!' (10711)

Consider now, you who are in love, whether there is still such love in the world. Surely not! Instead, a very different kind of love prevails. One woman loves a man for the gifts he gives: such love is repayment, not natural love. Another woman doesn't care about gifts, but loves a man for his beauty. There is disloyalty here also, for when she sees a more handsome man, she soon has a new sweetheart! I'll give you another example: a woman loves a man because he serves her, and when the service stops love also comes to an end. (10728)

Now I will speak about men, for I don't intend to leave them out. It is a man's way to inflame a woman with his fancy talk, and when he finds a silly woman he beguiles her by his tricks, deludes her, confuses her, despoils her and then chases her away – and then he sets out after another! Those who use such trickery give love a bad name. There are men who are inconstant and only out for what they can get, who are in love – for a moment! – beyond all reason and measure. If they don't get what they want, what sorrow! Their love turns to bitterness and they start to show hatred for what they used to love! And when they do get what they want, that causes sorrow too. As soon as they find someone to tell it to, they tell it! Love that begins and ends like that is not true love. The one who loves truly ought to take responsibility for all the consequences. Let him be careful that love finds no place for pride in him. And if love grants all his joy, let him keep the secret at all costs: as soon as love is flaunted, it is betrayed. (10764)

You who are loyal lovers, I commend you to the Lord in Heaven; I consign those who mock true love to burn in Hell. But Caradoc and his sweetheart Guinier do not belong there. Everything one could expect of true lovers was found in them, and each of them burned with love. Hear now what pleasures they had: one cried and the other fled, but the one who fled suffered for the one who remained behind. And do you think that she felt no pain, staying alone after he fled? I assure you that nothing could separate their hearts. Although one fled and the other remained behind, they stayed together: Caradoc stayed with Guinier and Guinier was with him in the woods. (10786)

King Arthur was in Nantes when he learned of this sorrow; but before he got there, a messenger came to him and announced that Caradoc had turned away from them and fled, and no one knew where he had gone. When the King heard this news, you may be sure that he was not pleased. If he felt sorrow before, now it was even greater. 'By Our Lord God,' he said, 'my sorrow is more than I can say! I do not know where to go. Ah, God! What do I want in Nantes if I cannot see my nephew there? Tell me now, my boy, is this really the truth? Take care not to deceive me.' (10804)

'I'm telling you the truth, my lord, I swear it by my eyes! Come and see, and you will believe it!' (10806)

The King went to Nantes; he did not find his nephew there, but he did find his sweetheart Guinier, quite despondent and eagerly calling for death. I tell you that they did not delay but went off at once in search of Caradoc. There was not a single castle or village, plain or wood in the whole region where they did not search for Caradoc. They even went to the hermitage where he was, but they did not discover him because he was so careful. In order not to be recognized, he had put on a long, wide, sleeveless cape which belonged to the hermit. He was wearing a white tunic and had covered his head with the hood, so that no one could see his face. He had put on rustic shoes and was wearing a cape. That time, he escaped by his precautions and his trick, and they did not recognize him at all. (10830)

Why should I make a long story of it for you? King Arthur, the counts, the lords, the castellans, princes and captains searched all Brittany. They searched thoroughly, but they did not find Caradoc, and his uncle felt great sorrow. Touraine, Anjou, Poitou, Maine, Normandy, Île-de-France, Burgundy, Germany, Saxony – they searched for him in all the countries on this side of the sea. Worn out by their searching, they crossed the sea and searched the land to the end of England. They were very sad when they couldn't find him. The King was so distraught that he wanted to die; he felt more pain than the others, and, after him, Sir Gawain, Yvain, Tor the son of Arés and all the King's household. For the King's sake and because they had not found Caradoc, they took up residence in Cardigan after their search. During their stay there, the King and all his companions felt such sorrow for Caradoc that it is surprising that life remained in their bodies. But when they could endure it no longer and weren't accomplishing anything by their grief, they gave it up and dispersed throughout the country, convinced that they could do nothing and tired of living in sadness. So they lived for two years and more, and no one heard anything of Caradoc. No one could learn any news about him. (10871)

As for Cador, I tell you truly, he searched many countries for his friend Caradoc, accompanied by his sister in his quest. He searched all over Brittany, then he crossed into Cornwall. Then, I tell you truly, though the others were exhausted with searching, Cador went on the road alone. He left his sister in Cornwall in great honour. Then, he explored England, Ireland, Wales, and Northumberland; from there he crossed to Spain and came straight back to Brittany. By the time he had looked everywhere with no reward but pain and fatigue, Cador had spent more than two years searching for Caradoc without resting. He swore again that he would never be disloyal to Caradoc and that he would stay faithful to him forever; he would not stop until he found him, wherever he might be. Do you know how he said this and how he spoke to the people in the countries where he was looking for Caradoc? 'In the name of God, dear people, have you seen a man with a snake attached tightly around his arm?' All those who heard this commended themselves to God and cried out: 'God have mercy, we have never seen him here and there is no trace of him in this country!' (10909)

That is the life which Cador led for the sake of his companion Caradoc. Caradoc lived on nothing more than grain, for that summer he had left the hermit with whom he had been living. He had gone in search of holy men, exploring the wilderness and eating raw grain. This harsh life was his penance. The snake tormented him, sucking away his flesh and blood. Do not believe that I am joking, but he was so oppressed, so feeble and emaciated that if Cador had seen him he would scarcely have recognized him, for Caradoc could hardly walk. Finally, he took up residence in a thicket in a wood near an agreeable hermitage. Many good people lived there, serving Our Lord in a church. The church was small and beautiful, on the bank of a small stream which flowed through a valley. Few people came there. The place was beautiful and solitary: God was well honoured there. (10940)

In a thicket in this wood Caradoc took up residence and lived there, awaiting his fate until his life might end. He did not expect any other remedy: he lived on nothing but roots, and went to drink at the stream. Each day of the week he went to God's chapel by a narrow path to pray and hear the holy service. The good men, out of generosity and for the love of the Creator, nourished him most sweetly and clothed him like themselves. They saw clearly the evil snake which was strangling his arm and heard the complaints of the poor man who endured such bitter penance. After eating a little, Caradoc would return to his thicket, not expecting any other solace except that God might send death to him. (10966)

Cador had searched for him through many a land and did not know where to go, when by chance he arrived at the hermitage where good Caradoc was living. I tell you that he spent the night there. Cador asked them for hospitality and they welcomed him. For food, they gave him what they had, and then Cador asked them if they knew or if they had ever seen or met a noble man who wore a vicious snake attached to his arm which was killing him cruelly. (10981)

'Dear lord,' said one of them, 'he comes around here every day! You will see him here tomorrow when he comes to hear mass.' (10985)

Cador was filled with joy! 'Tell me, dear sir, is he a tall, dark man?' (10987)

'That is correct, my dear friend. He was of a goodly size when he was in good health, but now he is in such a sorrowful state that he is nothing but skin and bones. But I do not know his name.' (10992)

Cador was overjoyed. He went to lie down, I tell you. How do you think he passed that long night? He made no complaints about the bed, though he found no comfort in it. The good men treated him as well as they could. So the night passed and finally it was day. Cador didn't stop searching for what he wanted, and Caradoc came without delay to the church in the morning. In order to watch for him, Cador stood in a corner where no one could see him, so that Caradoc would not be afraid of anything before he came into the church and Cador took him in his arms. Caradoc, who suspected nothing since he mistrusted no one, entered the church fearlessly and began to pray sweetly to God. Cador saw him and did not recognize him, but still decided to approach him. Caradoc began to pray and Cador leapt forward and spoke to him thus: 'God help me! Brother, brother, who could have shown you this abbey? Many times, in order to find you, I have covered my feet and legs in blood looking for you. I explored so many countries that I became exhausted; it has been at least two years, I think, since I saw you, my dear friend. Who put you in that habit? He must have loved you very little in order to clothe you in such garments!' (11030)

Caradoc was wearing two tunics and large shoes on his feet and was wrapped in a cape. Cador looked at him and wept with pity for him. But you may be sure that on the other hand he was full of joy because he had completed a voyage which he never would have ended before he found Caradoc. Why make a long story of it? Caradoc was so ashamed when he saw his companion Cador that even if someone had given him a valley full of gold – or the entire world – he would not have spoken a word. He lowered his hood and lay down on the ground by the chapel. Cador approached him, raised him up, and kissed him. 'My friend,' he said, 'you have suffered greatly for a long time because of the snake which is rending and destroying your body. Do not deny it. You have no need to hide it. We are in a church: do not disguise the truth, but tell me why you were so foolish as to leave your country. And Guinier, your beautiful sweetheart, why have you abandoned her?' (11064)

Caradoc sighed and began to weep when he heard Guinier's

name. 'Dear friend, it is because I was afraid that she might scorn me and be harsh to me when she saw my misfortune. I fled because I would rather be dead. I want nothing else, for my life is not worth anything.' (11074)

Such weeping and sighing you could have seen then! Caradoc's anguish moved Cador greatly. He begged Caradoc, but he refused; he approached him, but Caradoc pushed him away. No matter how often Cador came forward, Caradoc would not let himself be embraced. That is how they acted, one with the other, until they began to cry out in sorrow, and all the good men ran up. The conclusion of the discussion was that Caradoc would not leave that place, not for friendship or prayers, not for God or His beloved mother, not in the name of the apostles or the martyrs. When Cador saw that he could not accomplish anything and would have to leave Caradoc and occupy himself with other business, he implored and instructed the good men to take care of Caradoc and to provide him with food him according to his needs. 'And I promise you truly that you will be well rewarded for everything you give to him.' With that, he left his companion in the house with them. (11102)

Cador went to Nantes and found Caradoc's mother, for she hardly ever went away from there. He came to her, greeted her, and then blamed and reproached her for not caring about her son whom she cruelly allowed to suffer for so long: 'Wise or foolish, everyone says, my lady, that it is because of your wickedness and by your own actions that the snake seized his arm. Everyone accuses you and blames you. But I want to tell you one thing: you could easily recover your reputation by delivering him. A mother ought to correct her child by punishing him, and when she has beaten him she ought to think about easing his pain. She should not let him suffer but she ought to think about comforting him. After punishing him, she ought to draw him to her tenderly.' (11126)

The lady understood that Cador was speaking on Caradoc's behalf, but nevertheless she pretended that she had not understood: 'My friend Cador, come, explain to me what you are concerned about.' (11131)

'My lady, I will not be silent about it: I have spoken on behalf of Caradoc whom you have abandoned. A mother must be cruel and insensitive indeed to allow her child to suffer grievously when she can rescue him. May God never allow such a woman to enter Paradise!' (11139)

'Tell me, is Caradoc still alive?' (11140)

'Yes, certainly, he is alive, my lady.' (11141)

'By my soul, I never knew that he was alive! I thought he was dead, and I reproached myself for it. Great blame would come to me, and anyone who heard that my son was dying in such torment would consider me very cruel, if I had the power to cure him. Come back tomorrow and I will tell you if he can be cured or if he will die of it.' (11152)

Then Cador left the lady and waited for the next day, until he saw it was time to go and speak with the Queen. He came before her; she summoned him and took him into a chapel in a part of the house where they were alone. 'Cador,' she said, 'I feel great pain in my heart for the sake of my child; because I have pity for him, I tell you that I have managed to find a way for him to be cured.' (11165)

'My lady,' he said, 'we shall soon see.' (11166)

'By my faith,' she said, 'I do not think it is easy to find the way to cure him. But I tell you that if anyone could find a maiden who could be proven equal to Caradoc in nobility and in beauty and who would love him as much as her own body, he could then take two tubs, not too big or too small, and place them side by side exactly three feet apart during a full moon. One of the tubs should be full of vinegar, the other full of milk. When this has been done, Caradoc, who is so thin and eaten away, should enter the vinegar; at once, without hesitation or repugnance, the maiden should enter the milk and rest her right breast on the edge of the tub. Then she should conjure the serpent to leave her sweetheart and fasten on to her breast. When it hears the maiden conjuring it and feels the vinegar, and when the white and tender maiden offers her breast to it, I tell you that the snake will leap. A man who had a drawn sword could kill the snake on the spot before it drew back, if he dared to strike. I tell you Caradoc cannot be delivered from the viper any other way. But if you can do this, you can prove the truth of it.' (11208)

That is the advice which the lady gave, but she didn't say a word about where the plan came from. The truth was that the devil Eliavrés had come that night to visit the lady. When they were in bed, with great joy and pleasure, the lady said: 'My sweetheart, I am very afraid that my soul may be cruelly damned because of the hideous destruction we have brought upon our son, all because of my wickedness! I pray you, see if you can find a way and teach me how the snake which has bled him so horribly can be removed from him.' (11227)

Then Eliavrés told her the plan you have heard. 'My lady,' he said, 'do you know what? So help me God, the Great King, he had only three more months and it would have been his time to die: no one could have protected him from it.' And so you have learned where the plan the lady gave to Cador came from.* (11237)

Cador took his leave and went to find Caradoc and comfort him. He brought good news to him, and told him faultlessly how he could be cured. 'Companion,' he said, 'stay here in joy and hope. I will go and see what advice I can get from your dear sweetheart Guinier. I believe that she will not fail to risk her body for you.' (11249)

With that, Cador went away. He left Caradoc with the good men in the garden of the abbey. He asked them to protect him and serve him so well that he might lack nothing that he needed or wanted. 'For I will return soon,' he said, 'and I will reward you for it generously.' (11258)

With that, the faithful companion went away. He arrived at the sea, embarked, and crossed directly to Cornwall. There he found his sister, the unhappy Guinier, who was leading a harsh existence. When she saw him, she was eager to learn the truth. The beautiful maiden rejoiced greatly to see him again in good health, and he told her the news which lifted her spirits: 'Dear sister,' he said, 'I have found what you love most in all the world.' (11271)

'Found him? My lord, you are mocking me!' (11272)

'No, I assure you, my sister, I would not mock you for anything: I have found Caradoc.' (11275)

'Dear brother, where?' (11275)

'My sister, in a wood where he is living on grains and roots; he cannot find any remedy, dear sister, unless he gets it through you.' (11279)

'Through me? How?' (11279)

He told her. He revealed the plan to her, telling her how she could deliver her sweetheart from the wicked snake if she was willing to risk her body for him. (11284)

'Certainly,' she said, 'I will risk my body and I will deliver him, for I remember very well how he risked his body for the sake of mine.' (11288)

They did not delay very long: the next morning at daybreak they prepared themselves, went straight to the sea and crossed over to Brittany. In the forest, they found a forked road and followed the branch which led them to the abbey. One must admire such a companion, who endured great pain and suffering for his friend, and such a sweetheart, who gave such a gift as her own body for her sweetheart. God would be very unmerciful indeed if He did not reward her truly, this woman who gives herself up to such torment and harsh tortures for her sweetheart! It is a very difficult thing to endure death for one's sweetheart! For woman is tender and weak in the face of such a thing as death: Guinier had nothing of the woman in her, but possessed more virtue than I could tell you. (11313)

They ought to be full of shame and confusion, those false lovers, who do not know what love really is! One who is willing to serve love, even if he has no joy, will never fail: no one serves love in vain, without receiving a fine reward. But do you know what false lovers do? They show a false appearance of love; if love is put to the test, true love can be recognized. Love is able to unmask deceitful people, and those who are loyal to it acknowledge the great reward they receive. But these two, who endured so much pain for it, were never false to love. (11330)

They went to the abbey, out of love and companionship. As soon as they were seen, they were received in fine style. The good men took great pains to honour them and led them into the church. When Caradoc saw Guinier, his rosy-cheeked sweetheart, he felt such joy that he did not know what to do. He began to weep for joy and to show his joy as he wept. Shame prompted him to hide himself, but true love commanded him to rejoice ceaselessly because of the girl: that is the compromise he came to. The strife was ended; not for anyone would he have failed to get up and go to meet her as quickly as he could, though he was grievously afflicted. Once he was standing, I tell you that he appeared tall, thin and pale. He was wearing three large, ugly, dirty robes, like a hermit. On his feet he wore large shoes with no spurs, and his head was covered with two capes to protect himself from the cold. He was deformed and hideous: his forehead was flat and his eyes were sunken, his skin was stretched on his bones, his nose was pointy and his cheeks were high, his face was drawn and his voice was hoarse. His beard – flecked with dirt – stretched as far as his belt, and his long, matted hair fell down to his sides: his whole body, to tell the truth, was so dry that it could have been set on fire, because the snake he bore clamped on his arm had drawn so much out of him and because of lack of food. Through treachery, he had lost all the strength and beauty Nature had put in him. (11378)

Caradoc approached his sweetheart. When he saw her, he forgot the torment he had suffered for so long. I could not imagine the joy they experienced, for no one who has ever seen the joy two lovers feel could describe it. But I can tell you one thing: despite the blackness of his face, despite his beard and his hair, the girl felt no disgust, but kissed him tenderly and hugged him tightly. Why should I delay, since I cannot describe even half of the joy or sorrow which they both felt because of love? They felt great mutual joy and also great sorrow, it seems to me, because of the suffering and torment one had to inflict on the other. Caradoc was distraught for the sake of his sweetheart, who was willing to give up her body to torture to deliver him from the snake. (11404)

'My friend,' she said, 'do not be afraid. I have come here to help you, by Saint Peter the Apostle, and to risk my body for yours. There is nothing more to do but make the preparations!' (11409)

Caradoc tried to dissuade her: 'That must not happen,' he said, 'I would prefer to die all alone, rather than have you die with me,' (11413)

'Dear friend, by the faith which I owe to God the Celestial King, that is impossible! I could not endure seeing you die when I could cure you – either that or I myself will die with you. My heart would be too sad if I survived you. If you die, I will die also: I could never live without you.' (11424)

For his part, Cador kissed and embraced his companion and spoke: 'My friend,' he said, 'she is my sister, and I would not want either her or you to die, not for anything! Do only this much, to save yourself from death: I implore you and I beg you to agree to this. You will see two tubs; you will enter one of them, completely naked. Your sweetheart will enter the other and will conjure the snake. The wicked beast will jump to her, and as it jumps I will cut off its head: so will I deliver you and see you freed.' (11440)

Guinier said to Caradoc: 'Do as Cador tells you!' (11442)

'I won't!' (11443)

'You will!' (11443)

'I would rather die!' (11444)

'You will not die, so help me God in glory! I will never do anything for you if you do not do this for me.' (11447)

'Then look after everything, my dear; prepare everything necessary; but you may be sure that if you die to cure me, I must die for you. For in truth, I would hate any life I might have because of the death of my sweetheart.' (11454)

When Cador heard Caradoc's agreement, he looked for tubs and had them filled, one with vinegar, the other with milk. He had his sister go quickly into the milk, completely naked, and the maiden rested her breast on the edge of the tub. The other tub was placed exactly three feet away, and filled with clear vinegar free from all impurities. The valiant Caradoc entered it, and plunged his body into it as far as the neck, so that the snake was in the tub of vinegar. It did not like that at all, and almost left. As for the maiden, hear what she said and how she conjured the evil snake: 'Look now at my breasts, how white they are, and tender and beautiful. Look at my white chest, whiter than the flower of the hawthorn. Think about it: that wine is bitter, and Caradoc is so thin that there is nothing more to take from him. Do not let yourself be mistreated by him. You'd be wise to leave there. Come and attach yourself to me. I conjure you, come on, snake, in the name of Almighty God, detach yourself from my sweetheart's arm and hang on my breast. For I am white, I am plump and tender: with me you will have something to look forward to.' (11490)

For their part, the holy hermits recited a mass of the Holy Spirit with great devotion. Carrying the reliquaries in a grand procession, they came to where the maiden was conjuring and imploring the snake. They made their prayer to God to destroy the cruel snake without delay so that it would not harm either one of them. As for the snake, the vinegar was biting and burning it. It saw the milk and the maiden who was conjuring and calling to it; it could find nothing more in Caradoc to suck out. It unwrapped itself from him and jumped: it threw itself on the maiden's right breast. But behind her was her brother, his sword drawn in his hand. He struck the serpent skilfully and cut off its head. But with the same blow he cut off the tip of his sister's breast which the snake had bitten. Along with the snake's head he cut off the end of her nipple.* The snake fell to the ground; Cador rushed at it and cut it in pieces, fully avenging his companion. I tell you that Caradoc leaped out of the tub at once, very worried about the maiden who was wounded in the breast and very happy to feel himself liberated and delivered from the viper. Cador saw this and embraced him. He was so joyful he didn't know what to do, and Caradoc was so happy that he kissed him repeatedly. Caradoc rushed towards Guinier and embraced the beautiful maiden as she wept. Cador took her out of the tub, completely naked, and dressed her in beautiful precious clothing. Caradoc put on his clothes again – but not the poor and vile clothes which the hermits had lent him! They brought him other garments much more precious and more beautiful. (11543)

The hermits and the young lords cared for the maiden and dressed her breast. There was a holy hermit there who knew about medicine. He applied a poultice which healed her, and purged Caradoc of all the venom the snake had spread in him while it had been attached to him. They bathed and cared for Caradoc and Guinier, looking after them so well that in a week they were cured. How could Caradoc be unwell now that he was kissing and embracing the one he loved? But nothing could return to Guinier the tip of her breast. Caradoc lived a good life, enjoying himself with his sweetheart, and Guinier had everything that she wanted, now that she held her sweetheart in her arms. They enjoyed themselves in love and tenderness, without any impropriety. (11568)

Caradoc rubbed his body, had himself shaved, washed and combed, and I can tell you truly that there was such virtue in him that in less than a month he had recovered from the evil which the serpent had done to him. Only a single trace remained: where it had seized him, I tell you, the bone was twice as large, and because of the size of that arm, he had the name Caradoc

'Briebras'.* The snake had left a mark on his arm, but he was no weaker because of it. Cador had food brought from the lands around, and so they lived a pleasant existence there. (11585)

The news about them spread throughout the land until King Caradoc heard it, to his astonishment. He travelled through the forest until it happened that he came to the hermitage where Caradoc Briebras was living. When he saw him coming in the distance, Caradoc did not flee, but rushed to meet him, took him in his arms tenderly, and kissed and embraced him. (11598)

Everyone who was with the King rejoiced with Caradoc and with his golden-haired sweetheart and his companion Cador. They showed such joy for him that I could not describe it to you today, and I do not wish to delay over it. The King asked them to prepare themselves, and when they were ready they didn't remain there very long. But I tell you that when they left they endowed the hermitage so well that there was no abbey so rich in Brittany. For love of Caradoc, they gave it so much silver and gold, revenues, lands and fiefs that there was no more comfortable abbey in the world. Then they turned towards a hill called Carantin. (11618)

Why make a long story of it? All the barons and counts of Normandy, Brittany, Anjou, Poitou and Germany were so thrilled and joyful when they heard this news that none of them remained in city, town, manor, castle or fortress, unless because of sickness: not one of them relaxed or rested until he had seen Caradoc. There was such a crowd to see him that they didn't even let him sit down in peace: he had to stand up for each noble man who came! I tell you, he was so tired that he couldn't endure it any more. He escaped the crowd by night and went elsewhere: the snake which he had carried had so exhausted and enfeebled him that he could not endure great effort. The King showed great honour to Cador and his sister, and rode personally by her side. They rode straight to Nantes, for good Caradoc wanted to see his mother again: she had been a prisoner such a long time because of her misdeeds. She had been enclosed in the tower of Bofois, but then her son delivered her from it. Prostrating himself in front of her, he implored her humbly to pardon him for the great wrong which he had done her. She pardoned him for his misdeed and finally he arranged it that she would not be enclosed in the tower, but could go anywhere she wanted, on foot or on horseback. But by this I do not mean to say that afterwards she was anyone else's sweetheart or that she loved another man besides the King. I will speak no more about her for I have too many other things to say. (11665)

Caradoc did not rest at all, but went in great haste to see King Arthur. King Caradoc was also very eager to do that, so they decided to cross the sea. They arrived in England and did not have to go far to find the court, for King Arthur already knew that Caradoc had been found and that he was healthy and strong, and was rushing to see him: when he learned that Caradoc had crossed the sea, he felt more joy than any other day of his life! He was so eager to see him that he said he wouldn't stop travelling until he found him. They journeyed until they met, and when they recognized each other, they hurried towards each other; they rushed joyously to meet one another as fast as their horses could go. (11688)

No man in all the world could describe to you the great joy they felt when they met. All the people of the King's chosen retinue rushed there as best they could, weeping with joy. I tell you that they consoled themselves for the sadness they had felt: as great as the sorrow had been, the relief was even greater. It often happens that a great pain is the source of a great joy. I do not wish to use my skill to amplify the descriptions of their joy, for that could result in great shame. Nevertheless I tell you briefly that they stayed a long time with the good King in England. Valiant and brave warriors went in quest of adventures. Caradoc Briebras, I tell you, found many adventures where he proved his great valour. When his lord Caradoc of Vannes died, he left his kingdom to him as his heir. But before his death, I tell you truly, he summoned him to invest him with the kingdom in the presence of King Arthur, who was in full agreement. (11719)

But Caradoc answered in these words: 'Dear Lord,' he said, 'my well-beloved lord, my dear friend, I told you a long time ago that I was not your son. I am very sad that you are not my father, I assure you. So I wish to say something to you: I have no desire to possess the land or the riches of another. I certainly do not want to have a land unless I conquer it, for anyone who heard that I enjoy the rights of another would consider it dishonourable.' (11734)

These are the words he spoke and how he refused it; nevertheless, after some difficulty, he accepted the land in front of King Arthur – a fine windfall! King Caradoc, who had had enough of living, died. They buried him with great honour the same day. Caradoc Briebras showed great sorrow during the next forty days: King Caradoc, according to my calculations, died at the beginning of Lent. Then King Arthur announced that he would hold his court at Nantes for the feast of Rogations. (11749)

On that day so many people assembled that I could not number them all, and I do not even want to try. When they heard the King's summons and declaration that he wanted to crown Caradoc, they came from all over without delay. People of all occupations and arts came to serve the court and earn a reward. Knights, ladies, and maidens all assembled there, ugly and beautiful. Cador of Cornwall's sister, the beautiful Guinier, was there without fail, for Caradoc would not have wanted to be crowned without her for anything. She was his sweetheart and he was hers, and they had risked their bodies for each other in a deadly adventure. It is therefore just and proper that they should enjoy happiness together, and so they will, I am sure! (11772)

When day broke, Caradoc was richly dressed and looked most handsome. He wore a silken robe, subtly embroidered in gold with little doves, and a tunic and mantle over it. I tell you that he was so handsome and elegant that he captivated everyone. The ladies bathed Guinier, washed and combed her hair, and all of them took care to arrange her head-dress becomingly. Over her ermine dress they put on a mantle made of the same cloth as Caradoc Briebras wore. I tell you that her mantle was trimmed with fur and very beautiful. Its border was of sable, and the mantle itself was set with two precious stones; they had such power that no one who wore them could be hated by anyone, but on the contrary would find love and delight from everyone. The ladies prepared the beautiful Guinier, the King led her to the church, holding her by the hand, you may be sure, and on the other side Sir Gawain escorted the gracious maiden. Blushing with embarrassment, she was so charming that anyone who saw her would have thought that she had been made to steal their hearts away. (11804)

Caradoc was very handsome: I tell you truly that his appearance was very different from when he was in the forest. The lesser people said that he did not resemble a hermit at all! The chapel was very near. A bishop put on his vestments with great devotion to unite Caradoc with his sweetheart. You will never find anyone who could even tell you about anyone who ever witnessed the marriage of two people so well matched in appearance and deportment. Everyone said truly that God had made them for each other. They were united in marriage, and then they were blessed and anointed. (11824)

He was King and she was Queen, and the King put a costly crown on the girl's head. A very precious stone called an onyx, which comes from the river of Paradise, stood on the front of the crown. In the space below, there was a huge sapphire, and then a topaz, sapphires, jaspers, onyxes, precious emeralds, amethysts, jacinths, chrysolites, carbuncles and beryls. There were also many worthy and venerable relics. No one ever saw such a rich crown on the head of a king or anyone else. I tell you, without a word of a lie, that it was made completely of pure gold. The reliquary had been piously encased in gold and ornamented above with the gems I have told you about, the choicest of all. It would become tiresome for you, I think, if anyone described the crown in more detail. King Arthur placed it on the head of his niece, the beautiful Guinier, who had no need of any instruction. Then he crowned his nephew Caradoc with a golden crown so splendid that its value could not be calculated. (11862)

Everyone said that no one had ever seen such a magnificent coronation. After the reading of the Gospel and the singing of the Credo, the people pressed around the altar with such offerings in such numbers that the clerks grew tired of arranging everything that was brought. When the services were finished in all the principal churches, they went to the court to eat, and were served unsparingly. I do not know what more to say or how to make the story longer, for even a list could become tiresome. When they were finished eating and drinking, the eager young knights went out to joust and the others turned to games of chess or checkers. (11885)

But day does not last forever, and so it proceeded until night came. The day had seemed too long to Caradoc and Guinier, for they both were eager to enjoy the pleasures of the bed. But no matter: they finally came to the game of their desire. Now they have all that they want, and nothing that they don't want. Neither had cause to complain of the other, for they both had what they wanted. (11896)

Now I have recounted to you the marriage of Guinier with the faithful heart and good Caradoc Briebras who wore the snake on his arm: of these two especially have I told the story and described the coronation. My lord! What presents were distributed! Never at any king's coronation could you see such fine gifts as were given at that court, for the smallest present made the one who received it rich for all his life. I do not know what more to say to you: they were all satisfied with their gifts. (11911)

The marriage celebration lasted eight full days and then came to an end. The people went back to the regions where they lived, but the King and his closest companions stayed a long time with his nephew and his niece and did not leave Brittany. After he had stayed for a long time, he crossed the sea, taking Caradoc with him – but not without great difficulty, you may be sure. Caradoc was very sorry to leave his sweet lady whom he loved as much as himself. It was hard for him to leave her, but his good uncle warned him not to stay so long that jealous people would say he was neglecting chivalry.* Caradoc didn't delay for long, but went with his uncle and crossed to England with him. They amused themselves in the countryside, searching for adventures in the forest to win fame and participating in tournaments. Caradoc came to be considered one of the best knights at the King's court. He performed marvellous feats and accomplished so many acts of prowess that his reputation grew until it was said that Caradoc was the most glorious and valiant knight in King Arthur's household. (11948)

One Ascension Day, the King was at Caerlion. He had held a noble and powerful court and many people had come to admire its magnificence. After dinner, the King called his companions to assemble. He gathered the most valiant and spoke to them: 'My lords,' he said, 'at Pentecost, I would like to hold such a feast that no matter what happens I won't remember having had another one so fine. I invite you to spend tomorrow, from morning to night, shooting in the forest. We will leave immediately after we have heard mass.' (11967)

This news delighted everyone who heard it. They returned to their lodgings and went to bed, and slept until the watchmen roused them. They got up, heard mass and then set out on their way. They rode through the forest until they came upon a wild boar. They spent all day pursuing it, and followed it until nightfall. No matter, they thought they could harass the boar until they manoeuvred it into a place where they could manage to catch it. But the boar tricked them, and slipped into a thicket; it found a swamp where it could lie down and wallow about. Why should I take the trouble to tell you about the boar when the men taking all that trouble to catch it couldn't succeed? Between the night and the threatening thunder and lightning of a storm which broke at nightfall, they were forced to flee in great haste. There was so much thunder and lightning that it seemed to them that the skies were split, and it was so dark that none of them could see anything, except when a flash of lightning allowed them to see around themselves. They wished they were in the city, protected from such troubles. (12006)

The King and all his lords spurred their horses and went off in great haste. They would rather have been at Caerlion, for they had no better refuge. Caradoc became separated from them, and followed a different path, until he noticed a knight riding along alone on his horse. The knight was tall and handsome: strange to say, he was surrounded by a flock of birds singing different melodies. Caradoc saw all the birds, singing very sweetly, pressing around him. They made such a joyful noise that Caradoc never heard such bird songs in all his life. The man was surrounded with a bright light, like a brilliant ray of the sun. No rain was falling on him, and for him the weather was always fine. The whole road he travelled was illuminated. Caradoc was completely astonished: he marvelled at the tall knight, so elegant and so handsome, at the brightness and at the birds he saw surrounding the man. He began to hurry his horse, for he wanted to accompany the knight if he could. But no matter how much he spurred his horse, he could not get near him, and it was almost midnight. (12041)

Don't think that it didn't bother Caradoc that he couldn't catch up with this man he was pursuing so eagerly. And when he couldn't keep up with him, it bothered him that it was raining on him – and even more that it was not raining on the other man! They went along like that until they arrived at a great house. The door was open and there was a beautiful fire: it was a fine place! The knight went in and Caradoc followed. The hall was beautiful and there were many people there. When they saw their lord, the servants rushed to hold his stirrup. He dismounted and they welcomed him, and were surprised that Caradoc did not dismount. The knight took the reins of his horse: 'My friend,' he said, 'get down!' (12063)

'Hear me, Sir Knight! I do not want to dismount here until you have told me who you are and what your name is.' (12068)

'My friend, my name is Aalardin. My father's name is Guiniacalc and I am Aalardin du Lac. This house belongs to me, and now it would be right and proper for you to tell me your name.' (12073)

'It will never be concealed from you. I am Caradoc Briebras, whose arm was gripped by a snake for more than two full years, and I am King Arthur's nephew.' (12078)

Aalardin heard him and took him in his arms without letting him touch the stirrups. There were plenty of men to take his horse, care for it and give it plenty of oats. The two companions kissed each other and rejoiced with each other. They were so delighted to see each other, you may be sure, that they kissed and hugged each other over and over before either one could speak. Aalardin, still kissing and hugging Caradoc, spoke first: 'My companion, you have gone a long time without coming to see me. God knew what I wanted, and how to fulfil my desire! It's clear that He has had pity on me, for if He had not wished it to rain today and if He had not caused you to leave the road to the city, I would have never been able to have you here. But, God be praised, I have you now! You may be sure that this place is not close to Caerlion: no man on God's earth could get there in two days. So please stay with me a good long while, for I love you truly, God help me! This place is most delightful, as you will see tomorrow.' (12115)

They took Caradoc's cape and wrapped him in a mantle, and Aalardin led him off by the hand. The fire was big and the dinner and the room were beautiful and ample. All the knights and beautiful ladies rejoiced with Caradoc. Then Aalardin's wife, the beautiful Guigenor, came in, more beautiful than any other lady. She had come out of her room, most attractively clothed, and welcomed Caradoc joyfully. If I had all day I could not repeat to you all the words they spoke, and they could not be written down. I tell you that their joy was perfect, although they were not speaking about joyous things. I won't describe it all, but I know that nothing they had done since last they met went unreported. The dinner was ready and ladies and knights washed and took their places to eat and drink. The servants waited on them as they should, and the guests had plenty to eat. When they had finished eating and drinking, it was almost time to go to bed. They asked for wine, received it, and then they went to lie down, and slept until daybreak. Caradoc remained there an entire week. King Arthur was very sad, because he thought he had lost him. (12155)

Aalardin had a shield with a boss made of pure gold. No other treasure had such powers, for I can tell you that one could model that gold as if it were wax. Don't think it's a fantasy, but if a man had lost an ear or a nose, the gold had the property of adjusting itself perfectly to it so that nothing was lacking, as if Nature herself had fashioned it to the best of her ability. Aalardin called Caradoc aside and said to him, 'Companion, I love you, and if it were necessary, I would endure sufferings and pains for you. They say that your beautiful wife Guinier is missing the tip of one breast, for her brother cut it off when he took vengeance on the serpent for you. Do not be upset, but take the tip of the boss and apply it to her breast. You don't have to do anything more: you will see that the gold will take hold of it and stick there precisely as if Nature had put all her efforts into it.'* (12186)

He had his shield brought to him. It was made of pure gold with an azure band across it, and the cord was made of crimson silk. 'Caradoc,' said Aalardin, 'my dear friend, no craftsman in the country could fashion such a boss, no matter how much he tried. Just as gold is worth more than silver, the gold of this shield-boss is more valuable than any other, I am sure. It has a marvellous property: if a knight who has had half of his nose cut off should put the same amount of this gold on it, the gold would fasten there at once and never come loose: no one could ever take it away. You may have it, my lord, if you wish.' (12205)

'I will take it, dear sweet lord, with much gratitude!' (12207)

'Caradoc,' said Aalardin, 'you have spoken well. I am sure that she has a use for it!' He had the boss of the shield removed and gave it generously to the King. Caradoc took it and went away, and travelled until he reached the court. King Arthur was quite distraught, for he thought that Caradoc must be a prisoner somewhere and had searched for him throughout all the forest. When Caradoc came to the court, the King himself ran to meet him and kissed him, and everyone showed such joy for him that I don't believe I have ever heard the like. Now everything was turning out well for Caradoc. His wife Guinier came to the court without delay because he had summoned her to come to the great celebration that was planned. Far from being diminished, the splendour of the court was enhanced by her arrival. Caradoc escorted Guinier to a chamber by the sleeve of her ermine mantle and said to her: 'My lady, show me the breast whose tip you lost when you freed me from the great affliction of the snake.' (12233)

She showed it to him readily. Caradoc examined the breast; without hesitating, he took the golden tip from the boss and applied it to the wound softly and gently. The gold adhered to the delicate white flesh and the breast began to look just as it had before. When King Caradoc saw this, he felt great joy in his heart and said: 'As long as no one knows, my lady, that you have a breast of gold, you will always be sweet to me, my beautiful sweetheart, and do me no wrong. But you may be sure of one thing: if anyone other than the two of us should learn of it, my heart would be broken forever, for then you would have disobeyed my orders and crossed my will.'* (12253)

'Dear Lord, in God's name, tell me, I pray you, how can I protect myself?' (12257)

'I will tell you, my sweetheart. I will make a band and wrap your breast with it. No maiden, no young lady, no matter how close she may be to you, will help you with it when you get up or when you go to bed. At night, I will unwrap you with pleasure and joy, and I will wrap you up again in the morning, sweetly and tenderly.' The Queen thanked him, for he had advised her well. (12270)

King Arthur had a letter written and sent throughout his empire ordering and summoning all his knights and lords to be with him on the day of Pentecost. All his lords gathered at his command at Caerlion. After the great procession and the solemn mass, the valiant and courteous Arthur went to sit at high table according to the custom of the time in a great hall filled with knights, maidens, and noble and beautiful ladies. Kay came out of a room, approached the King and said to him: 'My lord, my lord, God help me, I will have the trumpets sounded for washing, if you please, for your meal is ready.' (12291)

'No, you will not, Kay, my dear friend. Don't talk about having the water distributed. You have known my custom for a long time: it has never happened, and, God willing, it won't happen today, that I should eat and hold court before seeing some great marvel or adventure.' (12299)

Even as he was speaking, a knight with a sword at his side and wearing no mantle came into the hall on a large horse. He was richly and elegantly dressed in fine crimson cloth. An ivory horn with bands of gold hung at his neck, encrusted with magnificent precious stones. He rode up to the King, dismounted and spoke to him loudly in front of everyone: 'My friend, my lord, I offer you this horn which is called "Blessed". It is precious for its gold and workmanship, but even more valuable for another reason. I tell you truly that if you have it filled with water from a spring or with other pure, sweet water, it will become the best and clearest wine to be found in all the world; everyone here can drink from it in turn and they will all have plenty of wine.' (12326)

'By the Lord who never lies,' said Kay, 'that is a fine present!' (12328)

The knight replied to him then: 'By God, dear sweet lord, no knight whose wife has deceived him or who has deceived his wife will be able to drink from this horn without spilling the wine on himself.'* (12334)

'Take it away!' cried Kay the Seneschal. 'God help me, Sir Knight, now your present is worth much less!' (12337)

In front of all his followers, the King had the horn filled at once. Guenevere could not restrain herself from saying, so that all the court could hear: 'Dear lord, do not drink from it: it's some kind of spell to bring shame on everyone! No wise man ought to drink from it, for he might easily deceive himself or someone else and be dishonoured and upset.' (12348)

The King laughed and replied: 'My lady, by the faith I owe to all the world, I will try it first, in the sight of all these knights.' (12352)

The Queen heard this and was very disturbed, but she laughed and answered him politely: 'If I have ever addressed a prayer to Almighty God which has been pleasing to Him, I beg Him now that if you try to drink from it you will soil yourself!' (12359)

Then the King took the horn; he thought that he would drink, but he spilled the wine all over himself and it could be seen throughout the hall. The Queen lowered her head, angry and ashamed. (12366)

Kay said, 'Things are going from bad to worse!' (12367)

The King was angry and started getting hot, but he could hide and cover his anger and displeasure so as not to trouble his followers. He answered Kay most amiably: 'Seneschal,' he said, 'my dear friend, I was a great fool to act against the Queen's wishes, for I wouldn't want to have her hatred for anything! Truly, I know for sure that Lord God loves her, since as you have seen He has heard her prayer. But so that I am not the only one to be mocked, you take it and try after me, Seneschal, by the friendship and loyalty you swore to me when you became my liege man.' (12386)

With that he gave the horn to him; Kay was very upset, but he took it because he didn't dare refuse. Full of anger, he brought it towards his mouth: but the wine spilled all over him. Everyone in the hall broke out in laughter and mocked him afterwards. The King himself laughed at this and said to him jokingly, 'Now, my Seneschal, now there are two of us!' (12397)

'Very true, my lord, and believe me there will soon be even more of us!' (12399)

'I do not know if it is an illusion or not, but every knight here must take this test, by the soul of my father Pendragon!' (12403)

'My lord,' said Kay, 'let's see! I will give it to anyone you wish. It is proper and just that the first to take the test after me should be your nephew, Sir Gawain.' (12408)

'Take it to him then,' said the King. (12409)

Kay took the horn at once, and put it in Gawain's hand, brimming with wine. He laughed and said to him: 'Don't be afraid, Sir Gawain, drink, by the love you owe to the King, for he orders you to do so.' (12417)

'Since my lord orders it, Sir Kay, I will try it, and find out if I can drink from it.' He raised the horn to his mouth, but as soon as he touched it the wine spilled all over him. (12422)

'My lord,' said Kay, 'pass the horn along!' (12424)

Then he began to laugh, and everyone, high and low, began to rejoice in turn throughout the hall. The King and Kay were both most delighted. I believe that Sir Gawain passed the horn to Sir Yvain, who was seated on his right, and said to him: 'My lord, let us see how it turns out for you!' (12434)

'It will surely turn out better for me than for you, I think,' replied Sir Yvain, taking the horn, 'if loyalty can be any use to me!' He raised the horn then, intending to drink, but he failed: the wine spilled all over his precious blue robe of cloth from Constantinople. Every noble knight of the Round Table took the test, it's no lie, but like it or not they all soiled themselves. The horn finally passed to Caradoc, and when he had it in his hand, you may be sure that he was very worried. He looked at his wife Guinier who was seated by the Queen, and she saw that her lord was worried about her. At soon as she saw him she said: 'My lord, you may drink confidently!' (12457)

He drank so cleanly that not a drop spilled. 'My lady,' he said, 'thank you! No lady has ever shown greater honour to her lord than you have shown to me, my sweetheart.' (12463)

Then the horn was passed throughout the hall, and every knight took the test in turn. I can bear witness that every single one of them was soiled, and every one of them was furious at Caradoc because he drank without soiling himself. The Queen was very sad, and so were many other noble ladies. They hated Guinier and were jealous of her because she said 'confidently'. They hated her more violently than any other living creature. (12479)

Then the trumpets sounded and they washed their hands and sat down. They were served generously and joyfully, in my opinion, and ate at their leisure. When the court had lasted three days, King Arthur gave the knights so much gold, silver, horses, cloths from the orient, precious brooches and splendid rings, belts, dogs, and birds that they returned to their countries in great joy. The King stayed with his closest companions, and I tell you truly that he kept Caradoc with him. Caradoc sent Guinier back to his country as soon as he could; he acted wisely, in my opinion, for he knew that the Queen felt mortal hatred for her because she had said: 'confidently'. The King lived for a long time in peace and repose. He spent the whole winter in his best forests to amuse himself and relax. (12506)

THE KNIGHT
WITH THE SWORD

If anyone loves entertainment and joy, let him come forward: listen, and hear an adventure which came to the Good Knight,* who upheld loyalty, prowess and honour and never loved any cowardly, false or churlish man. I tell of Sir Gawain, who was more well bred and prized for his deeds of arms than anyone could describe. If someone wanted to relate all his good qualities and set them down briefly, he would never reach the end of it. Although I can't relate them all, still I shouldn't keep silent on that account, and not at least have my say. One may not reasonably reproach Chrétien de Troyes,* in my opinion, who could tell stories of King Arthur and his court and retinue, which was praised and honoured so much: he recounts the deeds of the others but never took any account of Gawain. He was too fine a man to forget. For this reason, I am pleased to be first to recount an adventure which happened to the Good Knight. (28)

King Arthur was in his city of Cardueil one summer; he had with him the Queen and Gawain, Kay the Seneschal and Yvain, and only twenty of the others. Gawain was always moved by the desire to go out to entertain and amuse himself. He had his horse made ready, and dressed himself in courtly fashion: he fastened on spurs of gold over his cutaway hose of well-embroidered silken cloth. He had put on his breeches, extremely white and very delicate, and a short but ample shirt of finely pleated linen, and was wrapped in a fur-trimmed cloak: he was most elegantly attired. (46)

Then he set out from the town, travelling straight along the road until he entered the forest. He heard the song of the birds which were singing very sweetly, listening to them for so long – there were plenty of them to hear – that he began to think about an adventure that had once come to him. He stayed that way for such a long time that he went astray in the forest and lost his way completely. The sun was setting and he began to get worried. It was starting to get dark when he finally emerged from this musing, and he had no idea where he was: so he decided to turn back. He started along a cart-track which led him ever forward: the night was growing darker and darker, and he had no idea where to go. (69)

Then he began to scan the road that lay before him and, through a clearing, he saw a large fire burning. He proceeded in that direction, expecting to find some man who would send him on his way, a woodcutter or a charcoal-maker. Next to the fire he saw a charger which had been tied to a tree. He drew nearer to the fire and saw a knight sitting by it; he greeted him at once: 'May God who made the world and put the souls into our bodies, grant you His mercy, my dear lord.' (85)

'My friend,' he replied, 'may God protect you as well! But tell me where you are coming from, travelling alone at such an hour.' (88)

Gawain told him everything, the whole truth from beginning to end: how he had set out for entertainment, and then how he had gone astray in the forest because he had been so absorbed in his thoughts that he had lost his way. The knight then offered to set him back on his road the next morning, quite willingly, provided he would stay with him and keep him company until that night had passed; this request was granted. (102)

Gawain put down his lance and shield, dismounted from his horse, tied it to a little tree, and wrapped it in his mantle; then he sat down next to the fire. Then they asked each other how they had fared that day: Gawain told him everything and never stooped to lie to him, but the knight was false with him; he didn't tell him a single word of truth – you'll hear fully why he did so. When they had stayed awake a while, conversing about many different things, they fell asleep beside the fire. (117)

At daybreak Sir Gawain woke first; then the knight woke up and said, 'My house is very near here, two leagues away and no more; come there, I pray you, and you may be sure that you will soon receive friendly hospitality.' (125)

Then they mounted their chargers and took up their shields, lances and swords; then they set out at once on a paved road.

They hadn't travelled very far when they came out of the forest and were in open country. The knight spoke to him: 'Listen to this, my lord,' he said; 'it is always proper and accepted behaviour for a prudent and courtly knight who is bringing another along with him to send word ahead that his lodgings should be prepared, for if their arrival is not expected he might easily find something which might displease him. I have no one I can send there, as you can clearly see, except for myself. I hope it doesn't displease you if I ask you to travel along at your leisure while I ride on ahead in haste. Near an enclosure, straight ahead down in a valley, you will see my house.' Gawain realized that what he said was reasonable and polite, so he travelled on quite slowly and the other man galloped quickly ahead. (153)

Sir Gawain soon came upon four shepherds who had stopped beside the road. They greeted him most courteously; he returned their greeting in God's name and passed them by without saying anything more. 'Alas,' said one of them, 'what a disaster! Such a handsome knight, so fine and elegant! It certainly wouldn't be right for you to be wounded or mistreated.' (163)

Gawain heard these words distinctly and was completely baffled. He wondered why they were lamenting for him when they didn't know him at all. He returned to them quickly, greeted them all over again, and then asked them politely if they would tell him truly why they said it was a disaster. One of them replied to him; 'My lord,' he said, 'we feel pity because we see you following that knight who is riding ahead there on the grey horse. We've seen him take home many men but we have never yet seen one of them return.'* (181)

'My friend,' said Gawain, 'do you know if he does them any harm?' (183)

'My lord, they say in this region that if anyone contradicts him in anything, whatever it may be, good or bad, he has him killed in his house. We only know of it by hearsay, for no one ever saw anyone who came back from there. If you are willing to believe us, you will not follow him another foot, not if you care for your life. You are such a handsome knight that it would be a pity if he killed you.' (195)

Sir Gawain said to them: 'Shepherds, I commend you to God. But for a child's tale I am not willing to give up my journey through his lands.' If it were known in his own country that he had given it up for such a reason, he would have been reproached for it forever. He journeyed on, his horse ambling, musing on these things, as far as the valley which the knight had mentioned to him. (205)

He saw a beautiful castle beside a large enclosure, up on a hillock, which had recently been refortified. He noticed that the moat was wide and deep, and in the courtyard in front of the bridge there were many rich outbuildings: never in all his life had Gawain ever seen anything more impressive, unless it belonged to a king or a prince. But I have no wish to linger over a description of these buildings, except to say they were very beautiful and fine. He came up to the tournament yard, but went right through the gate, passed right through the courtyard and arrived at the end of the bridge. (221)

The lord of the castle rushed up to meet him, making a great show of pleasure at his arrival. A squire received his weapons, another took Gringalet,* and a third removed his spurs. Then his host took him by the hand and led him across the bridge. They found a very beautiful fire in the hall in front of the tower with lovely couches around it, all covered in purple silk. They stabled his horse for him off to one side, where he could see it, and oats and hay were brought to it in great abundance. Gawain thanked him for all of this, for he didn't want to contradict him in anything. (239)

'My dear lord,' said the host, 'your dinner is being prepared and you may be sure that the servants are hurrying to make it ready. Meanwhile you may amuse yourself: relax, and take things easy. If there is anything that displeases you, be sure to say so.' Gawain said that the lodging was all arranged exactly to his wishes. (249)

The lord went into the chamber to look for a daughter of his – in all the land there was no other young lady as worthy as she. I couldn't ever tell you all the beauty, or even half of it, with which she was endowed; but I do not wish to pass it over, so I will describe her in just a few words: Nature had gathered around her all the beauty and courtesy which ought to be pleasing for a human body. The host, who was no churl, took her by the right hand and led her into the hall. (265)

As Gawain gazed upon her great beauty, he was almost overwhelmed, but nevertheless he jumped up. When she looked at Gawain, the young lady was even more amazed at his great beauty and his good manners. Nevertheless, most courteously and in a few brief words, he greeted her. Right away, the host offered her to Sir Gawain by the hand, and said to him, 'May I present to you my daughter, if it doesn't displease you, for I have no more beautiful diversion to entertain and amuse you. If she is willing, she will surely be able to provide you with pleasing companionship. It is my will that she not be unwilling: there is such worth and discretion in you that if she were to fall in love with you she would have nothing but honour from it. As for myself, I grant you a gift, that I won't be a hindrance to you; rather, I command her, in your hearing, not to contradict you in anything.' (291)

Gawain thanked him politely for this, for he did not want to contradict him; the host then went to the kitchen at once to ask if they might dine soon. (296)

Gawain sat down beside the maiden, most concerned about his host, for he feared him greatly. Nevertheless, he began to talk with the fair-haired young lady most courteously, and without a trace of incivility, saying neither too much nor too little to her. He conversed with her most discreetly, offering her his service politely and telling her about his feelings until she, who was both wise and worthy, recognized and understood that if it was agreeable to her he would love her more than anything. She did not know which to choose, whether to refuse him or accept him. She heard him speaking so courteously, and she saw that he was so well mannered, that she would have fallen in love with him if only she dared to open up to him. Yet not for anything would she consent to lead him on, since he wouldn't be able to take any more. She knew that she would have been acting basely if she made him feel the pangs of love which she* would never bring to a conclusion; but it was hard for her to refuse him because her heart was so drawn to him. (325)

Then she spoke courteously to him. 'My lord,' she said, 'I have heard my father forbid me to contradict you in anything. Now I do not know what to say to you, except that if I should consent to do what you desire, I would never bring it to a conclusion, and so I would have betrayed and killed you. I must warn you of one thing, and I tell you this in all good faith: you must be careful not to act basely. Whatever my father may say to you, good or bad, it would be disastrous for you to contradict him, for you would be killed on the spot: you'd be doomed if you give any sign that you know anything at all about this.' (343)

Now the host, who had gone to the kitchen, came back; the food was all ready, and he called for the water – but I don't want to dwell on all that. When they had washed, they sat down, and the servants spread the cloths over the beautiful white tablecloths, laid out the salt-cellars and the knives, then the bread, and then the wine, in cups of silver and pure gold. But I do not wish to linger over a description of every single course: they had plenty of meat and fish, roasted birds and venison, and they ate their fill most happily. The host was most insistent that Gawain and the maiden should drink, and so he told the young lady that she should urge the knight and said, 'You may think very well of yourself that I should wish her to be your sweetheart.' Gawain thanked him for this politely. (366)

When they had eaten enough, the servants were prepared; some took away all the tablecloths and others brought them the water and the towel for drying. After dinner, the host said that he wanted to go out to inspect his woods, and asked Gawain to stay seated and amuse himself with the young lady. At the same time, he addressed Gawain, and told him – commanded him – not to go away before he returned. He gave orders to a servant that, if Gawain showed any indication, they should be ready to act at once. (381)

Gawain, who was worthy and courtly, recognized that he had to remain, and that it could not be otherwise; so he told him at once that he had no desire to go, if he was willing to give him lodgings. The host mounted his charger and set out at top speed, going out to seek another adventure: he was quite certain about this one, for he had it closed up inside his wall! (392)

Then the young lady took Gawain by the hand, and they sat down off to one side, in order to discuss how he might protect himself. She reassured him, sweetly and prettily, but she was distressed and undone because she did not know what plans her father had in mind. If she had known, she would have shown him some device by which he might escape: but her father would never tell her anything. He must take care not to contradict him, and so in that way he might be able to escape. (405)

'Let it be,' he said; 'he won't do me any harm. He brought me into his house, and he has been very pleasant to me here. Since he has treated me well and honourably, I will never have any fear of him from now on, unless I see or learn some reason why I ought to be afraid of him.' (414)

'Then it's no use,' she said. 'The common man has a proverb, and many people still repeat it: "Praise the day in the evening when you see that it has ended well, and praise your host in the morning." I hope that God will grant that you may take leave of your host joyfully and with no ill-will.' (423)

When they had conversed for a long time, chatting about this and that, the host returned to the castle. Gawain jumped up to meet him, hand in hand with the maiden, and they greeted him most politely. He told them that he had hurried back because he feared that if he delayed Gawain would have left already: that was why he didn't want to tarry. (433)

It was growing dark, and the host asked the servants if he could have supper. 'At your pleasure,' said his daughter, 'you may ask for wine and fruit, but nothing else would be proper, for you've already eaten plenty.' (440)

He ordered it at once. First they washed, and then the fruit was placed before them. The servants brought out an abundance of different kinds of wine. 'Be of good cheer, my lord,' he said to Sir Gawain, 'and be certain of one thing: it often grieves and troubles me when I have a guest who doesn't enjoy himself and who doesn't say what he wants.' (451)

'My lord, you may be sure,' said Gawain, 'that I am delighted.' (453)

When they had eaten the fruit, the host ordered the beds to be made ready, and said, 'I will lie in this room and this knight will lie in my bed. Don't make it up too narrow, though, for my daughter will lie with him. He is such a good knight that I think she will be well placed with him. She ought to be delighted with what has been granted to them.' Both of them thanked him for it, and acted as if it pleased them greatly. (465)

Now Gawain was very uncomfortable, for he was afraid that if he went to bed there, the host would have him cut to pieces, but he knew that if he contradicted him in his own house, he would kill him. (470)

The host was eager to go to bed; he took Gawain by the hand and led him straight into the bedroom. The young lady with the fair complexion went in with him. The room was arrayed with tapestries, and twelve candles were burning there, set up all around the bed and shining very brilliantly. The bed was beautifully covered with costly quilts and pure white sheets. But I do not wish to linger over a description of all the splendour of the silken cloth from the orient, from Palermo and from Romagna which decorated the room, or all the sables and furs, so I'll tell you everything in a word: anything that might be proper for a knight or to adorn the body of a lady, either in winter or in summer, all of it was there in profusion: there were many costly furnishings. Gawain was astonished at the wealth he saw. (495)

The knight addressed him: 'My lord,' he said, 'this room is very beautiful. You and this maiden will lie in it together, and there won't be anyone else. Close the door, young lady, and do his bidding; I know well that such folk have no need of a crowd. But I want to warn you about one thing: do not put out the candles, for I would be very angry at that. I have ordered this because I want him to see your great beauty when you are lying in his arms, so that he will have greater comfort, and I want you to see his fine body.' Then he withdrew from the bedroom, and the maiden closed the door. (513)

Sir Gawain lay down, and she came back to the bed and lay down beside him, naked: she didn't need to be asked. All night long she lay sweetly in his arms; he kissed and embraced her often, and he progressed so far that he was about to have his way with her when she said, 'Please, my lord! It can't go any farther: I'm not here with you without a guard.' (525)

Gawain looked all around, but saw no living creature there. 'My beauty,' he said, 'I ask you to tell me who is forbidding me to do what I desire with you.' (530)

'I'll tell you,' she answered, 'most willingly, all that I know. Do you see that sword hanging there, the one with the silver sword-knot and the pure gold hilt and pommel? This isn't just conjecture that you're about to hear me tell you, but something I've seen tested very well. My father loves it very much, for it has killed many good and worthy knights for him. You may be sure that it has killed more than twenty of them here alone – but I don't know where he got it from. No knight will ever come through this door and pull out alive. My father treats them most politely, but if he catches one in even the smallest fault he's sure to kill him. It is necessary to be on guard against baseness and to stick to the straight and narrow. He exacts his justice instantly if he catches him in any error: if a man acts so cautiously that he isn't caught in any wrong, he's sent to spend the night with me. Then he has come to his death.* Do you know why no one gets out? If he gives any sign of the desire that has come upon him to do it to me, all at once that sword strikes him through the body. If he tries to go and grab it to get rid of it, it jumps out of the scabbard all by itself and strikes him right through the body. You may be certain that the sword is enchanted in some fashion, so that it always protects me in this way. You would never have been warned by me, but you are so courtly and wise that it would be a great pity and would cause me grief forever if you were killed on my account.' (574)

Now Gawain did not know what to do. Never before in all his life had he heard tell of such a threat, and he suspected that she might be saying this in order to protect herself, so that he would not take his pleasure with her. But on the other hand he considered that it could not be concealed or be kept from being known everywhere that he had alone lain beside her in her bed, with both of them naked, and just because of something she said, he had failed to take his pleasure: it's better to die with honour than to live a long time in shame. (589)

'That's nothing, my beauty,' he said. 'Since I have come this far, I want to be your sweetheart now, and you really can't avoid it!' (593)

'Then you can't blame me,' she said, 'from now on.' (595)

He drew so close to her that she uttered a cry. The sword leaped out of its scabbard and struck a glancing blow to his side, cutting away a piece of his skin but not wounding him very much. It pierced right through the bedspread and all the sheets, as far as the mattress, and then it shot back into its scabbard. (604)

Gawain was left quite stunned, and had lost his desire completely: he lay there beside her, totally amazed. 'Stop, my lord!' she said, 'By God! You thought that I said it because I wished to protect myself against you with such a pretext. I have certainly never said anything about this to any knight but you, and you may be sure that I'm astonished that you were not inevitably killed, right at the first stroke. By God, now lie in peace and from now on be careful not to touch me again in such a fashion! Even a wise man can readily undertake a thing which turns out badly for him.' (621)

Gawain was left there pensive and mournful, for he didn't know how to behave. If God should grant that he ever return to his own country, it could never be concealed, but would be known everywhere that he had lain all alone all night long with such a charming and beautiful maiden and he still had done nothing to her, though she had opposed him with nothing but the threat of a sword which was wielded by no one at all! He would be shamed forever if he escaped from her* in that way! (636)

Now the candles which he saw around him caused him great annoyance; they spread a great brightness by which he saw her great beauty: blonde hair and a broad forehead, delicate eyebrows, sparkling eyes, well-shaped nose, bright and fresh complexion, a small and laughing mouth, long and graceful neck, long arms and white hands, soft, full sides, and under the sheets, white and tender flesh! Her body was so graceful and well fashioned that no one could have found any cause for complaint in her. (651)

He was no churl, and he drew closer to her very softly. He would have already been playing a certain game with her when the sword leaped out of the scabbard and attacked him once again: the flat of the sword struck his neck and he almost felt like a fool. But the sword wavered a little, turned towards his right shoulder, and cut off a slice of skin three fingers wide; it pierced the silken quilt, sliced off a piece of it, and then thrust itself back in its scabbard. (664)

When Gawain realized he was wounded in the shoulder and the side, he saw that he couldn't bring it to the finish. He was very sad and didn't know what to do, frustrated that he had been checked. (669)

'My lord,' she said, 'are you dead?' (670)

'Young lady,' he said, 'I am not; but I grant you this gift for the rest of the night: you have a truce from me.' (673)

'My lord,' she said, 'by my faith, if it had been granted when it was first requested, things would be much better for you now.' (677)

Gawain was extremely disconcerted, and the young lady was too. Neither of them slept, but rather they stayed awake, in such sorrow, all that night until the dawn. (682)

As soon as it was day the host rose quickly and promptly went to the bedroom. He was neither silent nor dumb, but called out very loudly, and the young lady hurriedly opened the door and then came back and lay down naked next to Gawain, and the knight followed along behind. He saw them both lying together peacefully, and asked them how they were. (693)

Sir Gawain replied: 'Very well, my lord, thank you.' (695)

When the knight heard him speaking so clearly, you may be sure that he was very sad, for he was very wicked and illtempered. 'What!' he said, 'Are you still alive?' (700)

'By my faith,' said Sir Gawain, 'I am perfectly safe and sound. You may be sure that I've done nothing for which I ought to be put to death. If you should do me any harm or mischief in your own home for no reason, it would be wrong.' (707)

'What,' he said, 'so you're not dead? It disturbs me very much that you're alive.' (709)

Then he drew a little closer and saw clearly that the bedspread had been cut and the linens were stained with blood.* 'Vassal,' he said, 'tell me at once where this blood came from!' (715)

Sir Gawain kept still, for he did not want to lie to him and he had no excuse by which he could conceal himself so that his host would not catch on. The host spoke again at once, saying, 'Listen to this, vassal. It's pointless trying to hide it from me. You were trying to have your way with this young lady, but you could not bring it to the finish because of the sword which prevented it.' (727)

Sir Gawain said to him, 'My lord, you are speaking the truth. The sword wounded me in two places but it didn't hurt me very much.' (731)

When the knight understood that Gawain had not been

mortally wounded, he said, 'My dear lord, you have arrived in a safe harbour. But tell me now, if you want to escape scot-free, your country and your name. You may well be of such a family, of such reputation and rank, that it will be necessary for me to fulfil your wishes: but I have to be completely sure.' (741)

'My lord,' he said, 'my name is Gawain and I am the nephew of good King Arthur. You may be certain of this, for I have never changed my name.' (745)

'By my faith,' said the host, 'I know well that in you the King has a fine knight; I wouldn't expect to hear of a better one! You have no peer from here to Majorca, nor could your equal be found in all the kingdom of Logres. Do you know how I have tested all the knights in the world who go out in search of adventures? They could all have lain in this bed and they all would have had to die, one by one, until it happened that the best man of all should come. The sword was to make the choice for me, for it wasn't supposed to kill the best man when he came here.* And now it has proven itself, for it has chosen you as the best. Since God has granted such honour to you, I don't know how I could find or select anyone more deserving of having my daughter. I give and grant her to you, and from now on you would be wrong to be on guard against me. And I grant to you, in all good faith and for all the days of your life, the lordship of this castle: do with it whatever you desire.' (773)

Gawain was delighted and joyful, and thanked him for it. 'My lord,' he said, 'I am well rewarded with just the maiden: I am not interested in your gold or your silver or this castle.' Then Gawain and the maiden got up. (781)

The news spread through the country that a knight had arrived who wanted to have the maiden and that the sword had been drawn against him twice, but didn't do him any harm. And so everyone arrived as soon as possible. The castle was filled with merriment; there were many ladies and knights and the father had a very costly feast prepared. I have no wish to linger over a description of what foods were served: they all had plenty to eat and drink. When they had eaten their fill and the tablecloths had been removed, there were hosts of entertainers and each one displayed his talents. One tuned his viol, one played his flute and another his pipes, and others sang part songs or strummed their harps and rotes. One read romances and another told fables, and the knights played backgammon or chess or dice or other games of chance. That is how they passed their time, all day long, until it was dusk. Then they supped, in great delight, with plenty of birds and fruit and an abundance of good wine. (811)

When they had joyfully finished their supper, they quickly went to bed. They led Gawain and the maiden straight to the bedroom where they had lain the night before. The host went along with them, and married them, with good will: he placed the maiden and the knight together without any hindrance, and then left the room and closed the door. (821)

What more can I tell you? That night Gawain did what he desired, and it wasn't a sword that was drawn there! If he returned to the fray with the courteous young lady, that doesn't bother me, and it didn't bother her at all. (827)

And so Sir Gawain remained at the castle for a long time in such joys and delights. Then he began to think that he had stayed there too long, and his relatives and friends might well think that he'd been killed. He went to his host to ask leave to go: 'My lord,' he said, 'I have stayed so long in this land that my friends and relations will think that I have died; so I ask you, please, to grant me your leave to go back. See to it that this young lady is arrayed in such a way that honour will come to me for bringing her and to you for having given her to me, so that when I come back to my country, they will say I have a beautiful lover and that she has come from a good place.' (848)

The host gave him his leave, and Gawain and the young lady set out together. Her palfrey was equipped with a fine bridle and saddle. The maiden climbed up on it, and Gawain mounted his horse. But why should I make a longer story of it? He took up the arms he had brought and set out, with his host's permission, happy and joyous for his adventure.* (860)

But when she was outside the gate, the young lady pulled back on the reins and Gawain asked her why. 'My lord,' she said, 'I'm right to do so, for I've forgotten something important. You may be sure that I will leave this country most unwillingly without the greyhounds I have raised. They are very good and beautiful: you never saw any so swift, and they are whiter than any flower.' (871)

So Gawain turned around and galloped back to get the greyhounds. The host saw him coming from a distance, and came out to meet him. 'Gawain,' he said, 'why have you returned so soon?' (877)

'My lord,' he said, 'because your daughter has forgotten her greyhounds, and she tells me that she cares for them so much that she will not go without them.' (881)

The host called to them at once and handed them over most willingly, and Gawain returned quickly with the greyhounds to the maiden who was waiting for him. Then they set out once again and entered the forest through which they had come. (889)

Then they saw a knight coming along the road towards them. This knight was travelling all alone, but he was very well armed, for he lacked not a single thing of all a knight needs. He was seated on a bay charger, which was strong and swift and spirited. The knight came on quickly until he came right up to them; Gawain intended to greet him peacefully and then to ask him who he was and where he came from. But the knight had something else in mind: he spurred his horse so sharply that it shot forward – he didn't say a word – right between the maiden and Gawain. He took her horse by the reins and then turned back at once. Without even being asked, she went away with him at once. (911)

There is no need to wonder whether Gawain was angry and upset when he saw him take her off like that, for he had brought no armour with him except a sword, a shield and a lance, and the other knight was fully armed and was a tall, strong, haughty man. So, compared to him, Gawain had the worst of the bargain. (919)

Nevertheless, Gawain spurred his charger boldly towards him to challenge him for the maiden. 'Vassal,' he said, 'you have acted very churlishly in seizing my sweetheart so roughly. But now do something bolder, as I will describe to you: you can see quite clearly that I have only my lance and shield and this sword hanging by my side. I order you to disarm, so that we may be on an equal footing, and then you will be acting courteously. And if you are able to win her from me through your chivalry, let her be yours, with no further strife. If you are not willing to do this, then be courtly and honourable enough to wait for me under these elm trees. I will go to borrow some arms back there, from a friend of mine, and when I am equipped with armour, I will come back at once. After that, if you are able to win her in a fight with me, I'll give her to you, with no ill-feeling: I pledge you this, truly.' (947)

The knight replied at once: 'You won't receive permission to go, and if I've done anything wrong, I won't ask your pardon for it. You're a powerful man indeed, if you think you can make me a gift of what's already mine! But since you are unarmed, and so that you won't feel mistreated, let's have a little contest. You say that she's your lover because she has travelled here with you, but I say that she is mine. Now let's place her in the road, and each of us will go off to one side, and let it be completely up to her which of us she loves better. If she wants to go with you, then I'll grant and give her to you; but if she wants to come with me, then it is right that she be mine.' (967)

Gawain agreed with him politely, for he loved her and trusted her so much that he thought for sure that she wouldn't leave him for all the world. And so they left her and went off, withdrawing a little aside. 'My beauty,' they said, 'there's nothing more to say: it is all a matter of your own desires as to which man you want to stay with, for that is what we have agreed.' (977)

She looked at one, and then at the other, first at the knight and then at Gawain; he was absolutely certain that he would have her and was only puzzled that she was thinking about it. (983)

But the maiden, who knew quite well how Gawain could perform, wanted to find out how worthy and valiant the knight was. All of you should know, great and small, no matter who laughs or groans about it, that there is hardly any woman in the world – even if she were the lover and the wife of the very best knight from here to India – who could ever have such love from him if he wasn't hardy at home – you know the kind of prowess I mean – that she would value him at a pinch of salt. (997)

Now listen to the ugly thing this young lady did: she put herself in the control of the man whom she didn't know at all. When Sir Gawain saw that, you may be sure that he was furious that she had abandoned him of her own free will. But he was so hardy and prudent, so courtly and reasonable, that he didn't say a single word, although it grieved him greatly. (1008)

The knight spoke to him, saying, 'My lord, without contradiction, the young lady should be mine.' (1011)

'May God,' said Gawain, 'turn away from me if I offer any opposition or if I ever start a fight over anything which does not care for me.' (1015)

The knight and the maiden set off in great haste, and Gawain went off towards his own country with the greyhounds. But the maiden came to a halt right at the edge of the plain, and the knight asked her why she had stopped. (1023)

'My lord,' she said, 'never in all my life will I be your lover until I have possession of my greyhounds which I see that vassal taking away with him.' (1028)

'You'll have them,' he replied, and then he shouted, 'Stop, stop, vassal! I forbid you to go any farther!' He came up to him at full speed, saying, 'Vassal, why are you taking the greyhounds, when they are not yours?' (1035)

Sir Gawain replied: 'My lord,' he said, 'I consider them mine, and if anyone makes a claim for them, I will have to defend them as my own. If you are willing to engage in the same contest as you offered me when you placed the young lady in the middle of the road to choose which man she wanted to go with, I would willingly allow it to you.' (1045)

The knight agreed with him that he would willingly accept that game. Wicked as he was, he thought that if the greyhounds came to him, they would stay with him without a fight; and he could be quite certain that if they went to Gawain, he could simply take them away, just as he was going to do anyway. So they left the hounds in the road. (1055)

When they had drawn apart, each knight called to them, and immediately they ran straight to Gawain, whom they knew simply because they had seen him at the home of the young lady's father. Gawain petted them and talked to them, for he was very happy to have them. (1063)

The maiden addressed the knight at once. 'My lord,' she said, 'as God is my witness I will not go another step with you until I have in my possession my greyhounds which I love so much.' (1069)

And he replied, 'Without my permission, he won't be able to take them away.' Then he said, 'Let them go, vassal! You will not take them away!' (1073)

'What villainy,' said Gawain, 'if you go back on your word. I have taken possession of these greyhounds, and they came to me of their own free will. May God in Majesty desert me if I ever give them up! I left the young lady to you just because she chose you, and she was mine and came with me: and so by rights you ought to leave the greyhounds with me, without hindrance, since they are mine, and came with me, and stayed with me of their own will. You may be sure of one thing, truly, and you can see the proof of it in me: if you want to fulfil all this maiden's desires, you'll have only temporary joy from her – I really want her to hear me now – for as long as she was mine, you know, I did everything for her: now see how she has treated me! It's not the same with a dog as with a woman, you can be sure. There's one thing you can be certain about with a dog: it will never leave the master who has raised it and go to a stranger. But a woman quickly abandons her master and so does not fulfil his desires:* the astonishing thing about such an exchange is that she leaves her own for a total stranger. The greyhounds haven't abandoned me, and so I can prove well – and I will not be refuted – that the nature and the love of a dog is worth more than a woman's.' (1109)

'Vassal,' he said, 'all your debating can't be of any use to you here. If you do not yield them at once, on guard! I challenge you!' (1113)

Then Gawain took up his shield and placed it in front of his breast. Each man charged at the other as swiftly as his horse could carry him; the knight struck him so vigorously, hitting his shield above the boss, that it pierced and shattered it and the splinters flew as far and high as an arrow-shot. Then Gawain struck him back on the first quarter of his shield, so powerfully, it seems to me, that he knocked both man and horse to the road. He fell into a pool of mud between his charger's legs. (1129)

Gawain drew his steel sword and immediately turned towards him. He dismounted as soon as he could and pinned him to the ground. He struck him hard, in the face and head, and stunned him completely: he hated him so much for his misdeed and for the grief that he caused him that he put all his strength into it. He wounded him, he maimed him, he pulled up the skirt of his hauberk and quickly thrust his good sword in his side. (1142)

Once he was avenged, he let him be. He paid no heed to the knight's horse or hauberk or shield, but called out to the greyhounds which he loved so much because they had proven true to him. He saw his charger wandering in the woods and ran to catch it. He reached it quickly, and seized it, and leaped into the saddle: he had no need at all for stirrups. (1153)

'My lord,' said the young lady, 'by God and honour, I pray you, do not leave me here! That would be most villainous. If I was stupid and foolish, you shouldn't hold it against me. I didn't dare to go with you, I was so frightened when I saw that you were so poorly equipped with armour and he was so well armed that nothing was lacking to him.' (1164)

'My beauty,' he said 'there's no point. Your pretences are doing you no good and this deception is worthless. Such faith, such love, such nature one can often find in a woman: anyone who hopes to reap a different crop than he has sown in his land and anyone who hopes to find in a woman something other than her nature is a fool! They have always been this way, ever since God made the first one. The more a man takes pains to serve them, and treats them well and honours them, the more he repents at the end; the more he respects and serves them, the more he is vexed and the more he loses. This concern of yours did not arise to preserve my honour or my life, but came to you from quite another thing.* The common man has a saying: "At the end one sees how everything turns out." If anyone finds woman false and deceitful and still cherishes, guards and loves her, then may God never protect him! Now you can look after yourself.' (1189)

He abandoned her there, all alone, and he never knew what happened to her.* (1191)

He returned to his proper road, and thought a lot about his adventure. He travelled through the forest until at dusk he arrived in his country. His friends were delighted to see him, for they thought that they had lost him. He recounted his adventure, just as it happened, from beginning to end – and they were willing listeners – how at first it was fine and dangerous, and afterwards ugly and vexing because of the sweetheart he had lost, and then how he fought at great risk for the greyhounds: and so it all came to an end. (1206)

THE PERILOUS GRAVEYARD

My lady has given me my instructions, asking me to tell her of an adventure which happened to the Good Knight. I must not fail to do so – when she has commanded it – because it pleases her and strikes her fancy. (6)

Hear now how it came about. One Pentecost, King Arthur held a very great feast. From the sea as far as Cornwall, every knight errant and every young lady of any worth came to that court. The King showed them great honour, giving them many costly gifts. When all the lords had arrived and were assembled after the hour of nones* on Saturday, and the King was relaxing and enjoying himself, they saw a very elegant and beautiful young lady come in, quite alone. She was beautifully dressed in a fresh new robe of precious crimson silk; I do not want to give a long description of the saddle and harness of her horse or the rest of her finery: she was so well adorned that it would take a great deal of effort. She entered the hall and didn't rein in her horse until she arrived right before the King. (28)

'Your Majesty,' she said, 'may the Lord who rules everything high and low – the sky, the sea and the land – preserve you! I have come from my country to ask you to grant me a boon: I will not ask for anything unjust, improper or base.' (41)

The King politely agreed that she could have the boon: 'Tell me what it will be,' he said, 'and you will surely have it, provided I am able to grant it.' (46)

'My lord,' she said, 'I thank you. Hear now what I ask of you: tomorrow I wish to be your butler, pouring from your best cup and serving at your meal. I would also like the most honoured, esteemed and accomplished knight here to protect, defend and honour me as long as I am at your court, so that I may not be mistreated: I wouldn't dare remain here without a very good guard.' (59)

The King looked at her amiably: 'My beauty,' he said, 'you may perform the service you desire; but I could not decide who is the best knight in this hall or in my retinue! You are so wise and well bred: perhaps there is a particular man you mean. If you please, name the one you want it to be. I will order him at once to protect and defend you and to place himself at your service for as long as you wish to stay here.' (73)

'My lord,' she said, 'it is not proper for me to give that honour to any one of them: I put this burden on you, who have granted me the boon. I would be afraid of being disliked if I made the choice myself.' (79)

'I'll be damned if I could pick the best!' said the King. 'I pray you, grant me something in return, if you think it good: without making a choice, I would like to place you under the protection of a knight who is handsome and bold, courtly and wise; if he were not one of my own kinsmen, I would find much to say about him!' (89)

The maiden was no fool, and said to him: 'My lord, please tell me his name before I agree.' (91)

'My beauty,' said the King, 'it is Gawain. You will be under his protection tomorrow and for as long as you wish.' (95)

'My lord,' she said, 'when I came here, Gawain was praised greatly, and with your agreement I will stay with him. I do not ask you for anyone but him.' So the boon was granted, just as I have just told you. (101)

Gawain escorted her joyfully to his lodgings, and you may be sure that no one could find any cause for reproach in what he did for her. He gave strict orders for her care to a servant girl and to his own sister, who was very beautiful, saying that they should serve her and keep her company. They passed that night most enjoyably, until the next day. (111)

Gawain arose most joyfully, as did the three maidens. Then he went to church with them to hear mass. The King was already in the church, along with the Queen and her maidens, when Gawain arrived from his lodgings with the young ladies. When the service was complete they all returned together. The best cup was presented to the maiden, I believe, just as had been promised, for the tables were already set. Then the food was served, with many beautiful rich dishes, for King Arthur was no fool and wanted everything to be perfect. But there is no need now for me to tell you everything he did, only what is appropriate here. (132)

The girl served from the cup. The Queen was seated beside the King, and after her sat the King of Wales; Gawain, Tor the son of Arés, and Erec sat on the other side, and Caradoc Briebras* was the fourth; all the others were seated after them. Many a worthy knight and many a pretty young lady was there, with many gold and silver goblets and plates spread before them. They hadn't been eating very long – they had only had one course – when they saw a knight coming through the door at full speed. You must know that if he hadn't been so tall there wouldn't have been a more handsome knight under Heaven: but he really was excessively large. He came into the hall in full armour – and very fine armour it was – except that he had put down his lance outside the hall. This knight was so haughty that he didn't rein in his horse until he was right in front of the King, and he was riding so recklessly that his bridle crashed into the table: no porter or constable said a word to stop him! (161)

When he had looked at them for a long time without addressing a single word to them, he turned towards the maiden, seized her by the shoulders, and set her in front of himself over his charger's neck. 'King,' he said, 'I don't want to hide it from you: this young lady is my sweetheart and I have followed her into many a court since I began to love her. Never before could I find her in a court where I dared to take her; but I see that your court is so feeble and lacking in brave knights – I say this because they're all confused, now that I have taken possession of her – that I will never lose her on their account. I will take her away without any difficulty: no knight seated here will ever take up his shield against me! (182)

'Lord King,' he went on, 'I am going away towards the woods, by the high road which will take me towards my own country. Do you know why I am telling you the way I plan to travel? So that if any knight here, in wisdom or in folly, wishes to dispute what I have just said in battle, he won't be able to claim that I escaped by another road. I make my declaration before all of you: that is the way I will go, and I'll travel slowly until nightfall: I want anyone who follows me to catch up with me easily, if he doesn't dawdle, before I arrive in the woods.' (200)

With these words he set out on his way. He went after his

lance and picked it up, for he didn't want to leave it behind. He rode his horse slowly out through the gate; in that way he carried the young lady off to his own country. (207)

Gawain, who was seated at table beside the King, was sad and pensive: he couldn't decide whether it was more honourable to leap over the table to pursue the knight or to stay seated until the meal was finished. He mulled it over for a long time, not eating or drinking; finally he decided it would be better for him to wait patiently: he knew that his horse was so swift that he would soon catch up with him.* (221)

Kay had seen it all, and called to his companions: 'My lords,' he said, 'see to it that you serve the court properly. I must follow that knight who has haughtily committed such a great outrage in the sight of all these lords, carrying off the young lady right in front of the King while he was at table. Not a single knight said anything to oppose him! You may be sure of one thing: there has never been such a disgrace since the King first held a feast: that coward the King assigned to protect her didn't even budge! May a hundred disasters strike the man who first said that he was a "good knight"!' (241)

With that, he went to his lodgings and prepared himself most splendidly. As soon as he was armed, he mounted his good horse and reached the road the knight had taken.* He scanned the ground in front of him and spotted his tracks; then he galloped off to catch up with him quickly. (251)

He hadn't been riding for very long when he saw him going up a small hill. He began to call out, 'Halt, vassal, halt! I will take that young lady and your horse away with me and deliver you in person to the King to exact full justice! You'll be sorry that you took that maiden away so haughtily, right in front of him! If I don't deliver you to him dead or captured, I'm not worth a fig!' (263)

The other man put the young lady down, turned his horse around and said: 'Is this Gawain who is following me so furiously?' (267)

'Certainly not!' he said; 'I am Kay, King Arthur's Seneschal!' (269)

'That's bad luck! You're not the one I was looking for: in my country, there hasn't been a lot of praise for you as a knight!' (273)

THE PERILOUS GRAVEYARD

Then they charged each other without any more discussion. Kay struck him with full force under the boss of his shield, piercing and splitting it, but his hauberk protected him – not a single link of it failed: Kay had struck well, but his lance broke. The knight struck back so vigorously that he threw both Kay and his horse to the ground: he fell into a ditch, battered and bruised all over, and his right arm was broken between the shoulder and the elbow; his horse leaped up and tore off down the road. The knight didn't say a word to Kay, but just left him lying there; he went straight back to the maiden and lifted her up in front of him again. 'My beauty,' he said, 'I don't believe that Master Kay will be taking you away!' Then he continued his route towards the woods, sporting joyfully with his sweetheart. (297)

Now I must return to King Arthur and his companions. He was still sitting at the table, deeply troubled by this adventure. As they all watched him, he picked up a knife and drove it into a loaf of bread, pushing so hard with his hand that the knife snapped in two. There wasn't a single knight who dared to ask or inquire why he was so upset. The King realized that they had seen him break the knife, and said, 'My lords, I am furious about today's disturbance, but I am even more upset by Gawain's failure. I never expected to be offended by just one knight without Gawain coming to my defence! If any other knight had the maiden in his care and through some cowardice didn't dare to defend her, it would have been up to Gawain to defend her for the sake of my honour. I am extremely troubled that such misfortune has come to me on such a fine day!' (323)

Then Yder the son of Nut said to him, 'My lord, have no fear: the Seneschal has gone after him and will avenge this shame!' (331)

'That will do no good,' said the King. 'Now my worries are twice as great: that man is so daring, powerful and haughty that Kay won't cause him any difficulty! He is a very valiant knight: never in all my life have I seen anyone more presumptuous!' (339)

'Please, my lord,' said Gawain. 'You have spoken as you pleased: but I did not want to leap over the table in the middle of the meal. I was afraid of being reproached if I jumped over it. You are such a great lord and God has exalted you so much that even if the Emperor of Rome came to your table to threaten you, no matter what he said – provided he did nothing worse to you – no one ought to cause any disturbance. Once the meal was finished, the man you selected for the task could go to avenge your shame and his own. I know that I have such a fine horse that I will catch up with him quickly! Do not think that he can carry off the young lady unchallenged. May God never grant me honour if I let him get away for any other reason! If I have done wrong in any way, I am ready to remedy it.' (365)

With that he rose from the table and asked for his arms, and two lads brought them to him; he was armed quickly and then he mounted his fine horse without even using the stirrups. When he had taken up his shield and had been given his lance, he hastened on his way. (374)

Gawain rode towards the forest; he was extremely annoyed because he couldn't see the knight anywhere. Then Kay the Seneschal's charger came rushing up at full speed; Gawain recognized the horse and caught it in a pass through the hills. It was wounded in its forehead and bleeding profusely; the saddle-bow in front was shattered and its reins were broken and ripped, so that nothing was left but the halter. 'By God!' said Gawain, 'a very valiant man has struck you!' He was dismayed and afraid that Kay had been captured or killed: 'Ah, God! It is my fault! What misfortune has struck me today: because of me the King has lost the knight he loved so much! Wherever I go it will always be thrown up to me! I will be shamefully reproached, and I can't say it will be wrong: he is dead because of my failure, for I had the maiden in my care.' (401)

In such great sorrow, he looked far down the road and saw Kay getting up, with great difficulty, from the place where the knight had left him. Gawain let his horse run, spurring it towards Kay. 'My lord,' he said, 'I am sad and distressed by your misfortune, for I am afraid that you will blame me and say that it was my fault.' (411)

'You coward,' Kay replied, 'it certainly did happen because of you! You're very proud and arrogant in the Queen's chambers: any woman you deign to speak with there is certainly not poor or wretched! Anyone who heard you boasting about your valour and prowess would never expect the King to be so insulted at his table by just one knight through any laziness, cowardice or

THE PERILOUS GRAVEYARD

deficiency in you! But today I've seen you stopped in your tracks.' (425)

'My lord,' said Gawain, 'I do not dispute that I was very wrong in this matter; but here, I've found your horse: mount up, if you please, and I will go to the forest to pursue the knight, for I must avenge the shame he has caused me without delay.' (433)

'A hundred curses on any man.' Kay said to him, 'who ever receives that horse from your hands or admires you enough to feel grateful to you for it!' (437)

Gawain paid no attention to his insults, but tied the horse to a nearby willow. Then he galloped towards the forest at full speed. Sir Kay struggled to reach the horse and led it over to a slope where he mounted it with some difficulty, and went back to his country in his misery. (447)

Gawain swiftly followed the knight, who was travelling easily and had already crossed the plain and entered the forest, and Gawain, still in pursuit, went into the woods behind him. He rode along like that for a long time, without seeing him anywhere. But then he heard three young ladies crying out in great need: 'Ah, God,' they said, 'have pity! What will we do, poor wretches, when all the joy in the world has turned to sorrow today! Maidens may truly say that they have utterly lost all hope of security.' Gawain left his path because of their great lamentations, rode towards them at full tilt, and found them at the edge of a meadow. After he had greeted them, he addressed them sweetly and asked why they were so distressed and why they were mourning so much. (471)

'Alas,' said one, 'if it were up to me all three of us would be dead! It is a pity that we are still alive when we have suffered such a loss, which could never be described or related by any human mouth.' With that she fainted on the ground and the lamentations began again. Gawain looked behind them and saw a young lord lying on the ground. He was handsome, tall, well built and elegantly clothed, but both of his eyes had been plucked out, and very recently: his face was still bloody. (486)

Gawain was very angry about this: the young lord was so handsome and well dressed that he seemed to be of high birth, and Gawain believed that this mourning must be on his account. 'My beauty,' he said, 'how and why was this lad here treated so brutally? I am very eager to know.' (495)

The second girl replied: 'May it not please God for me to live any longer, when I have seen honour, grace, generosity and nobility – the flower of chivalry – all die here together!' With these words her heart trembled so that she grew pale and fainted beside the first young lady. (504)

Gawain addressed the third young lady: 'My beauty,' he said, 'I pray you, in return for the service I will do for you at your request, tell me, if you can, what is the source of your mourning?' (510)

'My lord,' replied the young lady, 'since you have spoken so courteously, you will be told the full story of the sorrow and its cause. My lord, we are not mourning as much as we should: if everyone in the world knew of the sorrowful disaster that has happened today, they would all lament just as much! This loss is so great that when it is known everywhere it will be greater than anything that has ever been seen. Our sorrow does not equal the misfortune, for the man who was so brave and wise, who surpassed everyone in the world, has just been killed right in front of us in this forest. You can easily tell who it is that I mean.' (531)

'My beauty,' he said, 'since I didn't see him, I can't be certain.' (533)

'My lord,' she said, 'it is Gawain, the nephew of noble King Arthur, the best knight of all, who was praised and loved so much. Today he was travelling unarmed through this forest just for pleasure, lightly armed and with no companions or escort. He had brought no arms with him except his lance, his shield and his sword, and he travelled with no companions. Three knights – God damn them! – who had hated him for a long time, followed him here. When he came out of that valley, one of them let his horse run and charged straight at him; the two others lay in ambush while this third man was attacking him. The battle lasted until Gawain finally got the upper hand: the two men he had left in the woods couldn't abide that, and rushed to aid their companion. They subjected Gawain to such an attack that he couldn't defend himself, for he was alone and there were three of them, all well armed. The lad you see there was very brave, and rushed to help Gawain; he did all he could to help, but he had a formidable task, for the other men were big and strong: his efforts against them were useless, since he was completely unarmed. They plucked out the lad's eyes and cut Gawain into pieces. My lord, we tell you truly, we are sad and distressed not for the sake of this lad; we are most distraught because of the Good Knight, who is dead.' Then they began to lament again, so violently that no one could describe it to you. 'Alas,' they said, 'what can we do? Ah, Death, how greedy you are! We had no one but our brother here, and we have lost him! Wretched Death, why do you not kill us at once? But this is always your custom: when someone wants you to come and appeals for your aid, you refuse to help or assist them. You have killed the Good Knight, and the whole world will feel the grief. Ah, Death, how ignoble you are, so eager to take good men and leave cowards alive! There is no reason or moderation in you. Have you no consideration for these three unfortunate women who now have no use for their own lives?' (597)

'My beauties,' said Gawain, 'do not despair! There is no reason for your fear! I have come straight from the court, and just now I saw Sir Gawain seated at table: I assure you, I saw him in perfect health when I left.'* (605)

The lad replied to him: 'No, my dear lord; he is certainly dead!' (607)

'My friend, what do you know about it? How can you be certain of that?' (609)

'I was Gawain's squire at a tournament once,' he replied, 'and so I am absolutely certain he is the one who was cut to pieces.' (613)

'Then show him to me, my friend; I will surely recognize the body.' (615)

'My lord,' he said, 'the men who killed him are already out of the forest. After they took his head, they cut off all his limbs: they mutilated him so cruelly that neither foot nor fist remains. They are now a good three leagues away, taking the body off to their own country for safekeeping. They're not afraid of anyone now.' (625)

These's no need to wonder whether Gawain was furious and upset because of the lad who had been so tortured and the maidens he saw mourning over himself. He was enraged because of the lad, for a man who has had his eyes plucked out is wretched for the rest of his life. He also knew that it was because of him that this evil had been done to the lad. His anger with the knight who was carrying off the young lady was still fresh: so he didn't know what to do, whether to follow the first adventure or the new one. It seemed to him that he should complete the first adventure first, and later, if he could return safely and without difficulty, he would undertake this one and exact vengeance if he possibly could. (647)

'My friend,' he said, 'I must be going; I commend you to God. You may be sure that if I had been here earlier, my shield would have been pierced, my hauberk destroyed and my body grievously wounded before you would have been so mistreated! You will not know who I am until I come back; once I have returned, I will never stop until I am dead or you are avenged!' (660)

Gawain commended the maidens to God and then sped across the meadow until he was back on his proper road. He continued for a long time, until he had passed through the forest. On the other side of the valley he saw the knight riding in the distance. Night was beginning to fall, and Gawain urged his horse on until he too was on the other side of the valley. (670)

Then he saw before him a castle, entirely enclosed by rocks and squared stones, with a wall a hundred feet high: this castle was so strongly fortified that it did not fear any assault. He realized that it was too late to conclude his battle without difficulty, so he decided to wait and fight the next day with the knight he was pursuing: he was convinced that the knight would take lodgings in the castle, so he himself would stay there too and await the battle there. This is what he thought he would do, but it turned out quite otherwise. (687)

The other knight passed quickly through the outer enclosure, the sun set, and the gates were closed. He followed the road until he came up to the castle. The lord was seated with his people in a little field in front of the tower. The knight greeted him politely and then asked him for lodging. 'Dear friend,' said the lord, 'you will have it most willingly!' At once a knight rushed up to assist the young lady to dismount; the lord summoned his lads to help the knight off with his armour; then he had a tunic and a grey mantle brought for him. When he had seated the knight next to him, he asked him most politely about his situation and his plans, where he came from and where he was going; the knight told him, without stooping to lie to him. (711)

THE PERILOUS GRAVEYARD

I must return to Gawain who was still riding across the plain: nothing concerned him except finding lodgings while it was still day. He pushed his horse and came quickly up to the gate. He looked up through the strong town and examined the castle. He called to the porter, loud enough so that he heard him. 'Dear friend,' the porter replied, 'you're calling in vain, for the sun has set; no door will be opened tonight, no matter what the cost, nor in the morning before it is fully daylight. The lord of this fief, the clerks and knights, soldiers, townsmen and squires have all sworn that the gate will not be unbolted for any man alive once the sun has set, not until the next day.' (735)

'My friend,' replied Gawain, 'it is very late and I am exhausted. Tell me where I can find somewhere to lodge tonight.' (739)

'My lord,' he said, 'there is no house or cottage in this country for ten leagues in any direction. I do not know what to advise you: you could easily wander through the woods and moors all night.' (745)

'My friend,' said Gawain, 'I am going. I commend you to God.' He had not travelled the length of a bow shot when he saw a high and beautiful chapel beside the road, whose graveyard was surrounded by a wall. Gawain thought that he could pass the night safely there: but if there was ever a need for him to be bold, now it was even greater! Never in all his life had he escaped from anything so dreadful. He went up to the chapel and dismounted in the graveyard. He put down his lance and shield and leaned them against the wall of the chapel. He removed the saddle from his good charger, combed and groomed it well, and then left it to graze on the grass and sat down on a tomb. Just then that he heard a young lord* trotting along the road from the woods on his horse. He went out of the graveyard and asked him: 'Who are you, passing this way so late?' (771)

The lad shrieked and called out: 'Holy Lady Mary, save my life and my sanity! Glorious God, preserve me, so that I don't go insane and the devil doesn't get me!' (777)

Gawain was astonished. 'My friend,' he said, 'don't be afraid. May the True God whom you implore protect both you and me from evil.' (781)

When he heard Gawain speak of God, he turned his horse

towards him and came over at once to ask who he was and what country he came from. (786)

'Dear friend,' he said to him, 'I am Gawain, the nephew of the King. Why were you so terrified of me when I spoke to you?' (789)

'My lord,' he said, 'I will tell you. Don't you know that you have taken lodgings in the Perilous Graveyard? Every night – I swear it, and do not think that I am telling you fables – the devil comes to haunt it, or two or three of them, I don't know how many. For more than a hundred years any knight or any other man who stays here has been found dead in the morning. You have arrived in a dangerous harbour indeed, unless you look for other quarters. If you will take my advice, I will gladly provide you with fine lodgings, for the castle up there used to be mine; I gave it to a knight when he took my sister as his wife. They were all still sleeping when I went out today to hunt in this forest: that is a sport which pleases me greatly. Right away, I struck a deer: I followed it all day long, until one of my hounds caught it; I took a long time to render and butcher it. You can see it here where I have already loaded it on to my horse. We will have plenty of it for boiling and roasting. In God's name, my lord, I pray you not to stay here, if you value your life at all. Come up there to stay, for you will have fine lodgings.' (825)

'Well,' said Gawain, 'that is not what I heard. I just went up there to the gate and a servant told me that I was wasting my breath. He told me in no uncertain terms something which astonished me: every day, as soon as the sun has set the gates are barred and never opened until daylight.' (835)

'By my faith,' he said, 'that is a fact; he told you the truth. But we will soon come to the trench; I will throw my game into it and we ourselves will leap over it, and then we will scale the walls. My servants are in there, probably very worried right now; they will hoist us all up the wall, you and me and the venison.' (845)

'But my friend,' said Gawain, 'what provision could we make for our horses?' (847)

'My lord, we'll leave them to graze out here all night. Mine is very used to that: it won't go far away from the wall.' (851)

'But what about mine?' said Gawain. 'It doesn't know this region. If wolves or other wild animals should kill it, it couldn't be concealed; I would be blamed in my country as long as I live for abandoning it in such a cowardly fashion and letting wolves kill it! It will certainly not stay out here alone: I will endure both good and ill with it.' (863)

'You'd be a fool to let yourself be killed out here of your own free will for the sake of a horse,' he answered. 'You can easily get another horse. Trust me: come into that castle where I must go!' (870)

Gawain said to him: 'It is decided: I will not go anywhere with you unless my horse comes too. But I pray you, if it is possible, to grant me a boon. You will be well rewarded for it if I am able to escape from here.' (875)

'I promise it to you,' he replied, 'with all the loyalty I have: I will grant it to you if I can.' (880)

'My friend,' he said, 'now listen closely: a very tall knight – if he wasn't so tall, he'd be quite handsome – has taken lodging in this castle. He is carrying off a beautiful, noble, courtly young lady on his horse. He had the effrontery to take her away today from the King's court, when she was in my care. I was deeply humiliated by this, and I have pursued him all day without being able to catch up with him. I have never been as upset about anything as I would be if he kept her with him tonight! For my sake, if it can possibly be done, would you take on the responsibility of seeing that your sister takes charge of her tonight? You will be doing me a great favour. If the knight should have his way with her, my honour would be lost forever. Tomorrow, when it is day, he may take possession of her again. If you can do that, I don't care which way he goes after that, for he will have to fight me.' (904)

'It will be done,' he replied, and galloped off, since he didn't dare delay any longer. He came to the trench and called to his servants who were up on the walls, terrified that he was dead or wounded. He threw his venison into the trench and jumped in himself; he left his hunter in the field, after taking off its trappings. He carried it all with him, trappings and game. He didn't allow himself any other cause for delay: they quickly pulled him up the wall. (919)

The news of the lad's return came to the lord. He left the castle and rushed along the road to meet him, happy and joyful at his return. The lady herself ran to meet him, with all the people of the court: no porter or a guard remained behind. There was never such rejoicing for a single young man as was shown for him in the castle, for everyone knew that he had gone with his bow to hunt and amuse himself in the forest, and he had been gone so long that they were afraid that the devil who guarded the Perilous Graveyard might have attacked him. They were very afraid of this, for even the bravest of them would have turned coward at that. (940)

Then they went into the hall, and the lad looked at the knight and the maiden he saw seated there, concerning whom Gawain had made the request. He recognized the knight, who was so tall, by his appearance and demeanour. Then he addressed the lord: 'My lord,' he said, 'there has never been and there never will be such a sorrowful disaster in the Perilous Graveyard, you may be sure, as will happen tonight! The whole world should certainly weep for him, for he has no equal in the world in generosity or in courtesy, and yet he has not become arrogant because of his great chivalry. Curses on the Perilous Graveyard, since he has taken lodging there! When King Arthur learns of it, he will destroy our country completely! The powerful King will call us to account – and rightly so – for his nephew, whom he is losing right now. He is losing him and it is a great pity! God! How his kinsmen will grieve when they learn of it! Everyone in the entire world, even those who know him only by hearsay, will be sad and distressed for him, since he was honoured and loved so much. My lord,' he said, 'now hear the circumstances – the outrage and the wrong – which brought about his death. (976)

'The knight I see there came not long ago to court while the King was at table. This maiden had come there the day before to offer her service to the King: she was staying at the court and performing the service from the royal cup, and Gawain was protecting her against all shame and dishonour. Suddenly this knight had the audacity to seize her, in the King's presence. Gawain followed him all day long through the forest of Cardueil. I saw him in the Perilous Graveyard and I stayed with him there for a good long time, and he recounted to me, from beginning to end, how he had pursued him all day. I entreated him sweetly to come and take lodgings here, but he absolutely refused to come without his charger. If you value me or anything that I may do for you, see to it that I find you a good friend, for I have a request to make of you.' (1001)

'I will grant you anything that you wish to ask of me,' said the lord, 'even if it were all my land.' (1004)

'Thank you, my lord,' he said. 'I pray you that my sister may guard this maiden for the rest of the night: the knight who brought her may have her again, without dispute, in the morning. Sir Gawain requested me that she not be in the knight's control tonight.' (1011)

The knight looked at him brazenly and said to him: 'That will not happen! Rather let me be damned five hundred thousand times! I have followed her to many courts and just now I caused a commotion about her in front of the King as he ate, in the sight of many knights: I will never consent to have anyone else guard her, not as long as I can still stand!' (1020)

The lord was very refined, and asked him politely to be kind enough to yield her, and then the lady entreated him, as did all the people of the palace, saying that he would do well to agree. (1027)

'This is pointless,' he replied. 'I would not do it for anyone!' (1029)

'This is all there is to it,' said the lad: 'if what I want is not done, I will go back to Sir Gawain and tell him that I was unable to fulfil his request. It is more seemly for me to tell him, since it is necessary to do so, and to go back and share everything with him, good or ill, rather than have him think me disloyal!' (1040)

When the lord heard this and realized that he had made up his mind to go back, he said: 'My friend, if you cannot get what you want by a request, I will use violence rather than have you leave the castle tonight. My friend,' he said to the knight, 'it would be better for you to turn her over to me as a favour. You will gain greater honour than if she is taken from you by force: if she is taken from you in battle, she will never be returned to you, but if you entrust her to me amicably you will get her back tomorrow morning with no difficulty.' (1055)

The knight finally realized that he was wasting his efforts: he was forced to give her up, and there was no way to avoid it. 'My lord,' he said, 'I took lodging here with you in all good faith. Now you are going too far, saying that the maiden I love so much will be taken from me and not returned. This is a piece of treachery, and no one could defend you on the charge!' (1067)

'My friend,' said the lord, 'I'll make you understand that it must be so and can't be otherwise, if you will listen to reason. The maiden you are bringing is not yours: rather, you abducted her. It is therefore quite proper and correct for her not to lie with you: there is a knight spending the night outside in the chapel who is following you for the sake of this young lady; he says that he will fight with you tomorrow and maintains that you took possession of her wrongfully. If he can prove it in this way, it would be very wrong for you to have any joy or sport with her. You would be wrong to have any joy or pleasure with his sweetheart if he can defend his claims to her.' (1087)

'My lord,' replied the knight, 'his word is not enough to prove it! He could easily have overtaken and found me before I arrived here if he had seen any advantage in it, for I was travelling very slowly and the horse he rode pursuing me was not slow.' (1095)

'Your plea is pointless,' said the lord, 'it has been decided. Either she will be delivered to me amicably or I will take her, right before your eyes.' (1099)

The knight realized that he could not keep her by fighting and so he preferred to give her up peacefully than to be harmed and to lose her anyway. 'My lord,' he said, 'since I have to give her up, and since I'll have her back in the morning, then I'll put up with it.' (1107)

The lady took the maiden and escorted her to her room, which was very beautiful. She and the young lady ate together most happily. The lord and all his people ate in the hall, in great joy and happiness – except for the knight: the meal was unpleasant for him because he didn't see his young lady there. (1117)

The news spread throughout the town that because the sun had set Gawain was lodged outside in the Perilous Graveyard. Clerks, townsmen and knights all felt great anguish; everyone ran to the church to pray to God to protect him from death. You could have heard such great lamentation that it could not be described. Some of them mounted the battlements to hear what would happen and to find out how Gawain would fare. (1130)

Sir Gawain sat down on a tomb of grey marble between the

wall and the grating. The tomb was so splendid that I don't believe I could describe its form and I am afraid I could not succeed in recounting how it was sculpted: so I won't even try. He hadn't been sitting for very long when he felt the stone lid move under him and begin to rise: he was astonished, since he couldn't see a soul anywhere in the place! The stone continued to rise and his feet were lifted off the ground. He went to find another place to sit, for this one was not to his liking. He hadn't gone more than four steps when the tomb was completely open: there, stretched out in plain sight, he saw a young lady. She sat up, right before Sir Gawain's eyes, and he raised his right hand to make the sign of the cross over his face and head; nevertheless it seemed to him that ever since he was born and had first been able to recognize beauty, he had never seen such a beautiful woman. She was splendidly dressed in a parti-coloured samite robe of green and red, which left him gaping. 'Gawain,' she said, 'I am astonished that you are afraid of me.' (1165)

'Young lady,' he said, 'I see something I have never seen before: it not surprising that I am a bit anxious. There is no knight in King Arthur's kingdom brave enough to feel confident if he discovered you like this.' (1173)

'My lord,' she said, 'I assure you that I am one of God's creatures, and God has brought you here to free me from my captivity. I am sure of it: without your help, I will never be free from humiliation, pain and sorrow. But I will escape from it tonight, through you.' (1181)

'My beauty,' he said, 'tell me the truth about this Perilous Graveyard: I am very eager to know how it got this name in the first place. I would also like to know about you: how and why and for how long have you been here all alone?' (1188)

'My lord,' she replied, 'after my mother's death my father married a woman of a much higher rank than himself. She was very beautiful, but I was even more beautiful, and she was very jealous of me. She worked treacherous spells and enchantments, bewitching me so that I lost my mind. For a long time I acted like a madwoman, not knowing what I was doing. One day as I was going along a road alone, I met a devil in human form, who spoke to me at once: "My beauty," he said, "I can cure you this very day of your torment and the great sickness in which you have lived for so long if you are willing to be mine." (1208)

'I was very eager to be cured, and so I promised him at once that I would do everything he wished. He undertook to cure me, and afterwards I never had the least attack of this illness. He took me up onto his horse and brought me here, and I have been with him since that day. My life has been miserable, for I gave him his pleasure every night, and every day I would lie alone in this tomb; nevertheless, he did all he could to provide me with whatever I wanted. He catered to my every whim: beautiful dresses and jewels and whatever foods I wanted. But I hated him so much when I saw him coming every night, so ugly and hideous, that I would rather have died than belong to him. That is why this is the Perilous Graveyard, for it is here that he takes lodgings every night. (1233)

'My lord,' she said, 'now there is no other choice: you must fight against him, for I am certain that he is coming and that he is not far away from here. Do not be dismayed; have good hope in God: if your faith is firm, you would be wrong to fear him at all. You recognize the cross, whose sign I see up there; when you are most anxious about your battle, look up at it without fail, recover your breath, and you will at once be relieved of the greater part of your fatigue. If you do not pity me, dear lord, at least have pity on yourself: for you may be absolutely certain that either he will kill you or you will kill him. I will never be free from misery unless you deliver me tonight. Dear lord, now prepare yourself: mount your horse, for the disloyal traitor is not a half a league away!' (1259)

Gawain put on his helmet and mounted his good horse. The maiden with the charming body hastened to arm him; she handed him his shield and lance. By then the devil was by the wall: 'Now,' she said, 'have courage!' (1266)

The devil came through the gate: 'You whore!' he said. 'You are a dead woman, and your lechery has brought you shame! This little tryst will soon come to a bad end: he'll be sorry that he ever knew you!' (1272)

She replied courteously: 'It grieves me greatly, certainly, that I was ever your whore. But this is Sir Gawain, who is so praised and honoured! I firmly believe that God will come to his aid tonight and that I will no longer be your servant.' (1280)

When he learned that it was Gawain, he was furious, for he knew how renowned he was. They charged at each other as fast as their horses could carry them, and struck each other in the chest with their lances so violently that both their lances flew in pieces. They did not stop because of that; they charged again so fiercely with their horses, bodies and shields, that they were all thrown to the ground, horses and knights together. Gawain was shaking all over with fury and leaped to his feet at once; the devil was not at all dismayed, but had already seized his sword. Then single combat began: no one ever saw one so harsh! They didn't fear each other at all, to judge by the way they acted. The devil rushed at him and struck him on the helmet with his sword, splitting and breaking it in several places. Gawain took it boldly and paid him back as he ought to, for he hit him back savagely; he struck him a hundred times in a row before that assault was finished. It was a tremendous battle! (1310)

The devil struck him with his sword on the top of his shining helmet and broke its circlet. The blow glanced onto his shield and cut off more than a quarter of it. Gawain struck him with his steel blade on his helmet so hard that he knocked loose the precious stones on it: emeralds, sapphires and topazes all fell to the ground before him, and he struck down every bit of gold and enamel. The blow came down on his side and cut off the skirt of his shining mail coat. Both of them were battered, sore and exhausted, for each of them worked hard to wound or hurt the other. The devil was very angry, very strong and worthy: Gawain retreated to the archway at the entrance to the chapel. (1333)

'Gawain,' said the young lady, 'do you not believe in Glorious God, the King of Majesty? See the sign of the cross there!' (1336)

Gawain heard the girl's words and rushed against the devil so furiously that he pushed him back fifteen feet. The devil was enraged when he saw that he had to retreat; he ran at him as best he could and made a new assault. He struck him on the right side of his helmet from Pavia, cut off a quarter of it and unravelled a hundred links of his hauberk. The blow fell on his shoulder and wounded him in two places. He struck him again and again and pushed him back to the porch. Gawain brandished his sharp sword and defended himself as well as he could. The devil leaped at him and began a third attack, but the blood gushing from his wounds had weakened him greatly. For a long time he continued fighting and defending himself, with great difficulty. The powerful devil almost bent Gawain to his will, but Gawain fought no less vigorously, for the sake of the tearful maiden. Nevertheless he was forced to support himself against the wall, for he had many wounds to his head, his neck and his shoulders. The maiden was distraught when she saw him weakening: 'Alas,' she said, 'how can a devil be so powerful? Ah, good knight, what are you doing? Do you not remember the cross?' (1375)

Gawain's strength returned to him, along with his valour and bravery: he looked at the cross and then rushed quickly against him. He struck him such a sword-blow that he knocked him to his knees, and split his shield from top to bottom so that both pieces fell to the ground. Then he returned to the attack, for he could see that he had wounded him grievously. He forced him back towards a tomb behind him. The tomb was big and long, and he pushed him over the top of it. (1389)

What more can I tell you? The devil fell over it so hard that he didn't have the strength to get up. As he toppled and fell, his helmet struck the ground so that the laces snapped and it flew away. Gawain saw his head uncovered, and struck him in the middle of his face with his sword; from the eyes down, the blow cut away all his face and half of his chin. Then he struck him again and again until he had taken his head. Then the young lady sat down, for she had had a great fright. Then she said: 'God bless your arrival here! I have lived in despair for so long, in great anguish and torment! Now everyone can say that this man is the Good Knight, who always brings aid to young ladies in distress.' (1413)

The people on the battlements had heard the noise of battle and the clash of arms in the distance; they realized that one of the two had been defeated, but they did not know which one, and were very fearful for Gawain. They waited until day, troubled and anxious. Gawain took off his helmet and lay down in front of the young lady near the chapel. (1424)

As soon as it was day and the sun had risen, the lad rushed to the chapel. Every knight, young lady and townsman in the castle rushed after him to see Sir Gawain; they were eager to know how he had fared during the night. They were delighted to find him safe and sound, and they stared with astonishment at the devil who had been killed; since he used to ravage the whole countryside, they were thrilled about it. The news spread everywhere that the devil had been destroyed, and everyone knew then that the graveyard had lost its name. (1443)

The tall knight had arisen, and when he had had his horse saddled and had armed himself fully, he asked for his young lady, and set out on the high road which would lead him to his country. Gawain spoke to the young lord who had come to meet him: 'Dear friend,' he said, 'what has become of the maiden and the knight?' (1453)

'My lord,' he said, 'he was already on his charger when I came here, and I know that he is going to his country by the highway. But the request you made of me was fulfilled last night: just as you asked, my sister looked after her all night; then, after the knight was armed, she returned her to his care this morning.' (1463)

'Now, dear friend, look after me and my charger, and see to it that we have something to eat, and your kindness will have been perfect. I have had a very bad night, and I haven't eaten since yesterday morning.' (1469)

The lad mounted his horse, which was big, powerful and swift, and went quickly to the castle. He called two of his servants and provided them with plenty of bread and wine, a large piece of roast meat and a pasty made of two partridges. He gave many other things to them as well – white napkins, cups and salt – and provided them with oats and hay. Then he came quickly back to Gawain, who was waiting for him in the graveyard. There is nothing more to say about this, except that they ate happily. Gawain soon ordered that his horse should be saddled and bridled. (1485)

'My lord,' said the young lady, 'in God's name and for the sake of honour, I pray you not to leave me here, for I would be quite at a loss. I would like to go with you to your country, if that is agreeable to you.' (1491)

'My lord,' said the young lord, 'take both the maiden and me, and, if you please, I will go get a palfrey for her to ride; for a long time I have wanted to be in your service!' (1496)

'My dear friend,' he said, 'I would like this all to happen just as you wish.' (1499)

So the young lord returned to the castle quickly to get a

palfrey: you never saw one more handsome or more elegantly equipped. He brought it to the maiden and she mounted it; Gawain put on his helmet and mounted his horse, and so all three of them set out in that way after the knight. They rode for a long time as I've been telling you, until it was past midday. (1512)

Then they saw the knight riding far ahead of them, recognizing him by his charger and his shield, which was tinted red and glistened in the sun. They spotted him easily, since he had thrown his shield back because he was carrying the maiden. The young lady that Gawain had found in the tomb was very upset and her face turned fiery red when she realized who it was. 'My lord,' she said, 'is that the man you must fight? Even if three or four men attacked him, they would have great difficulty in doing him any harm. In all Britain there is no knight more arrogant, more cruel or more feared in his country; he has recklessly and outrageously killed many a knight! If you can turn back without shame or reproach, I dare say that you ought to give up this battle: none of your battles, not even the one last night, ever brought you as much pain as you will certainly receive from this man. I have heard so much about his strength and his valour that I am terribly afraid.' (1545)

'May it never please God,' said Gawain, 'that I should ever take flight as long as I am alive and healthy, or that he should have the young lady he is carrying off without a fight!' (1551)

'I would rather be dead,' she said, 'than see you forced to lose even a little finger, for you have delivered me from my misery! I am more afraid of this combat than I have ever been before. My lord, I learned who this man is and about his valour from the devil. Until the hour of nones, he has the strength of the three hardiest and most valiant knights that could be found anywhere; when the sun begins to decline, from nones on, he becomes a little weaker. He loses strength little by little until the hour of compline,* but he is still strong and hardy. You may be sure that he will never be so weak as to lack the strength to stand against the best knight who dares to bear arms against him. I'll tell you something more, so that you will know that this is true. Your mother was very wise, and she told you much of what she knew. I know that she was a fairy* and told you your destiny, revealing truthfully what was going to happen to you. She entreated you to be always brave, saying that you would never be defeated or killed by any man in all your life, no matter how strong he is: but she warned you to be on guard against this man, for she feared no one but him. I will tell you his name so that you will know whether I am lying or telling the truth. I know that she named him to you and said that there was no knight so wicked, so arrogant, so bold or so strong in all Britain: he is Escanor de la Montagne. She told you that she wasn't sure about this man: if you were forced to fight with him, she was doubtful about who would be victorious.' (1602)

'My beauty,' he said, 'that is the truth: she told me about him just as you have said. But God will never hate me so much that I would retreat in such a way! I would rather be dead than dishonoured: death is soon over, but shame lasts a long time, for everyone talks about it and spreads the story. As you can see, I could never turn back without shame. I must follow him until he kills me or I kill him.' (1615)

'I am very afraid,' she said, 'of some misfortune to you. But since it can't be otherwise, and since you know about his nature and his life, and since you are aware that he becomes weaker as the sun descends, if you follow my advice you will not begin a battle with him until after nones.' (1624)

'My beauty,' he said, 'I will do as you say: I will fight him after nones, as you have suggested.' (1627)

They travelled all day until they reached a hedgerow. The other knight, who was not going slowly, had passed it long before and entered a valley, and so for a long time Gawain lost sight of him: he could not see him and he didn't know which way the knight had gone. (1636)

So he began to go more quickly. Then he spotted him again, riding far in front of him through the middle of a field. He scanned the whole plain and saw a castle before him: he thought that he had never seen one so well protected, so fine, so strong or so well situated. Because it was growing dark, he was sure that the knight he was following would take lodgings in the castle. He realized that the knight was so far ahead that he couldn't possibly catch up with him before he reached the castle. 'Now, my lad,' he said, 'this is all there is to it! I can see that the knight is going to take lodging down there. How can we do the same?' (1655)

The young lord answered him nobly and affably: 'Most easily, my lord; you would be wrong to be concerned about anything as long as I am alive and healthy. That castle, all the surrounding lands and the large forest used to belong to me. I gave all of it and the lands around to another of my sisters and to a wise and valiant knight when he married her. I believe that the knight will seek lodging there, and we will go to the house of a rich and courteous townsman who has been my father's man and mine: he will give us fine lodgings. It would not be seemly, under any circumstances, for us to go to the castle and take lodgings alongside your mortal enemy.' (1676)

'Go quickly, then,' he said, 'to have a comfortable place for us to stay made ready at once.' (1679)

The lad spurred his horse and it carried him off rapidly. Then he saw the knight they were pursuing pass through the gate. The knight went along the streets until he approached the lord. 'May God,' he said, 'who allowed Himself to be hanged on the cross to save us, grant you honour, dear lord!' (1688)

'My friend,' the lord replied, 'may God protect you! You are tired, and it is late: I will not hesitate to give you lodgings in this castle, for it is certainly time to make a halt.' (1693)

'My lord,' he said, 'I want nothing more, and I thank you very much.' (1695)

Then a knight rushed to help the young lady down, a squire took the knight's horse, and two others ran to help him off with his arms. (1699)

I must now speak about the lad, who had gone to the townsman's house. As soon as the townsman saw him, he was very joyful: 'My lord,' he said, 'your journey is at its end, you may be sure; you have found your lodgings! You would be wrong even to ask for it: tomorrow you can visit your sister in the castle at your leisure.' (1709)

'My lord,' said the young lord, 'truly I have my lodgings, but now, mount up at once and we will go to meet a knight whom I am bringing to stay here; receive him with great honour, for no better man was ever born in all Britain and there is no one so accomplished from here to Germany. So you should be delighted that his arrival has brought such joy to you.' (1722)

The host was very pleased. At once he called his servants and ordered them to prepare the seats, the fire and the dinner, speedily and so well that no one could find any fault. Then he mounted his charger, which was large, swift and agile, and went out of the town. Gawain had already arrived at the gates of the castle. The townsman welcomed them very courteously and led Gawain into his own house. He had him dismount inside the hall, ordered rugs and embroidered cushions to be spread for sitting, and led Gawain to his place; a great fire was burning in front of them. The servants ran up at once to remove his armour, and the young lady with the blonde hair served him most politely. (1745)

'Wait a little,' said Gawain; 'I do not want to be disarmed just yet.' Then he called to the lad: 'My friend,' he said, 'run quickly up to the tower and do all you can to see that he has no joy or solace from the maiden he is escorting. If you love me, do everything you can to ensure that your sister looks after her tonight. Tell him that if he is not willing to agree to that, he has only to mount his horse: I will fight with him rather than allow him to keep her tonight against my will!' (1760)

The lad ran there quickly. Everyone had left the court to go to sit in the hall; as soon as they saw him, the knights all welcomed him warmly. Escanor looked at him and recognized him. 'Damn you for coming here,' he said, 'you meddlesome fool! I'll never be happy until I've taken vengeance on you. If I had you outside, I would avenge myself on you for keeping me away from my sweetheart against my will last night. My lords,' he said, 'you have never seen such a senseless, insolent boy!' (1777)

He told them the whole story of how the lad had treated him the evening before, and the lord replied: 'My lord, may God the Son of Mary never give you the strength or the power to harm him or do him any damage!' (1783)

'Let it pass for now,' Escanor said; 'he will soon die at my hands.' (1785)

The lad was no churl, and answered him peacefully: 'My lord, I can't do anything if you rail at me because of this deed. My lords,' he said, 'I will submit to your judgement concerning this crime: I was following the orders of Sir Gawain, whose man I am, and I will do so again today, not holding back because of this knight! My lords, I will tell you how this quarrel arose.' Then he told them the story from beginning to end: how the knight outrageously seized the maiden, right before the King, and how Gawain followed him and how he fought the devil in the graveyard. He left out nothing about how he had pursued him all day. Then he addressed the lord: 'My lord,' he said, 'I pray you, if you have any affection for me, grant me a boon!' (1809)

'By my faith,' he answered, 'it would not be right for me to deny you anything: I will never do so, concerning anything I am able to grant, as long as I live. I ought to serve you willingly, for you gave me this castle.' (1815)

'My lord,' said the young lord, 'Sir Gawain requested that my sister take care of this young lady tonight and that she should be returned to this knight in the morning with no dispute. I beg you to see that this is done.' (1823)

Escanor heard these words and could not keep silent: 'Do you want to keep me away from my sweetheart like last night? I would rather die on the spot than let her be under anyone's protection but mine for as long as I live! If you do what this boy says, my lord, you will have trouble and shame. I have taken lodging in your house at your request, and if I am not treated well it will turn out badly for you.' (1837)

'By my faith,' said the lord, 'it is true, I gave you lodgings; but I also promised this lad that I would do what he asked. I don't see how I can choose between the two.' (1843)

'My lord,' said the knight, 'it is right and proper for you to avoid treason. You would be blamed for it if I were harmed by you or with your knowledge. If I should be insulted or mistreated here you would be reproached for it all the days of your life.' (1853)

Then the lord agreed with him and told him to rest assured that he would not allow anyone, not even King Arthur, to do him any harm as long as he was in his castle. 'My friend,' he said to the young lord, 'I cannot take her from his control if he does not consent to it willingly, and it is not right for me to be openly treacherous towards him on account of you or your support, no matter what the cost.' (1865)

'By my faith,' he replied, 'I am astonished that you do not put my interests rather than his above all other obligations. But since you are unwilling to do so, the knight who is pursuing the young lady is still in full armour. He has not removed his horse's bridle or saddle, and is down there at a townsman's house. He will fight rather than allow this man to have control of her tonight against his will. On his behalf I tell this man to remount at once and make his preparations: the battle will take place in your court, right before your eyes.' Then he ran to Gawain at his lodgings. (1881)

'Now, Escanor,' said the lord, 'you have no choice. Since Gawain is coming here, you must fight with him. But I would suggest something different: this battle would be ugly and costly if it takes place at night; you will lose a great deal, I think, if you do not delay it.' (1889)

The other knights also told him that it would be very undignified. It was much more seemly for him to entrust his sweetheart to the lady's protection that night and take her back peacefully on the next day. The lady herself entreated him, and promised him that she would guard her loyally and that he would have her back in the morning. He finally agreed, not without difficulty, and the lady took her and escorted her into her room in the tower. She honoured her greatly with food and drink and a fine bed to sleep in. The host was very pleased with this and called one of his servants: 'Run and tell Gawain to rest until tomorrow, for the knight has entrusted the young lady to the lady's care for tonight, without putting up a fight.' (1911)

He ran off quickly and soon arrived at the townsman's house. He saw Sir Gawain in full armour and ready to set out at once for the court. He told him not to go to court, but to stay and rest for the night. (1919)

'My friend,' said Gawain, 'before I take off my armour, tell me truly if Escanor has agreed to the demand I made.' (1923)

'I swear it to you,' he replied, 'he has yielded to my lord; she has gone into the tower with milady, I saw it myself.' (1927)

Gawain didn't believe him and wanted to make sure, so he sent the lad to find out if what the servant said was true. The lad ran to the tower and found the young lady and his sister sitting on a bed and then he ran back to the lodging and reported to him that it was true. (1937)

Then Gawain went to sit down, and they disarmed him at once. His face had been wounded in several places and blood had spurted out, and he was rather unsightly because of the blood and sweat. The host had a beautiful, courtly sister, and he asked her to prepare a bath for Sir Gawain. She did so quickly, and it was soon ready. They took him into the room and bathed him and tended his wounds. The host's sister served him as sweetly as she could, and you may be sure that the girl he had brought with him took great pains to serve him. After he had a leisurely bath and wanted to get out of the tub, the host's sister brought him a linen robe and breeches, whiter than an April flower. As soon as he was bathed and dressed, the meal was ready. (1964)

Then they asked for water. Sir Gawain took a comfortable place next to the hearth; he had his host sit on his right with the young lady he brought from the chapel, and on the other side he seated the host's sister with the lad for whom he had such great affection. They had plenty of bread and wine, meat and fish, roast birds and game, and everything that they wanted; the host saw to it that they were well served amid great joy and pleasure. They ate a great deal of fruit. When they had finished eating, a bed was made for him by the fire, because they were exhausted. I could not describe for you all the honour which the townsman showed him, but he and everyone else did all they could for them. And so he rested and slept. (1989)

As soon as it was fully day, Escanor got ready, eager to be on his way. He was very irritated because he had lost possession of his mistress that night and the night before. A servant armed him rapidly and bridled and saddled his horse; he asked for his young lady, and the lady brought her to him. The news came to Gawain that Escanor was not delaying; he had already hung his shield on his neck, had passed through the gate a while before, and was taking the maiden away. (2004)

When Gawain heard this he was most displeased. He leaped up and dressed himself and asked for his arms. But they were very battered, so the townsman, who was eager to serve him, brought him a visored helmet from Senlis as well as a battle-hauberk and shining mailed greaves: you never saw any so magnificent. The sword they brought was dazzling and sharp, the shield was fresh and new and its belt and straps were inlaid with precious goldwork: never in all his life had Gawain seen such splendid armour. They brought him a powerful, spirited horse, strong, swift and lively, the best in the whole country. (2025)

Then Gawain said: 'May it never please God that this service should be wasted! May He grant me such strength, power and courage that I may find you in a situation where I can repay you for it, for you have shown me great honour indeed.' (2031)

'My lord,' he said, 'I honour you for the sake of my lord here and because I am sure that you are valiant and worthy. I do not know what more to offer you, but take anything else that could be useful to you: I place it all at your disposal.' (2039)

'That is a very generous gift,' said Gawain, 'and I would never have dared to ask it of you. I do not believe that such great honour has ever been shown to a stranger, and I certainly have need of it. But I do not want the sword or the horse, thank you; my horse is strong and hardy and my gilded sword is sharp, but I am most grateful to you for the rest. Now there is nothing to do but arm myself, for I am afraid of being late.' (2053)

The lad and the young ladies took pains to arm him; soon the saddles were put on and they brought out the horses. Without using the stirrups, Sir Gawain leaped onto his mount. Once he was in the saddle, the lad took up his shield and his lance. The host served him and assisted him: he helped the maiden they had brought with them to mount up, and they set out on their way. The good host escorted them until they came to the woods. (2067)

'My lord,' he said, 'I am turning back; I commend you to God.' (2069)

Then Gawain entered the woods on the road Escanor was following. He recognized him at once, riding along kissing his sweetheart. Sir Gawain couldn't allow that any longer and called out to him, 'Knight, put her down! You have been taking her away for too long! You will not keep her any longer without a fight: you have had her in your power long enough.' (2080)

'You have no one but yourself to blame for that,' answered Escanor. 'By Saint Lazarus of Avalon, you could have easily caught up with me yesterday if your horse wasn't so slow, for I wasn't riding very fast. But I don't believe you're really going to fight with me, and I'm certainly not going to ask you to. But you may be sure of one thing: I sent this young lady with the fair complexion from my country all alone to the King's court, and I burst in to seize her right before all those barons, just to find a pretext for fighting with you.' (2097)

'Then it's settled,' said Gawain; 'you will have a battle, since you have wanted it so much!' (2101)

The young lady and the lad were worried because the battle was going to take place so early in the day. 'My lord,' said the lad, 'it is not proper to fight on the road! I know of a meadow nearby and a large and beautiful field: it would be much more seemly for you to go there, if you please, and I would consider it proper for you to fight on open ground. You would be judged unfavourably if it took place on this path full of ruts and potholes.' (2114)

'That is true,' said Escanor. 'I will not refuse to go there if Gawain wishes.' (2117)

So the battle was delayed, and the lad was delighted. 'My friend,' they said, 'you go on ahead and we will follow you there.' (2121)

He set out on a path and rode through the woods until he came into a wide and beautiful field. Escanor put the young lady down in the shade of some elm trees and then put on his armour, and Gawain made ready. They charged each other and struck so hard that the shafts of their lances broke and flew off in pieces, but they stayed firm in their saddles. (2134)

When Gawain broke his lance, he drew his sword quickly and rushed at Escanor furiously. 'Gawain,' he said, 'in my country it is not the custom, if a knight has rashly undertaken to fight with another, for a sword to be drawn until one of them has fallen. They must first prove themselves in the joust and have more lances brought to them and continue jousting, no matter what it costs them, until one of them falls to the ground. The people of Normandy say that there is nothing in the world finer for knights than jousting. Let us have lances brought to us and our battle will be the better for it. Let us ask this lad, who has a strong, swift horse, to go back to the castle and bring us a load of lances.' (2157)

'My friend,' they said, 'do this for us and we will be very grateful to you.' (2159)

He took on the task most willingly and went off quickly, for he wanted to delay the battle until nones. The knights went to rest in the shade until the lad returned: he was extremely upset and very concerned. They sat down promptly, each one next to his young lady; they took off their shields, helmets and saddles in order to refresh themselves and their horses. (2172)

So they waited until the lad came back at a gallop carrying six strong and massive lances, which caused him a great deal of difficulty. One of them was exceptionally long, thick and quarter-cut: the bravest knight in Arthur's kingdom, no matter how big or strong or hardy he was and no matter how vigorously he struck, could never have broken it in a joust. (2184)

Gawain examined the lances and had a thought for which the whole world should praise him: 'Go to that knight,' he said, 'and take him these six lances on my behalf: let him consider which three of them he prefers, and bring me back the rest. I want him to have the choice.' (2193)

The lad spurred his horse along a path through the woods. He showed all the lances to Escanor, on Gawain's behalf, saying that he could send three back and keep the three he chose. Gawain saw that it was almost nones, and no matter what happened, if God allowed him to defeat Escanor, he didn't want him to have any excuse or to say that it was because Gawain had the choice of lances; so he preferred that Escanor should choose first. (2208)

'Ah, Gawain!' said Escanor. 'Just as gold surpasses all other metals, there has never been a report of a knight who has more good qualities than you. You ought to be very happy that you have so much honour that even your enemies are forced to speak well of you! I myself am sorry that I ever sought out this battle. I'm not saying this out of fear: whoever opposes or harms a knight of such great merit must feel very uneasy about it!' (2224)

He took the three thickest lances and gave the others back to the lad. He urged him to thank Gawain on his behalf for this generous present, and said that he should equip himself again at once, remount his horse, lower his ventail and return to the fray. Necessity is a harsh thing: now that they had begun it, neither one of them could renounce this battle without shame. The lad went back, very pensive and fearful for Gawain's sake, and Gawain made ready again. (2238)

Both men were fine vassals. Each one let his horse run and they struck each other with their lances in the chest so that splinters flew far and wide, for they had broken as far as the handgrip. Each one took up another lance and they struck each other under the nipples so that both lances broke in pieces. (2248)

Finally Escanor took up his large lance, his greatest treasure, which he had kept in reserve. Because it was as good as any four others, he expected to knock Gawain down with its force. Gawain took up his lance and they let their chargers race at each other. Because of the length of his lance, Escanor struck first, but he could neither break it nor knock Gawain off his horse, and so he was furious. Gawain held on well and didn't waver at all, and the lance flew from Escanor's grasp out onto the plain and fell in a thicket. Gawain struck him sharply on the boss of the shield, breaking and splitting it; his lance shattered, yet Escanor did not waver. They wheeled about quickly and came face to face. (2274)

Gawain drew his sword and returned quickly to the fray, striking him on the helmet. Escanor responded to him so well that Gawain was astonished. The battle between these two knights was very fierce and lasted for a very long time: shields, bodies and horses crashed into each other again and again, but they were so well armed and their hauberks were so strong that they couldn't do each other much harm. (2286)

Once when Gawain came to attack and wound Escanor, he happened to strike him so violently on his shining helmet that his blade glanced aside and fell on the shield: it split as far as the boss, and Gawain could not pull his sword out. Escanor twisted away powerfully and yanked the sword out of his hand: Gawain was very angry about that. (2300)

No one should be surprised if Gawain was frightened about the fight, since he had lost his sword. He spurred his charger, rushed in front of Escanor and quickly picked up the lance Escanor had just dropped. He wouldn't have traded it for all the gold from here to Antioch! He wheeled his charger around and returned bravely to face his enemy. While he was charging at him he realized that if he struck him on his helmet or shield, they were so strong that his lance would either shatter or fly from his hands: whatever happened, it would turn out badly for him. He knew for sure that if he lost this lance he could not find another weapon of any use to him in attacking or defending himself. Then he realized one thing: he couldn't do him any harm unless he struck his horse. (2328)

So he spurred his charger, and Escanor, holding his steel blade, waited for him boldly. In the encounter, Gawain struck the horse in the chest so that the iron tip came out through the middle of its left side. Then he drew up alongside Escanor, and as his horse fell he grabbed the edge of his shield, pulled it from his neck, and removed his own sword from it. (2339)

Escanor was furious when he saw that his horse was dead and he himself had fallen. He leaped quickly to his feet: 'Gawain,' he said, 'this attack hasn't killed or captured me, but my respect for you has fallen indeed! If my sword doesn't fail me now, you'll soon be on foot with me!' (2349)

Gawain knew that Escanor was so big and strong that if he attacked him he would soon kill his horse: he preferred to fight on foot, for he would have been sad to see Gringalet die. He rushed back to his squire, dismounted of his own free will and entrusted his horse to him, along with the shield he had taken from Escanor. Then he returned straight into the meadow where Escanor was waiting for him. Escanor ran more than a half an arpent to meet him. Then you could have seen the harsh assaults begin again, hauberks failing under the shock of steel swords; iron that had been whiter than a flower turned completely red! You could have seen a harsh combat between the two vassals, for you may be sure that each of them struck and wounded the other with all his strength. (2373)

The young lord and the maidens in the shade felt great sorrow. 'Alas,' said one of the maidens, 'I wish I were dead on the spot!' (2377)

The maiden Escanor was escorting fell into despair; she was so frightened that she fell to the ground in a faint. When she recovered, she began to moan and cry out in sorrow, 'Alas, wretch that I am! If I am losing all my comfort, my heart, my beloved, in this strange land, it is because it was wrong to come here! I have heard, and rightly so, that nothing good can come from an outrage. The fault is my sweetheart's and mine. In his country he was rich and powerful, and I myself had everything I needed. I was sent all alone to the King's court out of pride, and my sweetheart came to take me back, in the sight of all those lords, in order to have a reason to fight with Gawain. He was convinced that if he could defeat Gawain, no other knight in all the world would dare to face him.' (2405)

The other maiden, the blonde that Gawain found in the graveyard, was just as upset and sorrowful: 'Alas,' she said, 'I do not know what to say if I lose the Good Knight, the brave man who delivered me from my misery and is taking me with him to his country in such great honour. I'll be left here alone, wretched, sad and abandoned in my torment!' (2417)

The young lord tore his hair, cried out and lamented sorrowfully. Never did such great lamentations come from just three people, as the two knights tried to kill each other, more's the pity! Gawain had a great advantage in the shield which hung at his neck, but Escanor put up a good defence and didn't seem to fear him at all. Gawain came towards him furiously, striking his helmet with his good sword, splitting it and breaking its laces so that it flew off beside him onto the ground; then he struck him again immediately. Escanor had difficulty defending himself, but he struck him on the helmet, stunning him completely: the blow came down on Gawain's shield so hard that the blade stuck into it up to the hilt. Now Escanor was very frightened and had nothing else to protect himself with: he cried mercy and wanted to surrender, but Gawain was unwilling to accept it. He feared that Escanor wanted to deceive him because things had gone badly for him, and he was afraid that if Escanor got the upper hand he would kill him, because his mother had told him never to fear anyone but Escanor. That made him suspicious, and he felt such hatred in his heart for him that he would not allow him to get away safe and sound at any price. He struck him full in the face with all his might, right below the eyes, cutting off all of his nose and one of his cheeks. His blow left its mark: it split Escanor's head as far as his shoulders. With that blow he struck him dead. (2462)

Then the lad arrived at a gallop with the young lady Gawain had brought, feeling great joy. The young lady Escanor brought was showing great grief, but Gawain ran up and consoled her. He begged her sweetly to forget him and be comforted. 'My beauty,' he said, 'I shouldn't be blamed for killing him. It was caused by his own arrogance, for he made you leave his country to provoke this battle. But you may be sure that I will make your loss up to you if you are willing to follow my advice. I am not surprised that you are sad and bitter, but you may be confident that I will take you with me in great joy to the King's court where you will have the lover or husband of your choice, with great honour.' (2487)

'My lord,' she said, 'there is nothing more to say. Your command will be obeyed. Since I am placing myself on your mercy, behave now in a way that will bring profit to me and honour to you at the end.' (2492)

Then they prepared to travel. Gawain helped the young lady he had brought with him onto her good palfrey. He mounted his charger, and the lad, who was light and was glad to do it, took Escanor's young lady in front of him on his horse. Then they set out on their way. (2502)

The young lord took them to stay in the first castle, where they had fine lodgings; the lord was no fool and welcomed them joyfully for the sake of the lad who brought them, and he was delighted with Gawain. The knight was no churl, and in the morning, when he saw that they had to leave, generously provided another palfrey. All its equipment was new, reins, bridle and saddle. He gave it to the young lady whom the lad had been carrying on his horse. With that, they took to the road again. (2518)

Now Gawain travelled much more pleasantly, for the young lord carried his shield, helmet and lance. Gawain pressed onward and hastened his journey until he came near to his country. He crossed a copse and a small valley until he was less than seven short leagues from Cardueil. (2527)

An adventure came to him there which I must not pass over in silence. He heard the cries and screams of a maiden in great difficulty, so far away in the forest that he was scarcely able to hear her cry. 'Lad,' he said, 'did you hear what I heard?' (2534)

He and the young ladies answered that they had been hearing it for a long time. (2537)

'By my faith,' replied Gawain, 'not for anything in the world would I fail to go to find out why she is weeping and lamenting! I believe that this path will lead me straight to her. You wait here with these young ladies, lad, until I have news about why she is so distraught. When I know the truth about it I will come straight back here. You may be sure that it will be soon, if nothing else holds me back. My dear friend, if it happens that I find an adventure there so that I can't return at once, take this highway straight to Cardueil and tell the Queen on my behalf that I am sending her these maidens. Tell her from me, for my love, to look after them and entertain and honour them until I come to the court. And if she asks about yourself or about who these young ladies are, you may certainly tell her.' (2567)

'Gladly, my lord,' said the lad; 'there won't be a word of a lie about it.' (2569)

Then Gawain spurred Gringalet straight to where he had heard the maiden. When he had ridden for a while and crossed over a hillock, he saw the maiden. The dress she wore, so beautiful and becoming, her bridle and her saddle, her magnificent palfrey, whiter than a flower, so the story assures me, its bridle and equipment – if someone wanted to describe them all and do it properly, no clerk from here to Paris could tell the entire truth in a whole week, no matter how well he applied himself, without omitting something! (2589)

Sir Gawain saw clearly that no one was harming her; he spurred his horse straight towards her. 'May God who never lies, my beauty, grant you joy and honour! I pray you, if it's not too much trouble, and ask you to tell me the cause of your sorrow and why you are lamenting.' (2599)

She was noble and courtly, and answered him: 'My lord, most willingly. A handsome, valiant, wise and courtly knight brought me into these woods: he loved me and I loved him. I will tell you the cause of my distress. This morning, while my dear sweetheart and I were going along this road, we heard a maiden lamenting sorrowfully. He made up his mind and acted at once, leaving me on this road. He galloped off on his Gascon bay to seek the adventure. He told me to wait for him in this very spot, but before I separated from him he entrusted one of his sparrowhawks to me, which he loved and cherished more than any living thing in this world. I knew well that he loved it as much as he could love anything, except for myself, and he told me to guard it above everything. It was then that I, unfortunate wretch, made a foolish mistake. Knowing very little about birds, I began to feed the sparrowhawk, and while I was letting it eat a little bird which it had captured, the sparrowhawk, which was sitting on my hand, escaped from me. My sweetheart will go mad when he comes back; I have been destroyed by bad luck and folly. I know that he is so proud, bad-tempered and cruel that I am afraid he won't love me any more. I have no one to call back the bird, unless someone else will do it.' (2641)

Gawain promised her that he would bring her back the sparrowhawk, and would not leave her until she had it in her possession again. The young lady, happy with this promise, thanked him: 'My lord,' she said, 'may God grant that you get the sparrowhawk back! If you can return it to me, you will truly have saved me, and I will love you every day of my life.' (2653)

'Teach me its call,' he said, 'and I will summon it.' He called out to the bird, which was perched high in an oak tree, but it didn't do any good: the bird paid no attention at all. He moved forward and back, but it was all useless; the only good thing was that the bird was attached by a cord and didn't go any farther away. When he realized that nothing was working, Gawain removed his armour and climbed the oak quickly. (2667)

While he was up in the tree, the knight arrived. He saw the armour and the charger and asked who they belonged to. 'To the best knight in the world,' said the maiden, 'and the most valiant: I dare compare him to all the others, except for you, whom I will not include.' She told him at once how he had found her there, alone, distraught and tearful because she had lost the sparrowhawk. (2679)

Then the knight replied to her: 'You whore,' he said, 'you are lying, that's not how it happened! It was all quite different. I am well acquainted with the tricks of a man who wants to hide his deception. Do you think you can take me for a fool, and make a lie pass as the truth? I know this for certain, since I have plenty of proof: when she needs to, a woman can very quickly invent something to say.' (2691)

In order not to prolong my story, I don't want to describe their wiles. You have heard me say plenty about that on other occasions, so I will keep silent. The knight took the palfrey by the bridle at once and with his other hand he took the horse which Gawain had brought. Then he came back to her and told her that she would never be in his company again in all her life: he would leave her there all alone. She wouldn't go on deceiving him; she had been doing so for a long time, but he had never before seen her deceit so openly. (2706)

Then Sir Gawain spoke to him: 'My lord,' he said, 'do not think that I came here to dishonour you. It never happened! It never even entered my mind. I will never be so senseless as to plan such an outrage. Now hear my request: accept my explanation, and of my own free will I will swear on the spot, whenever you please, with nineteen other knights, that I never sought your shame. If you had heard it all, I never said anything to her because of which she should incur your hatred.' (2724)

'I will never accept your excuses,' the knight said to him, 'and I don't value your oath: I know how easily a man who wants to wash away such deceit is able to lie!' (2729)

Then he went off with the horses, and they had no idea what became of him. When Sir Gawain had caught the sparrowhawk, he came back to the young lady with the bright complexion and comforted her sweetly: 'Now, young lady, don't be upset,' said he, who was worth a thousand men in matters of love, honour and nobility. 'You may be sure that you will have my advice and help without fail; I will never leave you in all my life – except at your command – no matter what may happen to me.' (2745)

'My lord,' she said, 'may God protect you and preserve you from further misfortune. You may be sure that I am sad and upset about this adventure, since you are in difficulty because you acted well and honourably: you only came to me in order to comfort me in my distress.' (2753)

'My beauty,' he said, 'there is nothing more to say: there is no point in despair. Good and ill must come in turns to a brave man, and he should just forget it; if he has another chance to act honourably, he should not hold back because of that.' (2760)

Gawain took up his armour, which was lying under the elm trees, and left there at once with the young lady. He wanted to seek adventures, not knowing where or how or what sort, but if he could he would gladly choose those which would let him know where the knight who had taken away his horse had gone. This was his chief concern. (2773)

Then the weather became very bad: snow, rain, and hail fell down pell-mell, with thunder and lightning everywhere. He did not know what they could do or where they would find the nearest castle, town or lodging: there wasn't even a hermitage in all the forest! 'If you please, my lord,' she said, 'not far away, on the road I came by this morning I saw a covered cross; if we can reach there safely, with the Creator's help we could save ourselves.' (2791)

'My beauty,' he said, 'there is nothing to do but to go there quickly.' They hurried to the cross and both took refuge there. The maiden and Gawain suffered greatly there, for the storm lasted all that night until the next day; neither of them budged, and they had nothing to eat or drink. They stretched out on the bare ground, for they didn't have anything else. I won't say anything about the rest* – about whether they had any other delights – but I can tell you that their bed was very hard and uncomfortable! The wind did not die down, but caused them great pain and anguish, and Gawain, who could not give the maiden any greater comfort, held her in his arms all night. He lay against the wind and held his gilded shield along his back because of the storm which was battering him. He placed the sparrowhawk which he had taken from the oak on the arm of the cross. And so they had found a place to stay, but what they had was far from comfortable. (2821)

So they endured until morning, and when it was day, by the grace of the Creator, the weather was clear and pure. Good King Arthur's noble nephew was very upset and worried: he had to deal with the maiden, who was hungry. She hadn't eaten for three days and he couldn't help her. But her fear and dread of the great storm had made her forget about eating and lose her hunger. 'My beauty,' he said, 'what do you say? What would you like to do? We will not get any help by staying here in these woods.' (2839)

'My lord,' she replied, 'it is up to you, I will do whatever you wish. But I don't know whether we should stay here or move on: we don't have what we would need in order to stay, but travelling would be so hard on me that I don't know which to choose.' (2847)

'Maiden,' he said, 'I can see great difficulties for us if we stay here.' (2849)

Right then a knight came straight towards them along the road. This knight, who seemed to be bold and brave, was not alone: he had a squire leading another horse in front of him. Gawain and the maiden both spotted him together, and when he saw them he dismounted from his palfrey at once. He said to himself that they had great need of assistance and thought that since they seemed to be good people it would be proper to help them and bring them some aid. He turned towards them as quickly as possible. Sir Gawain and the maiden came to meet him, and both of them greeted him. He returned their greeting politely. (2871)

'Dear lord,' said Gawain, 'we had great need of your arrival!' (2873)

'Please tell me,' said the knight, 'how you are travelling, who you are, what country you come from and where you passed the night. Have you had anything to eat or drink since you came into the forest? Tell me, I pray you, why you have undertaken this journey.' (2881)

Gawain answered him quickly and told him everything I have already told you here. The knight was very well bred; he crossed himself because of the strange misfortune that had come to them. 'Now that I have come to you and you have told me your situation, you ought to profit from it. I will help you if I can, but I ask you for a gift before I give you my help: that you will repay me for it on the day when I ask you for it.' (2895)

'I will gladly give it to you whenever you please,' said Gawain, 'provided it is something I am able to grant.' (2898)

'Don't think,' said the knight, 'that I would be so base as to ask for anything you could not grant, for that would be acting badly.' (2903)

'Then it will be done,' said Gawain, 'since you make your request in such a way.' (2905)

'You may therefore ask for anything that you want,' the knight said. 'You can take my horse for yourself, I give it to you: I have seen your need and how much it dismays you, and so I am pleased that you should have it. I would also like this young lady, who seems to me beautiful and courtly, to accept, in her need, this palfrey with all its trappings. I will be repaid for it well when I am in need, and on the proper occasion, since you have given me your promise; I have no doubts about you on that account.' (2921)

'You have spoken well,' said Gawain. 'I thank you for it a thousand times. Since you have given me such a fine gift, you should not be refused your repayment; if I can find the opportunity, you will certainly obtain it.' (2928)

THE PERILOUS GRAVEYARD

Then the knight said: 'Certainly, I know that this covenant will be fulfilled in every way, if I make the request. But if this is not displeasing to the maiden or to you, I would like to ask you to give me the sparrowhawk I see on that cross, in expectation of something better. It would seem a good gift. Do you know why I ask you for it? So that if I ever see you again and I have the sparrowhawk with me, it would remind you that you owe me a reward: that is why I have asked you for it.' (2945)

Gawain then ordered the maiden to give it to him. (2947)

'My lord,' said the knight, 'God help me, because of the great merit which I see in you, if I could do even more for you, I would put all my efforts into it; but you may be sure that I cannot do more.' (2953)

'I do not ask for anything more than you have already done,' said Gawain. (2955)

'You do not know who I am,' said the knight, 'and you will not know until you are in a position to repay my favours.' Then he had his squire dismount, like a courtly man of good manners; and when he had taken his leave of them, he mounted on the packhorse. Then he went back along the road through the forest, just as he had come. (2966)

Gawain took the palfrey, which was very richly equipped with bridle and saddle; he set the maiden on it and then mounted the other horse, thinking again about the great favours that the knight had done for him. He pondered them over and over in his heart, and was very worried and concerned that he might never be able to reward him for them as he wished. The young lady with the bright complexion was happy and joyful because of the help which God had sent to her: they had been distraught, but now here they were on the right track and provided with good horses. So they set out together and followed a straight course, as adventure led them; they rode in this fashion until after midday, without having anything to eat or drink. (2991)

Then Gawain saw a charcoal-maker whom he didn't know at all, coming along the road towards them. He was leading two asses and a packhorse and was moving along very quickly. Gawain asked him if he could tell him where he could find the nearest hostel to take lodgings. (*9)

'My lord,' said the charcoal-maker, 'the Red Fortress is very near here, but don't even think of going there, no matter how great your difficulty or need may be. There is a cruel danger there!' (♦15)

'Dear friend,' said Gawain at once, 'tell me more about this danger that you have mentioned to me.' (♦19)

'My lord, the King of the fortress is very haughty and bold: he is the best knight from here to Germany. You will meet him up there near a fountain, already in full armour, for that is his custom. He comes to that fountain four times each week, bringing with him the most beautiful maiden anyone ever saw. I can't tell you any more about her, but if someone were to describe her appearance and her beauty, he could say truthfully that she is so charming and attractive that no other woman was ever a quarter so beautiful. You may be sure that this maiden will be in great pain: like it or not, he makes her enter the cold, dark fountain as far as her waist, totally naked, so that only her head and breast, whiter than a hawthorn flower, are left showing. She stays there all day in the cold fountain, and does not leave the water before nightfall: only then is she brought out.* Any noble king or count who said anything about it would die on the spot, for he would have to fight against the King. You must know that fifty-four knights have already fought with him: he defeated every one of them, and killed, decapitated and dismembered them, though they were the most renowned men in the whole kingdom! Everyone else has seen so many men killed that they are too frightened to say a word about it. He has sharp stakes fixed in the ground, and when he defeats and kills them he impales their heads and shining helmets on them. No matter how fine a man might be, no one could win any other ransom from him, for so the King has sworn, as you will see for yourself: if you go to the fortress you cannot avoid going past the King. Dear lord, take care and protect your life; if you choose to go in that direction, you will die without fail. You will never pass by without a battle, if you say anything at all about it.' (♦81)

Gawain said to him at once: 'My friend, you have told me enough. I commend you to God: but you may be sure that I will go there to see the maiden and the knight who has proudly set up those stakes on the road. I will tell him that if he is willing and consents, I want to learn what he is doing and why, for I am very curious to know about it.' (♦93)

With these words he left the charcoal-maker and set out on his way. He spurred his charger until he crossed the mountain. Then he saw the fountain, very near the city, and the armed knight on a strong and spirited charger: never in all the country had he seen a knight so handsome. You must know that his shield seemed to be of tanned hide, but it was so strong and so well made that it would be hard to tell you about it; his armour was so splendid that it is not easy to describe it, according to what the tale tells us. There was no white on it anywhere: his thick, strong lance was redder than any blood, with a fine steel tip, and his sharp and pointed sword a fiery red. He was very assured in his stirrups. (♦117)

Gawain rushed up at full speed and greeted the young lady who was astonishingly beautiful. Then Sir Gawain, who was full of nobility, spoke to the King: 'My lord,' he said, 'what is the misdeed for which you are mistreating milady so vilely?' (♦125)

'Knight, ask her to tell you herself, if you want to know; you will be acting very courteously if you can bring her out of there: but you will have to leave your life and your body as guarantees.' (♦131)

'You're talking outrageously,' said Gawain, 'and you ought to correct yourself. I will ask her, if she is willing to tell me: for love and courtesy, why, how and for how long has he been making you suffer this pain and discomfort?' (♦139)

'I will gladly tell you, my lord,' replied the young lady in the fountain. 'This knight is the King of the Red Fortress. He is so proud and wicked that he is not afraid of any man alive. Last year I went to amuse myself with him in a garden; he told me he was absolutely certain that there was no knight in King Arthur's realm whom he could not defeat in battle. I did not fail to reply to him, wretched fool that I was, that it was said in my country that the men of the Round Table were the best in the whole world. And my lord replied to me, "Young lady, I don't believe that there is anyone better than I." I said, "My lord, I believe that there are plenty of better men: anyone who thinks he is the best man in a kingdom or a fief is very foolish and arrogant." He answered me sharply: "Young lady, now I know that you hold me in very low esteem. I'm not surprised, for we have often seen this before: the mighty Samson, who had such great prowess, was betrayed by his wife. A woman by her very nature always values what someone else has more than her own. She thinks she has the country's leftovers, and that she has been cheated! Even if he were the best man in an army, she'd be quick to cover him with shame. Your heart is overheated when you scorn me, and I want to cool you down again. Because you have reproached me, this is the tribute you will have to pay until you have found someone who can take my weapons away from me and defeat me or kill me in battle: four days each week, in front of everyone, I will make you enter this black fountain. I swear and affirm it solemnly: you will stand there without any clothing at all until the sun sets. You can send for your friends, if you have any confidence in them. If anyone is foolish enough to claim that I have no right to inflict such treatment on you, and if I get the upper hand, this will be the punishment: I will impale their heads on sharp stakes beside you, even if a thousand of them come."' (†206)

While the wretched creature in the cold water was speaking with Sir Gawain, the King, who was no churl, called to the young lady whom Gawain had brought and asked her to tell him, in the name of friendship and courtesy, 'who is this armed knight who is so foolish and presumptuous as to come here to speak with my sweetheart so boldly, right in front of me? I would very much like to know all about him.' (†220)

She replied quite openly: 'My lord,' she said, 'God help me, I cannot tell you his name.' (†223)

'You do not know him?' (†224)

'No, by my head!' (†224)

'By Saint Thomas, how can that be?' (†225)

She told him at once how he had found her in the woods; she told him the whole adventure, without stooping to lie. (†229)

I must return to Gawain. The young lady of the fountain was telling him about the suffering and misery she had been enduring for more than three years. But she was even more upset about the loss of the noble and valiant knights he had conquered in combat. When he defeated them, he had sharp stakes set up and impaled their heads in their shining helmets on them. 'There is a stake in front of you with nothing fixed on it yet, but as you see he has leaned a shield against it, which belongs to the last man he defeated. You may be sure that this stake is waiting for your head. He waits for it to be fixed there, according to the declaration that he has made. When it is put there, another stake will be set up beside it, which will wait until another man comes. You must know, my lord, that I have told you all the truth about my situation, if you have understood it properly.' (↕255)

Then Gawain answered her: 'Young lady,' he said, 'come out of the fountain, according to a promise you will hear from me: you will never enter it again as long as I am alive and healthy.' (↕261)

At once she put on her clothes which were lying near the fountain. The knight took a deep breath and shouted to Gawain proudly: 'This conversation will cost you dearly, you may be sure!' (↕268)

'Knight,' said Gawain, 'threaten as much as you please! I am one who will never flee because of you or your threats: if someone wants to fight with me, he will find me on the spot, prepared to defend myself. I am ready!' (↕275)

They defied each other and rushed to strike as quickly as their horses could carry them. They struck sharp, cutting blows with their lances which pierced and cracked their shields. The lances broke and shattered and flew off in splinters, but neither of them left his saddle. The King of the Red Fortress was very upset and angered when he realized that he had not knocked Gawain down. He drew his good sharp blade, struck Gawain furiously on his sparkling helmet and broke it as far as the coiffe, almost knocking him over: but Gawain stayed firm and didn't fall. He turned on the King and struck him so forcefully on the top of his shield that he broke at the boss and cut off a good thousand links of his strong gold-embroidered hauberk. The blade came down between the saddle and the King: it cut the saddle-cloth and all the harness, as well as his good charger, so that the King was hurled to the ground between the two pieces. He was no mean soldier: he leaped quickly to his feet and said, 'By Saint Amant, knight, that blow was not child's play! Any man who came to attack me like that is no friend of mine! But when you leave me, don't beat your breast about it! Now be noble and courtly: get down on the ground like me; if you don't I can tell you that you'll be causing your horse to be killed – and acting like a churl!' (↕319)

Gawain realized then that he was speaking the truth: he knew for sure that the King was strong and fierce and could easily kill his charger. So he dismounted and came to attack his enemy. But the King defended himself so well that Gawain was quite dismayed; he struck him such a blow on the top of his gemmed helmet that he knocked the flowers, emerald and enamel off it. The blow glanced on to the shield and split it as far as the boss, and his hauberk was cut and pierced on the side. But certainly God was protecting Gawain, for his sword twisted back in his hand: if it had not veered aside it would have cut Gawain to the heart. He struck him with such force that he almost knocked him down. But Gawain was not dismayed: he paid back everything that he owed him! He made a new assault and thrust his drawn sword at him; but the King stood firm. Blows rained down on the gem-encrusted helmets. (♦349)

All the people in the fortress rushed to the spot: everyone who was able to walk – young or old, man or woman, straight or crippled, big or small, strong or weak – went there. Through all the streets of the fortress there was a great uproar, for nobles and commoners, clerics, townsmen, knights, ladies, maidens and squires all rushed there together to see what they were doing. They surrounded the fields. The King ordered them all not to speak a word, if they valued their lives, no matter what they saw or heard: 'I will kill any man who does with my own two hands, no matter how renowned he may be. I would not want any treachery against this man any more than against me, and I swear to him that if he can defend himself against me, he does not need to be on guard against anyone else; let him have no fear of that!' (♦356)

All the barons of the kingdom feared their lord. The King of the Red Fortress, who was no churl, spoke to Sir Gawain: 'Knight,' he said, 'what do you think? In front of the people of my country who have come to watch the battle, I promise and swear to you that you do not need to worry about defending yourself against anyone but me here, no matter what misfortune comes to me. I am in complete control of my people: no count or baron would dare disobey my orders even to save his beard, his nose or his teeth. I have given you my assurances and sworn and pledged it loyally.' (♦394)

'I thank you,' Gawain replied. 'Now, protect yourself! I defy you!' (♦396)

'And I defy you!' said the knight. (♦397)

But Gawain struck first, high on the red helmet. He cut the shield in front and broke the straps. He was expert in arms, and struck such a powerful blow that he tore and completely unravelled the hauberk above the armpit and cut off the flesh on his side by the nipple. The King was gravely wounded; the blood flowed down freely down as far as his spurs. (♦410)

When the King realized that he was wounded, he was furious, but he wasn't dismayed. He held his good steel blade and had full confidence in it, recovering his strength from it. He struck Gawain so forcefully that he broke his shield and thrust his sword into the helmet as far as the coiffe. The steel went as far as the skull, and the blade was so sharp that it cut the bone of his head, but it didn't reach his brain. Gawain felt the wound but he wasn't upset at all. He struck back valiantly, and the King defended himself well. They both skirmished well: the King struck Gawain and Gawain struck him, delivering a blow to the helmet that stunned him completely. He struck him back, slicing off half of his shield and a hundred links of his hauberk, so that the blade came down on Gawain's bare arm, cutting it to the bone; red blood gushed out and flowed down to his boots. (♦442)

Both knights were bold, and they were equally matched: no one who wanted to speak truthfully could say which one was better, more valiant or hardier, more enterprising or slower, except that Gawain always attacked first. Their hauberks were all unravelled and their shields were cut to pieces: nothing was left intact to give them protection. They often struck openly, battering and wounding each other. This battle lasted from the hour of tierce* until sunset. They both were so valiant that neither one could harm or defeat the other. Nevertheless Gawain fought very well, like a man who lacks neither prowess nor strength nor daring, and the King defended himself just as well, without seeming to be the least bit frightened. (♦468)

Gawain was upset that the battle was lasting so long. He charged at him furiously, battering and wounding him severely. He struck him so hard on the edge of his shield that the blow slipped all along it: the cold steel came down on his sword-hand, and would have cut off his thumb and two other fingers, but it stopped in time and they held on by the sinews. The

King's good sword flew from his hand, far away from him. He was furious and upset when he saw that he was wounded like that. In his anger he made an effort to run and get his sword; he took up a position behind his shield and out of necessity took up his sword in his left hand and rushed at Gawain. Then you could have seen a pitched battle begin again: the King struck Gawain with his steel blade, and Gawain struck him back, almost knocking him to the ground. The King covered himself with his shield and Gawain prepared to strike him on his head, which was uncovered; but the King had his sword drawn and struck Gawain so hard on the top of his steel helmet that he would have been seriously wounded by it, if God had not protected him. He fell to his knees. (♦506)

Then Gawain came and struck his shield so furiously that he broke it. He hit him again and again, striking twenty blows in a row. He completely shattered his helmet and pulled the ventail off his head. He would have cut off his head, but the King realized he had been beaten and said to him: 'Mercy! You have defeated me. Since I have no choice, take my sword, I surrender it to you.' (♦518)

But Gawain did not accept it. He swore by Saint Thomas, 'It wouldn't take much for me to kill you!' (♦521)

'Ah, noble knight, mercy! You would be committing a great crime if you killed me now when I have thrown myself on your mercy!' (♦525)

Gawain said to him at once, 'You must make yourself a prisoner, and tomorrow morning without delay you and this noble, courtly, beautiful maiden must go to the court of King Arthur. Tell him on my behalf that I am sending you to him as a present; you will tell the Queen and good King Arthur the whole story of the battle just as it happened.' (♦537)

'Agreed!' he answered. 'I will do everything that you wish; you need have no doubt that I will go there willingly. I will report to the King the truth about this battle you fought against me. But I would like to know your name. Who shall I say is sending me there when I arrive at the court?' (♦547)

'My friend, I have lost my name: I am the knight with no name.' (♦549)

'May I know nothing more?' (♦550)

'No, by my faith,' he said. 'Say it just this way, that the man with no name is sending you. Let them welcome and honour you until I come back to the court. Say that I will return when I have found my name. Now tell me your name.' (*557)

'I am called Brun without Pity; I am the King of the Red Fortress.' (*559)

'Your nickname suits you well,' said Gawain, 'you may be sure of that. But you must know one thing: you will rest tonight, and when day has risen, you and your maiden will have your horses saddled, just as you have promised me.' (*567)

The King swore to him at once that he would make himself a prisoner. Everyone around them, knights, townsmen, and vavasours, lamented greatly over their lord who was so grievously wounded, and then returned straight into the fortress. (*574)

Gawain said that he would go without any more delay. He ordered the young lady he had met in the meadow in the woods to mount her palfrey. (*579)

'By my faith,' said the King, 'I pray you in all generosity, if it is at all possible, to come and take lodging with me.' All the knights entreated Gawain, as did the courtly young lady who was so attractive and beautiful. But he told them that it was useless, and he wouldn't remain under any circumstances. He commended them all to God and they did the same. But the King promised and swore to him that he would set out without delay in the morning. (*593)

Gawain did not want to delay, and set out on his way. He had great need of ointment to care for his wounds. The young lady travelling with him could not stop weeping, so he said to her, 'Dear sweet friend, do not cry, I will be healed. You may be sure of one thing: never in all my life have I seen a man as valiant as that knight. I do not want to go to lodge with him, for that would not be appropriate. It would be most improper for me to accept his hospitality after causing him such pain. But I am very concerned that you have not had anything to eat or drink.' (*612)

'Ah, dear lord, I am not hungry: there is no bread in all the world so good that I could eat a bit of it now.' (*615)

So they rode along at a good clip – I don't know where – searching for adventure. But then a strong knight in armour spotted them; he had just finished killing another knight. There was still blood on his shining steel sword, which was well polished and, I think, very strong. Gawain greeted him courteously but instead of returning his greeting he cried out to him: 'Knight, you will not escort that lady any farther, God help me! I am going to make an attack on you, and you will pay for it dearly.' (*631)

That couldn't help but infuriate Gawain. They defied each other and charged. They both struck with all their force with the tips of their lances, shattering each other's shields, and fought each other valiantly. The knight struck Gawain first, on the top of his helmet, with such force that sparks flew from it. Gawain struck him in return full on his broken shield and cut him right to the heart. The charger leaped up and went off through the forest. Gawain was extremely upset at that and did not know what to do: he did not want to leave the young lady alone no matter what. The charger dragged its saddle and fled in panic. Gawain turned back so the maiden wouldn't be afraid. (*653)

That night until daybreak the two of them slept in the woods, and when it was day they both left there again. As a replacement for the damaged shield, which was of no use to him, Gawain took the knight's shield. Then they both mounted up and set out. They rode all that day until it was near midday, and you must know that it was the third day that they had not had anything to eat or drink. (*665)

They then saw a knight, very well and properly armed, who was coming straight towards them. The knight called loudly to them: 'Dear lord, may God save both you and your beautiful companion!' (2997)

'Knight, may God bless you and grant you honour,' said Gawain. 'I have been travelling all day, I don't know where, by adventure.' (3001)

And the knight replied at once, without letting him say anything more: 'Tell me your name, dear lord, if you are willing; I must know, if you please, who you are and where you come from: it seems to me that you are lost and that you have slept in these woods. If so, you had very bad lodgings last night: I am sure that you have not had any bread, salt, fish or anything else you might have needed. Even if you had as much wealth as the rich Sultan ever had, you could not have obtained a single loaf or a cup of wine for it.' (3019)

'You are a good prophet,' said Gawain. 'That is just what happened to us.' (3021)

The man who had met them said to him, 'Noble knight, my lodging was quite different last night. I can boast that the most courtly and beautiful maiden from here to the gates of Rome, the daughter of such a noble man that she is the lady of a castle, gave me the best treatment that any knight ever had. Nothing that I could desire was refused or denied to me.' (3033)

'Then you have been better cared for than I have been,' said Gawain; 'neither yesterday nor today have this maiden and I had the tiniest morsel of anything one could eat.' (3039)

'Dear lord,' said the knight, 'you would be wrong to worry about that any more. I promise you that before you leave me you will be well on the way to finding comfortable lodgings. I would very much like to be your friend and to be at your command. But before you have anything from me, listen to the story of how I have finally met success. (3050)

'Dear lord, about five or six years ago when I was still a young lad and inexperienced in arms, I happened to fall in love with the most courtly and beautiful maiden from here to Caerlion. Love imprisoned me in its bonds and made me as brave as a lion. It made me courtly and enterprising, so much so that I asked her for her love. I set forth my request to her, nervously but as prudently as I could. She placed no value on my words at all, and became quite irritated. Nevertheless, she asked me for time, saying that she would think it over and tell me what she wanted when she saw me again. Not wishing to endure a long wait, I came back to see her very soon. I asked her about her intentions and begged her to be courtly and gracious and to give me her reply. After I had lamented for a long time, telling her of my misery, she was not at a loss to give me a reasonable reply. She readily convinced me that her words were good and true. I never disputed what she said, for I saw that it was reasonable and that she was only looking for an opportunity to see if I would be discouraged. (3085)

'"My friend," she said, "if you love me and if you are telling the truth about the pain you say that you are in on my account, then I am certain that you will not seek to dishonour me. If any son of a powerful count in Wales or England dared to beseech or entreat me to love him, I would not grant his prayer, and he would not obtain any joy or comfort from me – not even a kiss – before he was a knight. If you should seek anything else from me, then I know well that you would be trying to bring shame upon me. But I assure you that when you are a knight and I hear you praised for your valour in arms so much that everyone speaks well of you, I will become your sweetheart. You would be wrong to have any doubt. You will have the proof of it before you leave me: with this ring from my finger, with this pure emerald, I grant you my love on the conditions I have set down. And I tell you, dear friend, that as part of this agreement, you must not entreat me any further: you may be sure that by excess* you would lose every bit of it." (3120)

'I was delighted to have that much; I took what I could from her, for I removed the ring from her finger, and with the ring and the promise she gave me our love was assured. When we separated, the young lady told me sweetly that if I ever wanted to enjoy her passionately, I must avoid all arrogance, baseness and excess. I told her that I would do so, because she had commanded it. When I had taken my leave, I went off to my country. Thanks to my father and friends, I was armed a knight within a fortnight. You may be sure that I devoted all my efforts to acquiring worth and honour. I was so successful that all the people of the fief, young and old, said that they had never seen a knight win so much renown in such a little time as I had done. I cannot recount to you each of my works and deeds, but I dare tell you that I suffered many a torment. At the end of the year, I returned to my young lady and reminded her of our conversation and the covenant she had made with me. She said that I was getting above myself: I did not yet have the worth, the reputation or the excellence to win her so quickly. (3159)

'If I had taken great pains to win fame during the first year, you may be sure that during the next year my efforts were four times greater! At the end of two years, I returned to my sweetheart and reminded her again of my request and her agreement. She said that I was going too far: I had still not accomplished so much in arms that I ought to entreat her. The third year, I set out to win fame and put all my strength into it. If I heard of any country or region where there was some gathering for a war or a tournament, I was there first if I could possibly get there. I never failed to show courtesy and honour.

Why should I make a long story of it? During that year I became so famous, courteous, joyful, handsome, valiant, noble and universally admired wherever I was known, and there was so much talk about it that it is still remembered. I may be acting like a churl to boast about it, but I am telling you the truth from beginning to end, just as it happened to me. At the end of three years I returned to my sweetheart. I told her that she had granted me her favours by her ring, and it was not seemly or proper for her to hold out against me any longer. (3199)

'The young lady told me that I was right; there was only one thing left which prevented me from having her. She knew for certain, since everyone said so and no one denied it, that I had won great fame in arms and should rightly have her, but there was still one obstacle. Then she said to me: "This is what delays you, the one thing which makes it difficult for me: the treachery which I see spread throughout the world. Everyone is so disloyal that when a man obtains his goal and does what he wants with his sweetheart, I've never seen one who doesn't go after another woman as soon as he has been satisfied." (3219)

'She said that she didn't want to love me in that way: if she was to be mine, she wanted to proclaim openly that I was hers; I would never possess her before she was completely assured of that. I replied at once that she would be wrong to have any doubts: I would reassure her by a promise or an oath. She said that such assurances would never make her feel confident; she wanted me to provide her with a guarantor: King Arthur's nephew, the noble, well-bred Gawain, who is so admired and praised.* You can see what a fool the poor wretch was, and how unlucky: it was known throughout the whole region that Gawain had been killed! I didn't want to tell her about his death, and I said at once that I wasn't acquainted with him and didn't know if he would be my guarantor when he didn't know me at all.' (3244)

When Gawain heard that, he remembered for the first time the young lad and the young ladies.* (3247)

'"Even though I am asking for him as guarantor," she said, "I don't know him either. Whatever I may do in the future, now I know him only by hearsay. But everywhere I hear him singled out as the most accomplished, loyal, esteemed, valiant and prudent knight of the Round Table. Since he is both loyal and brave – everyone says so, and not even those who envy him dare to contradict it or make any objections – I'm ready to accept him as a guarantor if you offer him. If you do not free him from the obligation I am sure he will do so himself. If he finds you lacking he will hand you over to me, like it or not. His renown is so great and he is so courtly and well bred that if you fail me in any way – if I have him as a guarantor from you and if I go to the court to summon him – he will come here for me and perform his duties as guarantor. If he can find you he will exert such force that you will have to make amends. I am so confident in his loyalty that I will accept him and not seek anything more." (3283)

'"I grant you that." I replied, though I knew well that Gawain was dead. (3285)

'So we were in agreement, my young lady and I. When she had my promise, my request was more pleasing to her. What more can I tell you? For the first time last night, I had what I wanted and I lay with her.' (3293)

Then Gawain asked him, 'Tell me where you are going. Since you are so worthy and you have such a beautiful sweetheart, I would like to know why you have left her so quickly.' (3298)

'I will tell you,' he said. 'I am going to see the most beautiful creature from here to Tours: I have been courting her for a long time and today she is to give me her answer.' (3303)

'God damn you on the spot,' said Gawain, 'you fool! You are repaying the maiden for her service in a very ugly way. You have just won her, after entreating her for three years, and for the first time you have had what you wanted from her. According to your covenant, you should be entirely hers, and you took the Good Knight as your guarantor. Yet here you are, going after another woman! I see nothing reasonable there, for she has given you no cause to hate her. By God, I pray you to be loyal to the young lady. Would to God that men who betray women who have done them no wrong were clearly labelled on their foreheads! There are so many of them throughout the world that they do great harm to those who are loyal.' (3327)

'What business are we of yours, my young lady and I?' replied the knight. 'The maiden who is to give me her reply is so charming, so beautiful, so noble and prudent, and of such high birth that the greatest barons from here to the ocean would devote themselves to loving her. The other one has put me through many trials and caused me many pains and sleepless nights, and now she has repaid me for it by giving me her love. I deserved it. I loved and served her so long and worked so hard that she couldn't have paid me for half of my service in a whole year. After being in such pain, now that I have managed to get the power to cause her some trouble, I want to make her know the suffering I endured for her: turnabout is fair play.' (3352)

'Noble knight,' said Gawain, 'by all the saints who are venerated in Rome, do not treat her this way, but be good and courtly and stick to your covenant. Even the most powerful king under Heaven who had done so much for her would be acting shamefully if he abandoned her like this.' (3361)

'You're talking nonsense,' replied the knight. 'I won't make you any promises I don't intend to keep. It pleases me to see her suffer, since she caused me so much trouble. This is the end of the dispute: I won't do anything for you.' (3369)

'Then it is decided,' said Gawain. 'I loved Sir Gawain very much, and I would be acting like a churl if I allowed him to incur any blame in my presence or if he were accused of any villainy, whether he is alive or dead. Since you will not listen to reason or act properly and will not do anything at my request, I have one thing to say to you: since you are going to carry on with this, you will have to defend yourself against me.' (3382)

'Now I am really caught!' he answered. 'You have defeated me very easily, if you think I would do anything because of you or your threats!' (3386)

What more can I tell you? The knights drew apart, prepared themselves carefully and then let their horses run. They struck each other with such force that both lances broke. But when they were passing each other, if the story doesn't lie to me, they charged so violently and struck each other in such a way that horses, bodies and shields crashed into each other and both they and their horses fell. The knights leaped up, and as soon as Gawain was on his feet, he drew his sword and attacked the knight quickly and well. He attacked him so well that the knight was completely stunned; nevertheless he paid him back well and rewarded him for every blow. He didn't treat it as a gift, but repaid him for it generously, striking back a good hundred and forty blows which would have dismayed anyone else. (3412)

But Gawain finally got the upper hand, and the knight could no longer defend himself; but when he wanted to yield his sword, Sir Gawain said that he would never take his sword or accept his surrender because the knight had refused to heed his request at any cost. If he wished to live and enjoy his fief, he would have to love the young lady faithfully as he had promised. He said that he would not have performed his duties as guarantor until the knight had made himself his lady's prisoner according to the covenant he had made with her. (3429)

The defeated man said, 'Willingly, dear lord.' (3431)

'Now you must tell me your name,' said Gawain; 'I wish to know it in order to relate the story at Cardueil.' (3424)

'My name is Espinogre de Wi. In all the kingdom of Logres I never expected to find anyone able to defeat me in combat. Tell me your name, and what country you come from: if it has happened that an unworthy man has defeated and captured me in battle and my sweetheart hears of it, I will never be joyful again. But if a better man than I has conquered me, my anger and distress will not be so great.' (3449)

'I cannot tell you my name,' said Gawain, 'for I have lost it and I do not know who took it from me. Now I must go in search of it, but I do not know where or in what country; you must come with me and do whatever I wish.' (3457)

'I consent to that,' said the knight; 'I will follow you willingly, for I belong entirely to you and you have rightfully conquered me.' (3461)

'When we have completed our search,' said Gawain, 'and we have finally succeeded in finding my name, I will tell it to you at once. You may be sure beyond all doubt, I promise you, that I will be a fine companion throughout the whole time. No knight in all your life ever made such efforts or was a more agreeable companion to you.' (3472)

The knight agreed to everything Gawain said without any protest. Gawain received his sword then according to their covenant: according to the story, the knight had to make amends for the misdeed. (3479)

Then they mounted their horses, which had been wandering nearby. The knight led them to the castle from which he had set out. They told the young lady everything they had done and said: how they met, how the knight told his story, how their quarrel reached the point that they fought in the forest, how the battle proceeded, and how they concluded the peace. Gawain brought about their reconciliation, making the knight swear at once that he would never love or desire any woman but her. (3497)

Then she wanted to know his name, but Espinogre said, 'That cannot be,' for he knew enough about Gawain's situation to realize that he could not tell it to anyone. Then she said, 'Dear sweet lord, you who do not have your name, I am certain that you are a worthy man and that I ought to love you. If it had been necessary for me to complain to Gawain about this knight, I am sure that my rights would have been upheld. I haven't heard it said that my sweetheart enjoyed any love but mine, only that he was on his way to court another woman. Now for love of Gawain this knight has brought my sweetheart back to me. He has battered him in combat and delivered him to me in person, making him pay dearly for his foolish plan. Gawain is certainly very worthy, and he should give thanks to God that he is esteemed and loved so much.' (3522)

The maiden, who was delighted with what had occurred, took their shields and had them dismount, and then she made sure that her servants served and honoured her guests. She took great pains to be worthy of the favour Gawain had done for her by putting himself at risk so that she could have her lover. She put her castle, her dwelling and all her property at his disposal and prayed him as a reward to treat them as if they were his own. They had fine lodgings and passed the night very comfortably: everything they could think of which might please them was done without objection. But in order not to prolong my story, I do not wish to describe every course they were so elegantly served – fine meat, fresh fish, game and birds, and other things too numerous to mention, along with many different wines. But the young lady's warm welcome was even dearer to them, as she offered them all that she had – and they received it willingly, enough for fourteen meals! (3552)

Why should I say any more? The young lady provided them with as much pleasure and honour as she could. In the morning at daybreak the two knights rose, armed themselves quickly and well, and set out on their way. The young lady with the clear complexion, the one who had come with them, set out with them; they commended their hostess to God and went into the forest, back the way they had come. Unless fortune separated them, they said, they would never stop their quest, but would travel over hills and valleys throughout the land in search of Gawain's horse Gringalet, wherever it might be. And when they had found it and had won it back in combat, they would go to seek the young ladies who had announced Gawain's own death to him. They decided that they would then go in pursuit of those who made the wicked boast that they had killed him; when they had found them, they would deny in combat that they had ever put him to death. They would fight with the two knights and then with the third if he could be found. Once Gawain had proved it against them, he said, he would look for Gawain: he will certainly find him, for he knows what had happened to him! (3587)

When they were back out in the plain, discussing where to go and what to do, a knight came out of the woods into a clearing before them. From the sea as far as Iceland there was no man so well equipped. The horse he rode was strong and swift and well rested. This knight didn't see the two knights who were approaching. Every piece of armour he wore suited him perfectly: he wore iron greaves whiter than any silver, he was tall, handsome and genteel, and he seemed to be both agile and brave. Under his hauberk, you must know, he wore a doublet decorated with fine silk. His hauberk was of fine mail, and everyone who saw it valued it even more than the iron greaves: it was very solid, light and sparkling. The knight's coat of arms was made of cloth from Constantinople and the belt he wore over his coat was elegant and well made; his sweetheart had sent it to him, and she had done her best to make it well, with threads of gold and silk. It would become tiresome if I wanted to describe in full even just the helmet he wore on his head, his circlet and his visor. This helmet bore a banner delicately embroidered with his coat of arms: his sweetheart had sent it to him as a love-token. His horse, powerful, swift and spirited, came from Lombardy. The only thing he desired, you must know, was to find his enemies, because he wanted to display and test his great courage. His valour, inspiring him to deeds of prowess, made him take up his shield by the straps; he couched his lance, steadied himself in his saddle, and spurred his horse. You should know that he had fastened an elegant golden clasp at his throat and wore a horn around his neck behind his shield. The shield was bright crimson with a rampant ermine lion. There was a banner hanging from his sturdy ashen lance, and he was wearing the finest sword in all the kingdom of Logres. (3649)

Gawain and Espinogre both gazed at him with great pleasure. The knight I am telling you about rode along in great joy, singing a love-song which he had recently learned. Suddenly, he grabbed his shield by the straps and took up his lance: then he threw them down in a rage, it seems to me, in the middle of the field. You may be sure that he was ready to begin to lament – to cry out and wail and bash his hands against each other: it seemed to everyone who saw him that he wished he were dead and couldn't be consoled by anything a man or a woman could do for him. He took up his shield and his lance, steadied himself in his saddle, and spurred his horse, letting it run at full speed, with his lance extended. And then he began his song again, starting up with the third verse. (3673)

'Is that knight bewitched,' said Gawain, 'to behave as he does?' (3675)

Then the knight threw his shield and lance to the ground again. 'Alas!' he said, 'this adventure I am seeking will be a disaster!' His lamentation began again, so violently that anyone who saw it would have pitied him. When he had lamented like a madman for a long time, he took up his arms again, seized his shield by the straps, and spurred his horse again, beginning to sing his song where he had left off. (3689)

'I can boast of having seen many an adventure,' said Gawain, 'but never before have I seen a knight behave in such a fashion! I can't help going to ask him where he comes from and what he is seeking.' They galloped towards him across the field. Sir Gawain greeted him amiably and courteously and then asked him to tell him, if he pleased, the source of the alternating joy and sorrow he was expressing. He could have searched throughout the whole world without finding such an adventure, so he urged him to tell him the cause of the sorrow and the joy he felt. (3709)

'My lord,' he said, 'not for the sake of any pain which might assail me could I tarry here or stay with you long enough to tell you my circumstances, where I come from or where I am going. There is a ford beyond these woods, more than five leagues away, and I absolutely must get there! I can only tell you truly that if I am not there before midday, I will have lost everything: I would rather have two lances pierce my body!' (3723)

'My lord,' replied Gawain, 'if you please, I will go along with you until you have told me the reasons for your pain and your joy. I have a great desire to hear it and to know all about this marvel.' (3731)

The knight then prepared to speak to him, still continuing on his way: hear now his story, just as he told it: 'My lord,' he said, 'it happened once that my lord was visiting a very powerful man. We had a fine welcome there, and the best lodgings I ever had, you may be sure. If anything I say to you is a lie, may I be dishonoured for it on the spot! Yet I tell you that although I stand before you as a strong man, I am now in danger of death. The master of the place treated my lord and all his companions with great honour. When it came time to eat, as a close friend of my lord I was seated next to the master's daughter, who was very courtly and elegant: there was no woman so beautiful in the whole region. I was then still a new knight. I spoke to her so sweetly and becomingly and my prayer was so pleasing to this beautiful young lady that she granted me her love. We promised each other that our love would always endure in all faith, with no trickery or deceit, and she would love no one but me: in return, I granted her that I would love no one but her. I can swear certainly that our love still endures: neither of us has failed to keep our covenant. This love continued until one day misfortune came to us. I do not know how it happened, where it came from or what caused it, but her mother realized that the young lady loved me, and became extremely displeased about it. (3778)

'She kept a close watch on her daughter because of me, and my sweetheart could no longer find a way for me to speak with her: she has been kept under guard for two and a half years. Now a rich man of the region has asked for her in marriage, and on her friends' advice and with the support of one of her brothers, her father promised her to him. He is to take her this very day, and she is so sad that she has almost died of sorrow, but she does not dare refuse because her father has commanded it. She sent word to me secretly that she will be taken away today. I tell you that the joy I feel, as you saw at first, is because I know I will see her there; the sorrow I feel next is because I will never see her after that, except in such anguish that I could never describe it: I would rather be dead! But then I feel consoled again, just from the fact that I know I will soon fight so well, right before her eyes, that no one could do better. When I see their people, I will strike them so vigorously and I will be so valiant and assured that no one except for good King Arthur and Gawain ... but I am mad and churlish to boast like this! I can say this much: I will be so brave and bold that, except for these two, no knight ever faced so many others and fought better than I will do! (3822)

'I am so sad because he is taking her away that no one could stand the harsh combat which I will suffer for her as long as I can endure it. I am delighted that she will see it, for no man who is not in love can take on the burden of combat like a man who is in the grip of love. I cannot help it if I then feel great anguish, for I have taken on a very difficult task: there are twenty hardy and bold knights accompanying him. The man who brought me the news told me that he counted them before he left them there. I am certain that I have gone too far, since I am all alone, and that I am going to my destruction. The messenger, who was prudent and courtly, told me further that they were very well armed. Now you will hear, if you don't know, why they are so well armed: no one can keep a thing secret, and so it is known that the young lady and I are lovers. They are afraid of my great rashness, and because of the rights I claim over her they are fearfully waiting for me to attack them when they are hemmed in. And they would have reason to be afraid, if I had a good troop with me! As soon as I saw them I would challenge them and it would be clear that she is mine! Even though I am alone, I can tell you that however it turns out there will be quite a fight for her. But no matter what I say, I know that I won't be able to endure it. There never was a knight – not even Roland or Oliver – who could stand such an assault without being finally killed or captured unless there were a miracle. But I have taken it on, and that is all there is to it: either I will die or I will deliver my sweetheart!' (3876)

'Espinogre,' said Gawain, 'anyone who sees another knight in such distress and doesn't help him in his need is surely cowardly and base.' (3881)

'My lord,' he replied, 'if you wish to take it on, I will not hesitate to assist you with all my strength. I am yours by right and nothing could ever happen to keep me from wanting to do my part in anything you wish to undertake. I will never desert you.' (3889)

Both of them promised that they would help the knight in his need. Then he answered them: 'My lords, I thank you; but although I have told you how far I have gone through my folly, you should not share in it. If I am going to face disaster which I cannot escape, I will not ask you to take part in it. It would be a great pity if one of you should be captured or killed because of my rash undertaking.' (3904)

When Sir Gawain, who was filled with nobility, heard these words, he was seized by great pity. He knew that the knight was only refusing them because of his generosity and that he was rejecting their help because he was afraid that they would suffer for it. 'My lord,' they said, 'no matter how it turns out, we have made up our minds: either we will be captured or killed or we will return your sweetheart to you.' (3915)

The knight thanked them, and was delighted with the promise that he heard. 'My lords,' he said, 'may God heed you so that you may bring me the joy for which I have languished so long! If a man takes pains to act honourably, God finally grants him honour and joy in return; no matter how much he strays he will be brought back to the proper path, for God aids and guides him.' (3927)

Then they set out on their way to perform their task. 'My lord,' said the young lady to Gawain, 'such a great hunger has come over me, God help me, that you will see me go mad unless I have something to eat soon. I assure you that if I don't get at least a piece of bread, I will eat my own hands! No one has ever been so famished!' (3939)

Gawain was extremely displeased when he heard this, and spoke to the young lady: 'By God, my beauty,' he said, 'please! We can't find anything we need here, not at any cost. You know that nothing can reasonably prevent Espinogre and me from helping this knight at once. We have made a covenant with him, and it would not be proper for us to fail him in his need when we have given him our promise. Anyone who failed now would be blamed forever when people found out about it. You have found me noble and honourable: see to it that I am not dishonoured. You would be reproached forever if it were known that you had done such damage. I pray you, don't be upset. Endure your troubles patiently until this business is finished.' (3967)

'I will never be such a fool,' she said, 'as to agree willingly to what you are saying! No matter who is upset or displeased about it, I would always choose someone else's discomfort rather than my own. Don't think that I am pretending: the hunger I feel is even greater than I can say. If someone gave me five hundred marks of gold just to endure it until midday, on my word I tell you that I couldn't bear it. Since I am under your protection, it would be very churlish of you to let me die because of your negligence. I have been here before, my lord, and I see a castle over there, just beyond this valley, not even a league and a half away. In your whole life you have never seen even six castles in all England or Wales so well situated or with such fine towers and splendid halls.' (3994)

I have other things to do besides recounting to you the description she gave him: she reported everything she had seen there to him, saying that the castle stood in a clearing and was provided with everything a worthy man might need. (4003)

'The straw that broke the camel's back!' said Gawain. 'But now I have to do it and I must go with you, since that is what you want.' (4008)

Solomon says in one of his books that the man who keeps company with a woman is not soon freed. For the man whom she captivates has a lot to complain about, once he is ruled by love – if he has the nerve to say a word about it! But no man is that brave. The more he loves her and takes pains to cater to her every whim and the more earnestly he honours her and does what she wishes, the more he repents in the end. But my heart draws me to other matters: I want to return to my story, for I have said enough about women, and no one will disagree that there are very few of them who don't deserve such a reputation. (4030)

'Espinogre,' said Gawain, 'now I am pleased that you have

two horns. Each of you has a loud one, and if you both blow of them so that four blasts can be heard, I will rush after you as soon as I have arranged for the maiden to have something to eat. I have to find her some food before I do anything else.' (4041)

'We will see to it,' he replied, 'since it cannot be otherwise.' (4043)

Then Gawain and the maiden turned a little to the left, riding along a path until they came to the castle. It was surrounded not by sharpened stakes but by a high wall and a ditch. It had a large forest beside it, and the keep and the tower were enclosed by a hedgerow so that there was only one entrance. The maiden, who knew the place, went inside; the man, who didn't know anyone there but was no fool, went straight through the gate up to the tower. He crossed the bridge on his horse without seeing anyone to stop him. The maiden stayed outside and the knight who had no name went into the hall at once. On a table he saw a clean cloth, whiter than snow on ice, and standing on it was a cup of pure gold filled with excellent wine. There he saw also flans, cakes, waffles and pastries, and fresh and spiced meat in a sparkling platter. He saw a young lady sitting at dinner: if beauty can be an adornment to a young lady when it is not combined with nobility, she could boast that Nature had never made a more beautiful woman – if only she had been friendly. But she was so proud and vain that no one who knew her could say anything good about her at all. The body is loved when there is courtesy and loyalty in the heart, but I tell you truly that pride is a wicked guest: beauty which keeps company with pride is often completely destroyed. (4089)

The knight greeted her very politely and asked her to give him some food. 'Listen to me, maiden,' he said; 'outside in the courtyard there is a young lady on a horse; unless someone helps her at once and brings her something to eat, she will never leave these gates: she will surely die. She is in front of the tower and prays you to be generous and helpful enough to aid me in this necessity.' (4103)

'My lord,' she said, 'I'll be damned before I'd give you anything! What audacity, what haughtiness, even to imagine that I ought to do anything for you! You are not such a great person that you should even think of it! You'd be sorry that you asked if my brothers were here – I have seven of them, all hardy and brave – but they are out in the forest.' (4115)

'Maiden,' he said, 'if you want me to give you a large reward for a very small gift, it will be given to you, if you will just give me a single cake and a pasty.' (4121)

'By my head,' said the young girl, 'I will not waste what I have like that!' (4123)

'You will never get what you want,' said a dwarf who was serving her. 'As they say, "A man who chases after dogs is wasting his words." I know what she is like: you will never have any success with her by polite requests; but if you are proud and insolent she will do as you please. Tell me, since you live at court: doesn't pride conquer pride? Answer arrogance with arrogance, I tell you, since your need is so great. The food is right there and you can take plenty of it.' (4139)

'It is necessary to guard against all outrage,' said the nameless one, 'and I would be afraid of acting badly. I wanted to do it peacefully, if I could, and not cause her to be angry with me.' (4144)

'That will never happen,' said the dwarf. (4145)

Then the knight drew nearer and picked up a pasty and some bread, and then some meat from the full platter in his other hand. The dwarf led his horse by the reins to the maiden who was waiting for him outside. He offered her the food and begged her to hurry because they had no time to lose: it was vital for him to move quickly to assist the knight he was supposed to help, according to the promise he had made to him. She answered him at once: 'My lord, as God is my witness, I will soon leave with you, but first I must think about protecting my life, for I have been sorely tried. This food has certainly saved my life. Don't think me churlish to mention my needs, but now I must have something to drink. Such a great thirst has come over me since this morning that I cannot stand it. I will not last for long unless I drink: I will set out on the road with you as soon as I have had something to drink.' (4177)

She didn't need to ask again: the nameless one set out and went back to the hall. He went to the table to take the cup, but when he stretched out his hand to it, the young lady seated at the table took the cup before he could and spoke angrily: 'There would have been a quarrel over this wine and food if all my brothers who are amusing themselves in the meadow and the woods had been here in the hall! But you have found me all alone, and you have shown what a brave man you are: what a great honour, to humiliate a solitary young lady!' (4195)

The dwarf called to him angrily: 'Sir Knight,' he said, 'you will not get even a morsel of bread from her without dispute!' (4199)

Whether she liked it or not, the knight seized the cup from her hand and took it to the young lady who was waiting for him at the gate. The maiden who was seated at the table said to him: 'You are senseless, Sir Knight, and ill-bred, to take my meal against my will. If the man whom everyone envied for his excellence were still alive, I would have my rights! Ah Death! You are so ruinous, treacherous and contrary that you never spare a good man! There is no young lady as far as Rome or from there to Spain who has not been left desolate! Ah, Gawain, if you were alive my cup would never have been taken from my hand and my food would not be carried off before my very eyes! I would not even have to worry about it! Now there is no one who maintains and stands up for what is right.' (4223)

He paid no attention to her complaints, but returned the cup to the dwarf; and the young lady, who had finished the food and the wine, took to the road with him. They hadn't gone very far after crossing the bridge when they met the knight who had given him the charger and the palfrey with its saddle and all its equipment when he needed it so much.* He had on his fist the sparrowhawk which had been given to him there; he was so well and properly armed that a more elegant knight couldn't be found in any land. He greeted him and then, like a man in need, asked for his reward and reminded him of the gift for which the reward was due: if he delayed at all and didn't repay him at once, it would never be possible to do so. 'I will tell you why,' he said: 'the castle up there is perfectly peaceful now, and there is no one there who can do you any harm. I learned today that the knights of the place are all sporting in the woods. There is a maiden enclosed in that castle whom I have loved for more than three years; I pray you to give her to me.' (4259)

'By my faith,' he answered, 'it is only just that you have her, if I can accomplish it! If I find her in the castle you will see how loyal I can be.' (4263)

He wheeled his horse about and went back into the hall. The maiden spoke to him scathingly, cursing him repeatedly and saying arrogantly that he had returned to his misfortune. He went towards her, seized her by the right arm, and put her in front of him on his horse and went back, not waiting in the hall any longer. She wept tenderly and cursed him, beseeching God to bring him misfortune. When she saw that she was getting far away and was already beyond the gate, she fell into deep despair. She wrung her hands, screamed and lamented, crying out: 'Alas, poor me, to be so hated by God! Alas, doesn't my brave brother Codrovain know about this! Ah, Gawain, how much we miss you now! The outrage that this knight is doing to me could never have happened if you were alive and well!' (4291)

Despite all this, he took her away and delivered her to the man who loved her so much. All this time she was shouting out, swearing that such an affront would never have been committed if Gawain were alive. (4297)

One of her brothers who was stationed behind a tree preparing to shoot his bow heard the young lady screaming: he could scarcely hear her. The maiden cried out again, but he was so far away that he couldn't understand her, but he knew that she was in difficulty and was calling out to Codrovain. (4305)

The knight who loved her now had her in his power, and said to her: 'Beautiful dear sweetheart, I am Raguidel de l'Angarde; since you are now under my protection, you should rejoice. You may be sure that it is I, your sweetheart: you have always promised me that you would love no one but me. If I can trust the pledge you made to me with your right hand, I ought to be able to feel confident now.' (4318)

When she heard these words, the young lady was overjoyed: 'Sir Knight,' she said, 'I refused to give you any of my food, but now I am obliged to you, and I thank you for what you have done, since you have repaid me so generously. Just a moment ago, I was sad and troubled and completely at a loss: I thought I was going to be handed over to a man I did not love. If that had happened, I would never have eaten again! Blessings on this knight, for paying his debt so well today! If he pleases, I willingly consent that he give me to you, and I pray him to pardon me and to pay no attention to the way I railed at him.' (4338)

'My beauty,' he said, 'I forgive you. But in addition to giving you to this knight who holds you, I must also ask your forgiveness for what I did to you before, for I know well that I acted badly.' (4345)

'My lord,' she said, 'I grant it to you.' (4346)

Her brother had heard her and came to the castle as quickly as he could. He found a servant in the court and asked him about the uproar he had heard; without delay he told him the whole truth about what had happened. 'Then I am no longer master of my own house,' said the brother, 'if he can take her away like that!' One of his men brought Gringalet to him from the stable, put on its bridle and saddle, and then went up to a turret above the main gate to bring his master his shield, sword and lance. As soon as he had mounted the charger, he rushed out of the enclosure: it was the knight who had left Gawain with his sweetheart out in the woods because of his jealousy, taking away their horses.* Once he was out of the castle he rode so vigorously that he soon saw the knights and the young ladies. Though he was a great knight with the whole country at his command, if he couldn't break up this little band and do some damage, then he thought he wasn't worth a penny! (4381)

The one with no name heard him galloping along the road through a valley, and he had never been as happy as when he recognized the horse he was riding. He was so angry that he didn't ask any questions: he drove straight at him, and the other man let his horse run at full speed until they struck each other. The knight struck the first blow, full on the shield: his lance splintered and the pieces scattered in the wind. The nameless one struck the boss of his shield, without any intention of sparing him, causing his shield to twist on his arm and pushing his arm to the side: he threw him stretched out on the ground. He drew his sword then, and would have cut off his head, but the young lady begged him not to kill him: 'My lord,' she said, 'I believe that if you kill him I will never have any joy again.' (4407)

The knight yielded to her and said that he would do as she wished, provided that the other man would do the same for him. 'My lord,' said Codrovain the Red, 'you are so valiant, generous and noble that you should not be blamed for anything that you have done to me, for it was all caused by my arrogance. I agree to do whatever you wish.' (4418)

'My lord,' he answered, 'I thank you. I pray you first to put aside your anger with this young lady. But I would like to say something more to you: I urge you to agree to give your sister to this knight, for he loves her with all his heart and I believe that she loves him. Make peace with your sweetheart, without any rancour or baseness. The other day when I climbed up to get the sparrowhawk, I offered to swear by holy relics that I said nothing to the maiden that would be a cause for reproach, even if I had been the holiest and most virtuous hermit or recluse from here to Rome.' (4439)

'I believe you,' he said, 'that you didn't say anything of the sort to her.' Then peace was concluded, according to their discussion and agreement. Then the one with no name took back Gringalet without any delay or further argument, and gave his horse to Codrovain: I can tell you that this horse was fine and worthy. (4450)

His brothers had heard the uproar and spurred their mounts at once, crossing hills and valleys. They did not spare their horses, but spurred them as well as they could and didn't find them slow or sluggish. Then, without even taking off their saddles, they asked for news from a lad they met. He told them just what had happened, and they went into the hall and called for their arms, and those who received the orders carried them out. They armed themselves, mounted their good horses and left in a great fury. They swore that even if it was the King himself who had undertaken such an outrage, he would soon be dealt with in such a way that he would die and nothing could protect him from it. (4472)

It wasn't very long before they saw them. They drove their horses hard, stretched out their lances and seized their shields by the straps, ready to attack them. Codrovain the Red, who was already mounted on his horse, rushed forward at once to meet them. He told them boldly that if they harmed a single one of the knights he would never love them again. He swore that he would do for these men what no one had ever done: if his brothers continued their attack, he would turn against them and fight for these knights. 'Listen to me, my lords,' he said. 'I have met two knights who are bold and valiant and courteous. This man, who has traded horses with me, is so renowned, brave and loyal, that no one could recount even half of the virtues that are in him.' (4497)

But it would be tedious to tell you again the story which Codrovain related: he told them how the knight had climbed the oak and captured the sparrowhawk and how he himself had surprised him. He recounted everything from beginning to end, and then he told them how the knight had ended their quarrel. He went on speaking to them until peace was made and the whole business was settled. (4510)

Then they begged the nameless one to stay and invited him to come to their manor with them and become its lord. He answered very politely that it was impossible: he had just left a knight in urgent need of help two leagues away, to the left. He told them the story he heard from the knight who was going to deliver his sweetheart. They swore that he would not go there unless they went with him, and he said to them: 'My lords, I think I have delayed here too long. Since I have given him my promise, I'd rather be killed than be a traitor and fail to help him. I owe you great thanks for the offer you have made me: I would be glad to allow you to accompany me, and I promise you that if you are willing to come with me I will always be in your debt.' (4536)

They promised him that they would go with him and affirmed that they would do everything they could to help in the rescue. Codrovain the Redhead said to him, 'My lord, if you don't mind, I will take my sweetheart back; if Raguidel agrees, I will take both his and mine, for they have no part in this. It shouldn't displease him for me to take her, for I swear to you faithfully that I will keep our bargain and I will give her back to him with no dispute as soon as we return.' (4551)

Then he explained to them that he knew every track and trail in the forest and that he would follow them as soon as he was armed. But first he must go to get his arms: if he were ill-equipped in such an important undertaking where it was necessary to do his best, his shame would be so great that he would never feel joy again. (4562)

He went back and the others set out in the manner I have described, eager to fight well. You can't tell me that the nameless one was not delighted to acquire the assistance of these men who were so well equipped and so eager to do well. Helmets lowered, they raced along paths and roads at a fast gallop until they found in a meadow the tracks of the two knights who were riding before them; they followed them in tight formation. (4579)

Espinogre and Cadret had ridden at full speed and had already arrived at the pass and were awaiting the arrival of the knight and Cadret's lover. For that was his name, Cadret, the worthy and famous knight who had made this undertaking. So he and Espinogre waited, and there were just the two of them there when they saw the others coming. The man who was escorting Cadret's lover arrived at the pass first. Cadret let his horse run as swiftly as it could and struck him so violently on the boss of his shield that he knocked down both horse and rider in a heap. Espinogre, it seems to me, struck another man so hard that he knocked him from his horse on a path at the maiden's feet. Then he harshly defied the others and charged again swiftly, striking with lance and sword. Never before had two knights alone endured such an attack with no damage or loss! They suffered a harsh assault, and yet I tell you that two knights never confronted twenty and succeeded in such an exploit, holding a narrow pass so well that not one of the twenty could pass through it. Cadret moved boldly, and in a particularly powerful attack he struck the first man he met full in the breast between the nipples, and his lance flew in splinters; the other knight fell with a single blow. With the stump that remained, he struck another man so violently on the vizor that he knocked him backwards on the saddle: he would have fallen from his horse if a squire had not helped him stay on. Cadret didn't drop the butt of his lance, but returned quickly to the attack and struck a third and a fourth. Espinogre for his part did not fail to excel. Each of them fought so well that all the others were kept in check, but they finally regrouped, feeling greatly shamed to be so mistreated by just two knights. Even the worst of the twenty thought that if he confronted either of the knights in single combat he could easily kill or capture him. They were so ashamed of the beating that they were getting that they charged the two knights *en masse* and took the pass from them, forcing them to leave it. (4651)

Then Espinogre remembered what his companion said to him

before he left him. He took his horn and blew it so that all the forest resounded, and the knights who were following him heard it. The nameless one was delighted, for he understood from the call of the horn that they were defending themselves well and could hold out long enough for him to reach them in time. He spurred his horse and said to his companions: 'Now, my lords, follow me! That horn you heard was blown by one of the knights who are waiting for us, and they are defending themselves against great odds.' (4668)

Then they let their horses run. As they came over the top of a hill, they saw the knights: Espinogre had been caught by the bridle, and the skirmish in the valley centred on him. Cadret easily recognized the nameless one and saw that he was coming fearlessly to help Espinogre, with his lance couched. The knights following him had their lances extended and their shields on their arms, all determined to help them. When they saw these reinforcements coming swiftly to their aid, the two knights were delighted. Encouraged by this increase in strength, each of them reached out and grabbed an opponent's horse by the bridle. (4688)

The nameless one charged boldly, as quickly as his horse could carry him, rushing into the thickest part of the battle and making a great effort to stop the opposing knights. He struck one man with his sturdy lance and hurled him from his horse to the ground. The knights who were following him held their lances extended: they were men quite able to knock down any knight they struck. They harassed them boldly and pushed them back, charging at them without reining in their horses: they almost went right through the pass. By force of arms they drove all twenty into a group, and when they reached them, they had the honour of capturing two of them and forcing them to surrender. Then they pressed their advantage and came back to the skirmish. These eight men were a great help to the two knights, who had been in a bad way, and together they routed their opponents. When those who were fleeing arrived at the pass, they reined in their horses before entering it. They looked behind them and realized that only ten men were pursuing them. They looked all around, near and far, but they couldn't see any further reinforcements coming against them. They were all perplexed, and then they took courage and attacked them boldly. If the book where I found this story written tells the truth, no knight ever saw such a fine battle waged by as many knights: they advanced boldly, but the ten valiant and hardy companions met them bravely. Many bits and pieces of lances fell on the fresh grass and many a knight was caught by the bridle. Cadret, who was far from fainthearted, had been looking around for a long time and saw his sweetheart watching him. He turned his horse violently and went to seize the bridle of the man who that very day was supposed to possess her. When he saw that, the nameless one, whose lance was broken, spurred his horse and rushed between that knight and his troops. His own companions were not far off: they rushed after him and cut off their opponents. The knight's companions didn't flee: seeing that their enemies had trapped their lord by catching his bridle, they drove boldly towards him to help him and deliver him. They did everything they could to rescue him, but they had no success. Cadret had already ripped the helmet from his head, and, holding him tightly by the neck, like an expert in war, he slipped to the ground. (4764)

Once Cadret was holding him on the ground, the man had to surrender, for he had no defence. The battle had reached the point, as you can hear me tell you, that his men were maddened with rage when they saw their lord captured. They undertook boldly to free him, preferring to be caught along with him rather than let Cadret take him away as a prisoner. (4776)

Right then Codrovain the Red rushed out of the woods, coming as quickly as he could. He entered the fray at full speed and struck one of their knights such a blow that he sent both him and his charger crashing to the ground. Then he charged boldly towards a second man and struck him with what was left of his lance so that he almost broke his head: he fell unconscious to the ground. Codrovain fought with a third man and cut off his hand: it flew off into the field, far from the sword it had been holding. When they saw him attacking so furiously, they couldn't believe that he was alone: they thought that so many people must be following him that they could never hold them off, and that none of them would be able to escape if they were found in the field. Their courage failed and they thought that they would be finished if these knights got the upper hand. There was no more defence: they left their lord in the field and fled as fast as their horses could go. Then the nameless one, who wanted to fulfil the promise he had made, took the young lady's horse by the reins – she did not put up any resistance – and turned her over at once to Cadret. (4810)

Now Cadret was overjoyed: by his prowess he had rescued his beautiful, courtly sweetheart whom he loved so much, and he had captured the knight who had undertaken to lead her away to his own country against her will. Cadret had truly found a fine helper in the man who had kept his promise to him. (4825)

Then the seven brothers returned, after chasing those who were fleeing shamefully for a long time. They questioned the nameless one, and when they had heard all about him they begged him to stay with them. He said, on his own behalf and Espinogre's, that they would seek out the adventure they had taken on through all the kingdom of Logres and would finally find it somewhere. When they had found it, he promised them that he would come straight back without fail; after his return, he would not leave them until he had told them all about himself. Not for anything could his story be told to them until he had found his name and the adventure he was seeking. (4841)

Each one begged and urged him to let them go with him; but he assured them that the two of them had to go without any other company, it could not be otherwise: he asked them not to consider this excessive, proud or insulting. Then he asked them, I believe, to stay all together and to wait in Codrovain's castle until they saw him again or heard tell of him: he knew that he would find many joys and many torments to endure in the adventure he was seeking before he returned. That is why he asked them to stay together until they saw him again, and they promised him courteously that they would do so. But they were very upset that he would not allow them to come with him: they would have gladly helped him in any need. Then Gawain left the knights, and he and his companion went to seek his name. (4868)

Cadret and Raguidel came together to the castle, escorted by Codrovain who entertained and honoured them greatly. Each of the brothers did all he could to treat them well, and nothing was lacking. Their stay was very pleasant: every single day both of them were invited to go hunting game by the river or in the forest as they preferred. They could do as they pleased, hunt with hounds or with bows, for the lord was very powerful, and his country, you must know, was provided with all good things. There were plenty of birds and hounds, bows and arrows, rivers, forests and enclosures, and all of it was put at their disposal. The promise which had been made to Raguidel – that he would have his sweetheart when he returned – was kept most loyally. (4893)

Now I must tell how the knight who was adventuring through all the earth in quest of his name was able to complete his undertaking. I could not tell you everything about his comings and goings, but one day as he was riding through the woods it happened that he found a hermitage. A knight came out of the hermitage who had heard a mass sung there by the hermit. He was wearing a mantle of fine ermine-trimmed scarlet cloth, embroidered with zibeline – at that time people did not wear sleeves. His shirt and his breeches were white, cut in the Welsh fashion, and he wore a pair of cut-off leggings over spurs of gold which were delicately worked. You must know that this knight rode a fine charger and had no armour except his sword. He had met a maiden who was very beautiful and charming, and he was telling her about something that had happened in the country. The one who did not have his name greeted him politely. (4922)

'My lord,' he replied, 'may God grant you what you are seeking.' Then he said: 'I would like you to grant me a favour: would you and this knight stay and amuse yourselves with me tonight? You will have a lodging as good as if it was your own or his, for everything will be exactly as you choose.' (4933)

'My lord,' he replied, 'I have undertaken to seek an adventure; and so I pray you, do not be upset if I don't come with you. I will seek it through forests, towns and castles until it has been found.' (4939)

'Knight,' he said, 'if you are unwilling to take lodgings with me, I will ask you for something else, and you should not refuse it or you will be acting very improperly.' (4945)

'Since you ask me so insistently, this gift will be given to you without any ugliness or treachery.' (4948)

'I thank you,' he replied. 'I have a castle very near here, a little beyond this valley, and a fine dinner has already been prepared for me there. You won't be diverted from your course more than a bow shot, and so that I may be your friend, I invite you to come without delay to dine with me.' (4958)

'I grant you that,' he replied. (4959)

Then all three of them turned and went to the castle. The tables were set before they had even dismounted and the servants had taken up towels and basins. The cloths, the bread, and the wine were all soon prepared and set out. Then they sat down at the table, as soon as water had been presented to them, without waiting any longer. You may be sure that the food was superb and plentiful and was both served and eaten most pleasantly. After they had been sitting for a long time at the table, the lord of the house addressed his two guests: 'My lords,' he said, 'I would like to tell you about a sad and sorrowful thing which has recently occurred and will bring torment to everyone when it is known. The other night, I set out to look after some business ... Ah, if it only were possible to keep what I am going to tell you a secret, no one ought to reveal it! But it is now generally known, and cannot be hidden. It grieves me greatly that it is known. God! Fortune hates the ladies and the damsels so much! When they learn the news you are going to hear me report, they will have good cause to despair. The man in whom God placed loyalty, prowess and nobility, whom He made courteous and prudent, with no baseness or arrogance, without pride or excess – careful to avoid all outrage, he cherished only justice and honour – he has been killed under evil circumstances. And since I have told you this much, you may know the source of this misadventure. When it is known at the court, the King will be very disturbed. Alas, who will dare tell him about the Good Knight who has been so unjustly killed and dismembered? I am speaking about his nephew.' (5011)

'By all the saints on earth, dear host,' said the nameless one, 'what do you know about it?' (5013)

'I am absolutely certain of it.' (5014)

'How do you know?' (5015)

'I will tell you, without a word of a lie. The other night I wanted to go out to amuse myself and to inspect my woods. As I was about to go through the gate, I saw three knights in full armour coming up on their chargers. The first armed man came along the road towards me, all alone, leaving the other two behind; we greeted each other and then he said to me: "My lord, I believe that you are the lord of this dwelling; I would be forever obliged to you if you would give me lodgings for the night." (5030)

'"I willingly grant you that," I replied. (5031)

'The knight came inside with me, we dismounted, and I myself took off his armour and put it in a safe place, ordering my squires to stable his horse. But if I had been more sensible and courtly, I would have asked him first who he was and where he came from and what adventure he was seeking: when I learned of the wickedness he had committed after I had offered him hospitality, I couldn't throw him out or chase him from my house. One of the knights accompanying him arrived then, with a body; the third one, who was following him, was carrying the limbs and the head, rejoicing and delighted with the adventure. Right away I asked him who this man was whose death made him so happy, and why they had killed him. (5057)

'"Because I promised his head to a sweetheart of mine," said the first. (5059)

'"And I," said the second, 'God bless me, promised the body to mine." (5061)

'Then I asked them again about the reason why they had killed him as they said. One of them began then a story, and I am sad and ashamed to repeat it to anyone.' (5067)

'My host,' said the nameless one, 'by all the saints of Rome, tell me, for I assure you in all good faith, this is the adventure I have been seeking; I pray you, tell me the whole truth.' (5073)

'I will tell you all about it,' said the host, 'have no doubt about that, just as he told it to me. The two knights were courting two remarkably beautiful young ladies whom they loved. They wooed the maidens for three years with no success at all. One day it happened that they were entreating them with all their hearts. The young ladies were sisters and the knights were companions. The elder sister said that she had already made a gift of her love and that it wouldn't be withdrawn for any knight alive. The man to whom she had given her love was so handsome and worthy that she would never love any knight but him. Maddened with sadness and anger, he asked his name. "I could proclaim it in any court, for he is so famous and renowned that it couldn't be hidden anywhere: it is Sir Gawain, whom everyone in all the world, courtier and churl, places above all other knights."* (5102)

'The second knight soon asked about the thoughts and feelings of the one he loved so much. "I have given it a great deal of thought," she said, "you may be sure. I cannot say his name or tell you who he is or when I will make him my sweetheart. I only know one thing: as you have heard, my sister has made Sir Gawain her sweetheart and is only waiting for the opportunity to go and find him at the King's court and ask him to be her lover. I will go with her. I tell you this: if my sister comes to an arrangement with him I will give myself there also, in that I will love a knight, with his approval: it will be the Red Knight whom I will make my sweetheart. I am speaking, you must know, of the good and worthy knight who came last year to King Arthur's court to be made a knight. He won his arms and his charger all by himself, through his bravery, without any armour. King Arthur had granted them to him: they belonged to the knight who had taken the King's cup right under his nose."* (5135)

'The two men who were courting the maidens were very upset. They told them that they were better knights than Gawain and the Red Knight. The young ladies swore that unless they could prove their words by meeting Gawain and the Red Knight in single combat and defeating them, they would never love either of them: if they didn't do so very soon, they would make their journey to the court. (5148)

'The knights said, "If we who have entreated you so long can defeat him, will we have your love?" (5151)

'"We will become your sweethearts," they said, "when that happens: but it will never happen, God willing, for that would be too great a loss." (5155)

'The knights were outraged and furious, and set out in search of Gawain. They travelled through the country until one day they happened to meet him. The men who were seeking to kill him found him alone and unarmed. It is a great sorrow to have to say it, but his defence was useless. And that is the way that the King's nephew died, you must know. I was never so saddened by anything, and I do not think I could feel such great sorrow for anything that could happen. (5168)

'Since this had happened and the men who had dismembered

him had come here, I asked them for his right arm – which they had cut off – and they gave it to me. They took all the rest to their own country the next morning. If I can live long enough, you may be sure that the arm will be preserved in gold and silver so well – if the goldsmith doesn't fail – that no arm from any saint's body was ever so richly treated. I have made this vow, and it is right for me to have it richly preserved, for that fine man showed great honour to the knights in this region, and everyone who is able should undertake to reward him for it.' (5188)

'Dear host,' said the nameless one, 'by God and His redemption, did you know Gawain well?' (5191)

'I will show you his hand,' said the host, 'may God protect me!' At once he sent for the hand which was wrapped in a piece of silk and enclosed in a coffer. When the arm was removed from it, wrapped in costly fabric, they gazed at it in astonishment. Then they asked him to guard it honourably until it was known whose body the arm belonged to. He told them he would do so: everything of his, arm or hand, would be honoured, wherever it was found. He was sure that it was Gawain's and so it ought to be cherished. The man who had come there without a name said to him, 'My lord, God help me, you are wrong to be concerned about that. Not four days ago, I saw Gawain safe and sound near Cardueil, as he was going out in search of adventure. Now I wish to ask you, out of friendship, to grant me one thing in return: I will not ask for anything unreasonable.' (5217)

'Then it will be done,' said the host, 'if it is something I am able to do.' (5219)

'Tell me where I may find the men who boasted that they defeated Sir Gawain and that he was killed by them. You may be sure that they are wrong: he never met his death from them. The truth is that they found a knight alone and unarmed, and he is dead. They acted very basely when they killed him without saying a word to him, when he had nothing to do with them at all. Every man of sense and reason in the world would believe that they killed him by treachery: was it valiant to kill him? Then they boasted that they killed Gawain. I have heard about it many times, but I haven't been able to learn the knight's name or where he came from, not at any cost, only that he carried a shield like Sir Gawain's.' (5239)

The host was greatly comforted to hear such fine and pleasant news. 'God help me, my lord,' he said, 'I will set you on the way most gladly whenever you wish, for it is only proper for me to guide you. I would like to accompany you until I have helped you on the way: I will go along with you to show you the road.' He soon told them everything they wanted to know about the knights, including their names and countries. 'My lord,' he said, 'have you ever seen the Faé Orgueilleux? I do not know his real name, but I know that he was given this nickname after the Roche Faée – that is the name of his town. That is what the first knight is called, and everyone calls the other knight Gomeret Sans Measure.' (5263)

'I'm not impressed by that nickname,' said the nameless one, 'for it doesn't bode well.' (5265)

'Yet it is appropriate to him,' said the host, 'for he is arrogant and uncontrolled enough – but I am not saying it correctly, and I can contradict it myself, for as it has been said and proven, "enough" has never meant "excessively". I don't know who the third man was, just that he was with them. I heard him say that he only came to keep them company, not in order to do anything wrong.' (5277)

'Did either of them get possession of his sweetheart,' said the nameless one, 'because of this?' (5280)

'According to what I have heard, they did not. The women objected, reminding their sweethearts that they had promised to bring Gawain dead or alive. There was a great quarrel, for the young ladies said that they had seen Gawain before and this body was certainly not his. The knights replied that it certainly was, and that they would prove it. They had it proclaimed in every castle in the land that they had killed Gawain: if anyone dared to dispute it, they announced that they were ready to prove it. They haven't yet been able to find anyone to contradict them. There is no one who is as worthy as the two knights who have said this, and so they want to prove it in battle. Things have gone so far that unless someone comes forward tomorrow who can prove that it is not true, they will finally have the maidens without delay. The maidens are so upset that they cannot find anyone who dares to disprove it or contradict the knights in battle that they are almost dead of sorrow. Do you know why they are dismayed? They are terrified that the knights may have them in the way I am telling you. They say that they will kill themselves if the knights have them for this reason: it will be their own fault that Gawain was killed, and they will never be consoled.' (5320)

'My host,' he said, 'if it's not too much trouble, could we travel far enough tonight and tomorrow before midday? I assure you of one thing, and I do not say this as a boast: if the Lord God speeds us and we arrive there in time tomorrow, I would like us to avenge the great wrong they are talking about. The two of us will refute it in battle; no matter how it turns out, there will be a fight!' (5332)

Then the host said to him: 'I do not believe that you will find the knights you are seeking together. If you defeat them in battle in this task which you have undertaken, you will have won great honour. If you do not delay too long, you will arrive in plenty of time. I will tell you how Gomeret Sans Measure is waiting. He has his tent set up in a meadow, and he has been waiting a long time. He keeps asking if anyone wishes to contradict what he has proclaimed, that Gawain was killed by the two of them. He is so strong and bold and hardy that he hasn't found anyone to contradict him, and he expects that he will have his sweetheart tomorrow. The Faé Orgueilleux is in his own castle, waiting to see if anyone will come and dare to undertake to test or refute what he says, that he killed Gawain. Unless someone comes to deny it in battle tomorrow, he too will finally have his sweetheart.' (5362)

Then they rose from the meal, each one mounted his charger and they set out on the road. The host was courtly and well bred: he escorted them for a long time and informed them about all the landmarks so that they could not possibly fail to find what they were seeking. When they had ridden until the time when the host had to return, Espinogre realized that they had made quite a mistake. He was very concerned about it and told his companion that they had not asked their host's name. (5378)

Then they spoke to him politely: 'My lord, we are your friends and rightly so, for you certainly have deserved our friendship. And so, dear host, we ask you to tell us your name. You are a fine, upstanding man, and we are pleased that we have made your acquaintance. You may be sure without any doubt that we will always be your friends.' (5391)

'My name is Tristan Who Does Not Laugh,' he answered, 'I do not seek to hide it. My lords, I beseech you, out of friendship, to grant me a gift in return. I will not ask you for anything outrageous or base, have no fear on that subject.' (5399)

'By my faith,' said Gawain, 'it is proper for us to grant you what you wish: you may always consider us as in your debt from now on.' (5403)

'My lords,' he said, 'I ask you in return, and out of friendship, to come back this way. I do not know, and you do not know, what will come to you from the adventure you are seeking; but when you return I would like to know how you have fared. You may tell me everything on your return: who you are, where you are from and what it is that makes you seek this adventure. If you defeat the men you have been seeking for so long, you will have won great glory.' (5418)

They consented politely. When he had escorted them far enough, the host turned back. They continued on, following the route he had shown them. They travelled until one of them noticed a beautiful tower in a valley, which belonged to a vavasour. The place was very prosperous and the lord who owned it was a worthy and very powerful man. In his manners it was clear that he was a man of great power. The two men took lodgings that night with the good vavasour, and may God give him as much joy and honour as he showed to them! He took great pleasure in telling them about his adventures that evening, and in return, I believe, they told him some of theirs. In the morning, when it was day and the knights had been armed, they mounted their horses. (5441)

When they had taken their leave, they set out on their way and soon reached a paved road. They hadn't travelled very far, and it was still very early, when they came to a fork in the road that Tristan had told them about; one path led, as Tristan had said, to the place where Gomeret was waiting, and the other led to the castle where the Orgueilleux was proclaiming that he had killed Gawain: he expected that he would take possession of his sweetheart that day without a fight. The two knights had to choose their separate ways, and the nameless one generously gave the choice to his companion: 'My lord,' he said, 'you decide. You will take one of these two roads and carry out your task. If God grants that we conduct ourselves well enough to

THE PERILOUS GRAVEYARD

prove in battle that they have lied, we will meet again at Tristan's. Whoever arrives first will wait until he hears news of his companion there.' (5471)

'Since I have the choice of one of the two roads – and I have to do it, it can't be otherwise,' said Espinogre, 'I will follow the one to the left which will lead me to Gomeret.' (5477)

'Then I will take the other,' said the nameless one. 'I commend you to the Glorious Almighty King: may He protect you from all shame and evil!' (5481)

Each one spurred his horse and they rode off at great speed. Espinogre had scarcely gone a half a league when he reached a forest. He rode for a long time without leaving the forest until he came to the meadow where Gomeret was waiting, the man he was seeking, as has already been said. It would be pointless to repeat it, for it was all well told and heard: Gomeret was sure that he would have his sweetheart and that no one would forbid it. He didn't think that anyone would undertake to dispute his claim. While he was rambling on about it with his proud and foolish speeches, as you have heard – and it's not worth retelling, for you remember it well – up came Espinogre. He spoke to him quietly and courteously: 'Sir Knight, stop saying that you have killed Gawain; you have acted very basely by saying so.' (5509)

'And why, knight,' replied Gomeret, 'would I not dare to make it known when it is the truth?' (5512)

'No,' he said, 'it never happened. If Gawain fought twenty men like you, one after the other, he could cut off all their heads!' (5516)

Then Gomeret replied: 'By my faith, I have his body! It doesn't have any arms or legs, but I am ready to prove that I have it and that the Faé Orgueilleux has taken the limbs!' (5522)

'You are a barefaced liar!' replied Espinogre. 'I am ready to refute it and kill or capture you before I leave this plain.' (5527)

Gomeret asked for his arms at once, and they brought him sturdy iron greaves, whiter than pure silver, then a hauberk, solid, light, and shining, and a helmet which came from Senlis; all the rest of the armour was black. When he was properly armed, he didn't waste any time. His horse was blacker that a blackberry, and when he was well armed, he mounted his good horse, ready to prove at once the claim which Espinogre was disputing. (5542)

No hill or valley stood between them: each of them let his horse run as fast as it could go. In the joust, they struck such hard blows that they broke and pierced the shields; the iron tips went through them and reached the hauberks – but found them strong and solid. The knights struck with their lances so powerfully and angrily that neither horse could stay upright. No one should blame the riders, when their horses were struck down, for falling with their chargers: they had to leave the stirrups. They jumped up at once and attacked each other quickly and confidently. You may be sure that no one who observed this combat could tell which one was the plaintiff: each one claimed the title. Espinogre ran towards Gomeret and struck him again and again, a hundred times in a row, but Gomeret was not in the least dismayed, and paid him back boldly for every blow he received. The helmet was split in several places, the hauberk was all unravelled; neither wood nor iron prevented the blood from spurting out in a hundred places. The battle was so fierce that no one could tell you which man was better or worse, but you may be sure that this harsh battle continued the same way until midday, and they wounded each other seriously. The battle lasted so long and they endured so many blows that their helmets were split, their hauberks were unravelled and hot red blood could be seen spurting out. Finally it happened that Gomeret rushed and struck him so hard with his sword that it drove a good foot and a half into Espinogre's shield. The blow was so violent that he almost cut right through it. He pulled with all his might, but before he could get it out the sword broke at the hilt, and only the pommel and the golden hand-guard were left in his hand. Espinogre attacked violently and struck him again and again, until Gomeret finally said to him: 'No more, my lord! Show some mercy in your victory! Since I have nothing more to defend myself with, I have no choice but to surrender: I throw myself on your mercy.' (5609)

Espinogre answered most nobly: 'I grant it to you, but only if you go with me at once to the King's court and make yourself his prisoner. You will learn your mistake about the knight you have killed. You are certainly wrong to say that it was Gawain; Gawain is safe and sound, you may be sure, and you will see him at the court when you arrive.' (5622)

Gomeret agreed to this; then they took their horses and set out on their way. (5625)

The nameless one, who had undertaken to search for the Faé Orgueilleux, had ridden and travelled until he had reached his castle. He was repeating his proclamation very loudly, just as Tristan the courteous knight had said. The nameless one contradicted him, without saying anything immoderate: 'Knight,' he said, 'it would be a great loss if Gawain had been killed. He never did anything wrong to you or anyone else, according to what I have heard. He was never irritated enough to do anything excessive that anyone ever saw – that anyone could have seen! It is not very wise of you to boast of such a thing. I am the man who dares to dispute it, and I will prove in battle and demonstrate that Gawain is still alive.' (5648)

The Faé replied: 'I will prove what I claim, no matter whom it may displease!' (5651)

Then he had his armour brought and armed himself rapidly. He was very attractive and gracious, once he was mounted on his charger. If he had not been in the wrong, he could have defeated any knight under Heaven. The common people made a large circle around them. The knights wasted no time over threats and didn't rein in their mounts; each one spurred his horse as fast as it could go. The Faé struck him first with his good lance, right in the breast, and it flew off in splinters. The nameless one struck back; he broke the wood of the shield and the lance pierced the hauberk. He drove it right through his shoulder, and it went a foot and more out his back. It cut everything, wood, iron and bone, and he pushed it so violently that he knocked down both the knight and his charger in a heap. Then he seized his steel sword and returned furiously to the attack. The man lying wounded on the ground said to him at once: 'Sir Knight, I surrender! Since I find you so strong and valiant, I cannot resist you: I throw myself on your mercy.' (5685)

The nameless one replied willingly: 'I accept your surrender. But before I receive it – because I do not want to deceive you – I warn you that you will be coming with me to the King's court as his prisoner and you will bring your sweetheart with you. If the King gives her to you, you will have her, but you may be sure that you cannot have her if it is not completely to the King's liking.' (5697)

The knight was silent: these words bothered him greatly. The nameless one raised his sword and made as if to strike. The man who was so wounded that he couldn't defend himself surrendered his sword. 'Ah, knight!' he said. 'Mercy! Act in such a way that I will thank you for it and that I will not have to agree to such conditions. If I should lose my sweetheart I would lose my life, for there is nothing in the world I love so much! You seem so valiant and worthy, well bred and courteous, that I am sure the King will grant her to me if you ask him.' (5715)

'Knight, do not be dismayed,' said the nameless one; 'you may be sure that you won't be left without a sweetheart.' (5717)

The knight was overjoyed. He and his lover made ready, and he had his wounds bandaged; then he wanted to go to the court with the knight who had captured him. As they were travelling along the road, he spoke to him politely: 'Dear lord,' he said, 'from what I can see of you, I would guess – and I don't know if my thoughts are accurate, but this is what I feel in my heart – that you are one of the King's men. And so I pray you, if it is possible, to tell me about yourself so that I may be certain.' (5733)

'By my faith,' he said, 'I am Gawain. My name will not be hidden now that I have proved in battle that I am alive and healthy. It would be tiresome and churlish if I concealed who I am from you or from anyone else. Since I have been travelling everywhere until I recovered my name I had lost for a time, it should be known by everyone. The story of the outrage you committed against the knight must be told everywhere, that you went into the woods to cut him up and then carried off his body. Before you left the woods, you plucked out both the eyes of a lad, who was not alone: he had with him three noble and beautiful maidens, who lamented deeply over him. Each one of them would gladly have died on the spot, and they wept so much that their faces were all pale and discoloured. When I heard their lamentation, I hastened towards them. It was then that I saw, lying at their feet, a noble young lord who was in a very bad way, for his eyes had just been plucked from his head. When I saw him so grievously wounded, with both his eyes plucked out, I believed that all the sorrow the young ladies were displaying was on his account. I then asked the cause of their great sorrow and anguish. The first maiden answered me at once: "My lord, we have seen a valiant knight dismembered here, and we couldn't help him at all." I asked who he was, and the second maiden* informed me that it was Sir Gawain, who had been riding there, hale and hearty, but he hadn't been wearing a hauberk and had no armour but his shield and a lance. He was travelling alone, with no servant or squire. Then two armed knights arrived on Spanish chargers, crossing a field and catching him in this valley. They let their horses run, in order to kill him and cut him to pieces. Then they called to him: "Halt, halt, Sir Knight!" He waited for them solidly, holding his lance in his hand. One of the knights said to him loudly, "Gawain, you will not escape!" (5799)

'Then the battle began, but it was not on equal terms. The cowardly traitors killed Gawain and cut up his body. Whether rightly or wrongly, the bold and valiant lad ran up, thinking he could help Gawain. But he was no use to him: he had already been dismembered. The lad had his eyes plucked out for trying to help him. One of the knights put the body on his charger and they set out on the road through the forest at full speed. I promised the young ladies on the spot that the lad would be avenged. I took my leave and set out without being recognized. I have searched and followed you, and now I am in a position to see that you make amends for this outrageous wickedness. When you committed this misdeed, you thought it was me!' (5825)

'I assure you, dear lord,' said the Faé Orgueilleux, 'that things were really quite different.' He told him how and why it happened, from beginning to end. 'It shouldn't be considered a disaster, since it can be corrected. In the presence of all the people of your land, I will return this knight to you, with his arms and his charger, as healthy as he has ever been. And I tell you truly that the lad you mentioned will see as clearly as anyone, once I have simply passed my right hand in front of his face: he will be completely healed.'* (5842)

Gawain said to him: 'Dear friend, if I could arrange for the lad to have his eyes and the knight to be unharmed by your treachery against him, it may still happen that you will be scot-free, with my assistance.' (5849)

'Then have no worries, my lords,' said the Faé Orgueilleux: 'neither the knight nor the lad was ever in such good health as they will be, dear sweet lord, when I return them to you at the court; don't be concerned about it at all.' (5856)

They continued on their way in conversation until they reached the spot where Gawain left his good friend Espinogre, and dismounted at the crossroads. Then a knight mounted on a horse blacker than a blackberry rode up at full speed. His charger was incredibly swift; anyone who wanted to tell you the truth could not have found its equal in all King Arthur's lands. The knight was very confident, and he was so well armed that he did not care a whit for any blow from a sword or any other weapon. He dismounted beneath an elm tree to resaddle his horse more tightly. The Faé Orgueilleux saw him and said to Gawain: 'My lord, as I look at that knight saddling his horse and lacing on his gemmed helmet, I think you may be sure that he is planning to do you some harm. Since I wish to be in your service, I will go as your envoy to find out where he comes from and what he wants.' (5886)

While he was speaking to Gawain, two knights armed from head to foot came across the plain. It was clear from their shields that they had been in a fierce fight, for they were all covered with blood. One rode a white charger and the other a bay; he was Gomeret the Moor, a knight of great valour. It was Espinogre who was riding before him on the white charger. The Black Knight saw him as they were crossing the field. He mounted his swift charger and took up his shield and lance, spurring his horse and rushing to meet them. He came to joust with Espinogre, who saw him coming and went out furiously to meet him. Without a word of defiance, they struck each other's shields with their lances, piercing and breaking the shields; but their lances were massive and solid and didn't break. The Black Knight attacked Espinogre so violently that he knocked him in the dust, like it or not. He charged again and struck Gomeret on his grey shield and sent him crashing to the ground over his charger's rump. Then he took the two horses and, leaving the two knights, he rode at full speed towards the men who had been watching everything from the shade of the trees. The courtly Sir Gawain recognized the white horse and knew at once that it was his companion Espinogre whom the Black Knight had knocked to the ground. He took his good charger to go and joust with the Black Knight, who had so arrogantly undertaken such an adventure all alone. He could not believe that any man was valiant enough to endure his attack, and didn't intend to let the horses be taken away by any knight alive. (*3)

'My lord,' said the Faé Orgueilleux, 'I will tell him to come to you. If he is too proud to come at my request, I swear to you that it will come to a fight: I will fix my sharp sword in his brain. I beg you to allow me this.' (*13)

Gawain was very pleased, for it was the custom at the time that if a knight came to joust or fight, only one man should come to meet him, and if two men attacked him, I believe that they were considered recreant and shamed: if it became known in the King's court, no one would ever serve them. Therefore the Faé Orgueilleux set out first to joust with the Black Knight, although he was concerned that Gawain might consider him presumptuous. (*27)

He set out on his dappled horse and went straight at the Black Knight, who had no wish to argue about it and charged him at full speed. The Faé Orgueilleux struck him violently on his black shield, and I tell you I believe that if the lance hadn't broken he would have left his saddle, but the lance broke at once. The Black Knight met him at a gallop and struck his painted shield. He was so furious and he struck so hard that he shattered his shield and unravelled his hauberk: the carefully made doublet he was wearing saved his life that day! Nevertheless, the Black Knight knocked him from his horse so violently that he broke his right arm. He did not want to stay there, and left him at once, taking away his swift charger along with Espinogre's and Gomeret's. Then he left and rode off. (*55)

Gawain was very displeased that the Faé Orgueilleux had fallen. He came to Gringalet, mounted by the left stirrup, and took his lance in his right hand. Then he said to the Faé Orgueilleux's sweetheart: 'My beautiful young lady, don't be afraid. Stay here in the shade of this elm and I will go to assist your sweetheart. I will get his charger for him, which that knight is taking away. God help me, I will endure great pain rather than let him take it!' (5947)

He left her under the elm and crossed the plain to meet him. The Black Knight asked him who the young lady was. 'If you wish, my lord,' he said, 'she could be both mine and yours.' 'By the apostle Saint Paul, you will never share her with me!'*

Gawain said to him, 'My lord, I ask you to be noble and generous enough to return that white charger to me, as well as the one that belongs to the knight you unhorsed in the plain. The young lady asks you to return it to him, out of friendship: it will be an act of courtesy and honour. I pray you further to give me the third charger, and you will have done me a great honour which will be reported in a place where many fine men will hear of it.' (5969)

'By all the saints of Rome,' replied the wicked knight, 'you are churlish and tiresome! You have asked me for something I wouldn't ever do because of you or your request. You will never get them that way! You may be sure, Sir Knight, that if you want to do anything about it, either you will have to fight me or I'll take all four horses, for yours will go with them! And I'll take your sweetheart I see there under the elm, and you'll take lodgings with the others who are lying flat over there, all four of you together.' (5987)

Then Gawain said: 'I think you are very false and ill-behaved, and I know that you won't do anything for me at my request. If I can get the upper hand, I am sure that I will take vengeance for all of them.' (5993)

'Stop your threats, knight,' said the Black Knight. 'We will have a fair fight. There is no one here but you and me; the others are lying there peaceful and senseless. I challenge you!' (6000)

Without a moment's delay, each one took up his shield and lance. They struck each other so harshly that both lances broke on the shields protecting their breasts and flew off in splinters. Since their lances were broken, they drew their swords quickly and began the attack. They were excellent skirmishers and very bold. The one who was black as ink struck Sir Gawain on the top of the helmet, splitting it completely as far as the gold circlet. The blow descended on the corner of the green-tinted shield. Gawain attacked so violently that both horses fell. The two knights leaped up. Gawain jumped up quickly, eager to avenge himself. He charged at the Black Knight who was running to meet him. Each man wanted to do the other great harm. But Gawain, in order to avenge himself for the blow the other man had struck, returned the favour. He struck back freely and hit his helmet on the side and sliced off the top. He cut it as far as the coiffe and almost knocked him down. The

Black Knight passed by him, and splitting and breaking his shield. The blow was so violent that it went past the shield and cut the skirt of his hauberk, leaving a mark on the belt. If he had attacked him straight on and struck his helmet, I think that he would have knocked him down. But Gawain did not retreat: rather he came at him swiftly and struck him violently on his helmet. His sword rang out on the polished helmet. The Black Knight was a master of the art and received it well: he feared no one's chivalry. He struck Gawain furiously on the shield, doing such damage that he broke a hundred links of his shining hauberk and made his coat of arms slide down a good foot towards his belt. He was very lucky that his body wasn't cut, but the blade slipped behind his shield. Gawain struck back furiously on the black shield. (6065)

No one watching this combat could have told which was the better man. They fought without weakening until evening, when day failed, and the three who were under the alders could not tell who was better: they rushed over to them. The Black Knight, who had destroyed Gawain's armour as far as the belt, said to him: 'Noble, valiant knight, must I be on guard against these three armed men who are coming towards me?' (6078)

Gawain replied to him at once: 'By my faith – and this is no joke – I pledge to you loyally that if any friend of mine even touched you against my will, I would strike him on the spot: no one will ever reproach me for such a thing!' (6085)

Then he ordered his three companions to draw back. They did exactly as Gawain commanded, and none of them said a word, no matter what might happen. The Black Knight spoke: 'Knight,' he said, 'I would advise you to go away, safe and sound, with these three men, and leave me these four horses and the maiden who is waiting for you under the elm; it will be much better for you, since you will save your life!' (6101)

'God help me,' said Gawain, 'you are talking nonsense. If this sword does not fail me, I will give you such a battle before we separate that I will have the lady and the horses.' (6107)

Then the knights attacked each other so vigorously and furiously that they would have seriously wounded each other before one recognized the other. Gawain struck a blow to the top of the engraved helmet and his sword cut it: the blade went in as far as the brain as he twisted it violently. This blow knocked the Black Knight to his knees, but he got up quickly and returned to attack Gawain. Never in any country have two men done each other so much harm in any land! The three knights who were nearby watching them said that it was astonishing that they were still fighting at so late an hour. Then the Black Knight said to Sir Gawain: 'Knight, don't be a churl: let us rest now, and tomorrow when it is day we can face each other again. You can see that night has fallen. You keep these horses with you, on condition that we will bring them here tomorrow, along with the young lady: I want to be certain about that.' (6139)

'By my faith,' Gawain said to him, 'I do not want to take them unless I can win them from you. You are too cruel and devious!' (6143)

'Sir Knight, it is very late,' said the dark Black Knight, 'but rest assured: I will come here tomorrow.' (6147)

'That will never happen,' said Gawain, 'God willing! We will not separate until I know whether I can take the horses, the maiden and the knights without any dispute or argument.' (6155)

'It seems that you have very little regard for me, Sir Knight, because I was first to propose a truce! You will not find me slow to fight: I will provide you with a battle! In all my life you will never get anything of mine at all unless you can take it from me by force. Still I am certain that you are courtly and valiant, and so I ask you to tell me your name: it is proper that I should know it and that you know mine. Then, I pray you, do your best! But I do want to know your name and something about you: my master of arms taught me not to fight with anyone without asking his name, or else I would be false and churlish.' (6177)

'By my faith,' he said, 'my name is Gawain.' (6178)

'Truly, Gawain, the King's nephew?' (6179)

'That is my name, by my faith,' said Gawain; 'you have spoken correctly. God help me, I will never hide my name from any knight.' (6193)

The other man wanted to kneel before him to ask for mercy: 'I could swear,' he said, 'I would never have believed it if I had not seen you with my own eyes! They say that the Faé Orgueilleux, in his mad pride, killed and dismembered you. Do not consider me a coward, noble and valiant knight: by the faith which I owe to King Arthur, who is my lord and my friend, you have defeated and conquered me. Here is my sword, I surrender it to you. I am very angry and upset that I did not recognize you. I know well that I have caused you pain, and I repent for it, God help me! I declare that I have been completely defeated in this assault, and I tell you that I don't believe I could endure any more, not for a hundred marks or even more! Since I have been beaten, I surrender: take my sword, I yield it to you.' (6209)

Gawain said to him at once, 'Dear friend, keep your sword: you are so bold and daring that you deserve it. What is your name?' (6214)

'My lord, my name is Le Laid Hardi, and it is certainly no slander to call me "ugly". The other evening I left my country to go and see if I could hear any news about you. You may be sure that I would have kept searching for you and I would not have been willing to return until I had heard about you. Now I have fought you and it has turned out very well for me: if the battle had lasted any longer I would have feared for my life.' (6226)

When Gawain realized that he was his very dear friend,* he threw aside his shield and unlaced his helmet. They hugged each other and felt great joy. I do not think that anyone ever saw two such fine knights: each of them was extremely worthy. A moment before they were ferocious with each other, but now they were sweet and peaceful. Both of them rushed to the young lady who was still waiting and lifted her onto her horse, and then they set out on their way. Gawain, the Faé Orgueilleux and Espinogre escorted Gomeret to his young lady. Espinogre reported to Gawain how he had fought with Gomeret, and how Gomeret had surrendered and begged him for mercy. (6247)

'My friend,' Gawain said to him, 'you have done me a great service. May good fortune attend you, as I would wish.' (6251)

So they rode on, for it was very close to vespers. Each of them told Gawain what he had done and how he had fared. They continued talking until they arrived at the castle of Tristan Who Does Not Laugh, who had shown such honour to Gawain and Espinogre. (6261)

As soon as Tristan saw them, he jumped up to meet them: 'My lords,' he said, 'welcome!' Tristan was very prudent, and he was not very old, but still a handsome and elegant knight. He rushed to take Gawain's stirrup and helped him to dismount. Many courtly squires ran up to take his horse and helped the other three knights to dismount, and here were many of them to help the two young ladies down: you may be sure that Le Laid Hardi was soon beside them, eager to serve Sir Gawain. Tristan took him by the hand and escorted him into the hall as courtesy demanded, and took great pains to serve him. For dinner that evening, they had plenty of bread and wine, roast birds, plovers, pheasants, partridges and large swans for their dinner, for there was an abundance of them in the park. Tristan, who was well provided with everything appropriate to a wealthy man, showed such honour to each of them that night that I could not easily recount the honour which he showed to each of them. He found good beds for all of them, so that they could sleep and rest, for they were tired out by their wanderings, harassed and exhausted; it was clear from their shields that they had endured harsh combat. (6299)

Tristan was delighted at the honour of taking Gawain by the right hand, and you may be sure that he was very proud that he had twice been his host. He turned towards Le Laid Hardi, who was noble and generous: 'My lord,' he said, 'I believe that you are exhausted. I can see that you have been struck and wounded under your white coiffe. I have a very charming daughter who will apply a salve to it and ease your pain: once it has been applied, you will never suffer from it again. The wound will be healed forever!' (6315)

The Black Knight was delighted with this promise and thanked him; Sir Gawain asked Tristan to help him as much as he possibly could. Tristan went at once to the room where his daughter was and asked her to help this knight without delay if she could. She answered him courteously, 'God help me, that wound could not possibly be completely cured today!' (6327)

She anointed the wound with a powerful herb called *toscane*; he slept peacefully until God brought the day. Then the knights arose and made their preparations. They passed all that day in the castle, resting until the next day. Then Sir Gawain spoke, seriously and with deep concern. He addressed his host: 'Dear host, so noble and generous, you know all about our affairs and our travels. Now I would like you to bring us the arm and the coffer which you showed me that evening when I first took lodgings here.' (6345)

Then Tristan looked to the one who was named Faé Orgueilleux. 'My lord,' said the Faé Orgueilleux, 'he has every right to ask: he fought against me so well that my sweetheart and I had to submit to his wishes. But we have a covenant: if I live long enough to restore to you safe and sound the body which I entrusted to you, I have an agreement with Gawain that in exchange for giving him to you healthy and strong, I will have his friendship and he will give me my sweetheart, provided that I also return the young man to him, with perfect sight and absolutely healthy. I made this promise when we fought and Gawain agreed to it.' (6365)

'Truly, that is what I promised you,' said Gawain, 'do not be worried about that.' (6368)

'My lord,' said the Faé Orgueilleux, 'let the arm, the body and the reliquary* be brought out.' (6371)

Tristan went and brought them back at once; he placed the coffer before him and the Faé Orgueilleux untied it. The coffer holding the knight's arm was already there; without delay the Faé Orgueilleux took out the arm and put it beside the body. Then he was more alive than any fish. They had given this gift to the Faé Orgueilleux, who was magical. Then the knight told them how the Faé Orgueilleux found him in the woods and attacked him, how he fought with him and died without realizing it, how he then rested enclosed in the hide of a deer. Gawain was astonished and crossed himself because of this marvel, as did Le Laid Hardi. Tristan and all his household who had seen the marvel hastened to ask him who had given him such a destiny, and he replied, 'It was given to me on the night when I was born.'* (6399)

Then Gawain asked the name of the knight who had been killed. 'My lord,' he replied, 'those who know me call me the Courtois de Huberlant, I give you my word.' (6405)

They were all overjoyed. The entire court shook with joy and rejoiced all that day until the night, and they all went to bed. (6409)

In the morning when it was bright, they put bridles and saddles on the horses and helped the two young ladies to mount up – one was Gomeret's sweetheart, the other the Faé Orgueilleux

– then they all took to the road. Tristan their host accompanied them through the valley and then said to them: 'My lord, if it pleased you, I would like to go to court with you and bring my daughter with us, who is so beautiful and noble, in whom Nature has used all her art. I have her prepared already: see her there, mounted on her mule.' (6424)

Gawain heard what he said and was delighted. 'My lord,' he said, 'God help me, you have spoken most courteously.' (6427)

According to the story, there were now three young ladies and the knights numbered seven. They travelled and rode until around midday they reached the castle of Codrovain the Red, who was very bold and courageous. The men who had been in the battle with Cadret when he rescued his sweetheart, who received welcome assistance, were staying there, and Raguidel de l'Angarde was there. The maiden who refused Gawain the wine, the meat and the bread saw him coming, and when he arrived there everyone who was waiting for him recognized him also. You may be sure that this was very pleasing to him. He told them all his story, just as I have told it to you: how he had fared, how he fought with the Faé Orgueilleux, how Espinogre fought with Gomeret, and how they had been reconciled. (6453)

Everyone was very pleased. They all showed him great honour and said that for love of him they should all stay there for the whole day. 'My lords,' said Gawain, 'you have spoken well, thank you; but before midday tomorrow I would like to be in Caerlion with my companions, and I will take my beautiful, courteous maidens along with me.' (6464)

'My lord, my lord,' said Cadret, 'I will give you lodgings tonight in Codrovain's castle and tomorrow when you see the day we will go in your company.' (6469)

Gawain said, 'I do not reject such company or such a journey.' (6471)

I will not recount to you all the joy they felt, nor all the foods that were there – pike, spiced meat, breads, fish from the ocean – or the wines they drank at supper. That night there was great rejoicing. In the morning, they all mounted their horses promptly. For love of Sir Gawain, Codrovain had his people, sixty-four fully armed knights, mount their chargers. (6483)

The knights travelled at full speed and rode until they came to the forest where the Faé Orgueilleux had plucked out the

THE PERILOUS GRAVEYARD

lad's eyes. Gawain made inquiries until he found the maidens who told him about the Faé Orgueilleux, as the story has told: their manor was in the forest. Everyone there was mournful and sad in heart because of Sir Gawain: they all believed that he had been killed and dismembered. Gawain then asked how the lad was faring. 'My lord,' she said, 'just as you would expect of one who no longer sees either the sky or the earth.' (6501)

'Get him for me,' said Gawain, 'and bring him to me at once.' (6503)

She left quickly and brought back the lad, who had a very fine appearance. He was wise and courteous: if he had been the son of a count or a king, he couldn't have been more handsome or attractive. The Faé Orgueilleux passed his hand along his face and returned his sight to him: the young man could see more clearly than a buck or a doe. As soon as he saw Gawain, he recognized him. 'Welcome, my lord,' said the young man most sweetly. 'God help me, I believed that you had been dismembered; I know now that this knight who is here, the Courtois of Huberlant, who never wanted to belong to a court, had been substituted for you.' (6527)

The lad recounted his whole story, just as the book has told it. But the Lord God had taken care of him and had returned his sight to him. (6527)

They did not stay there long but remounted quickly. Sir Gawain helped the three young ladies to mount without delay and didn't forget the young man, whose name was Martin; he had him mount on a horse. They rode at a quick pace. (6535)

They went straight to Caerlion, in time for supper; the horn had already been sounded for water and everyone was at the table. Then a knight arrived who gave them the news, much to the delight of the King and everyone else at court. All the people rushed to meet Gawain, as did the King and the Queen; every maiden and maidservant displayed great joy for him. The King laughed and kissed him, delighted at his arrival. (6550)

Gawain told him all about his travels: he told him the whole story, everything that had happened to him. Then they all dismounted, and every count, baron, king and prince in the house took pains to serve those who came with Gawain. The King honoured the knights properly and spoke with them, and the Queen escorted all the young ladies into her curtained chambers. She showed them great honour, out of generosity and for the love she felt for Sir Gawain. That night until the next day they all rested peacefully. (6569)

In the morning, the King rose and entered the hall. Gawain came down the steps and stood near him. He told him how he had rescued the young lady he found in the graveyard from great pain. Then he told him how he had won the young lady whom Escanor was escorting. He related all the harsh and hard adventures which he had encountered. Then he suggested that the King ought to reward the honour everyone had showed him, which he had just reported. (6584)

The King was overjoyed: he was not slow to pass out favours, but was very pleased and delighted when he could act honourably and generously. He said to him: 'I wish to act in this matter according to your desires. But first I want to be avenged on the man who upset me so much by boasting to people wrongly that he had killed you. I want to have vengeance for that.' (6595)

'My lord,' replied Gawain, 'I would not like that at all! They have come in my company, and I have a covenant with them: they have done everything I wished and so they are therefore completely secure.' (6601)

'By my faith,' King Arthur said to him, 'it will be as you wish.' (6603)

'My lord,' said Gawain, 'you will give the two knights their sweethearts; never, since the time of Jeremiah, have you seen two more courtly men. You will also give Espinogre his sweetheart, and Cadret will marry his, and Raguidel will not fail to have his, for he gave me a good charger when I needed it.' (6612)

The King told him how the King of the Red Fortress surrendered to him and joined the court, though he had never belonged to it before, and how he had sworn to him that he would cherish his sweetheart. Sir Gawain asked him that the two lads he had brought be dubbed as soon as possible: let him make them new knights and gives them lands and castles! Everything was done as Gawain and the King had said. They celebrated the marriages without opposition or dispute. They soon escorted them to the church; the procession was as impressive as such matters should be. Bishop Reniés of Chester soon married the young ladies to the knights to whom they had been granted on the King's advice. (6635)

The church was far from silent: everyone, great and small, felt great joy. Minstrels from various countries sang and played their fiddles, bagpipes, harps, organs, tympanies and psalteries, viols and flutes, trumpets and pipes, and everyone felt great joy. The court was filled with joy, for King Arthur was very rich and was never greedy or stingy. He did everything to give them all that they needed. And each one lay with his wife, just as was pleasing to him. (6652)

In the morning when it was day, the minstrels were paid: some received fine palfreys, beautiful robes and equipment, and the others were rewarded according to who they were. Everyone had clothes and money, and all were paid as they wished: even the poorest had plenty. When the minstrels had been paid, they returned to their countries and the court broke up. Each knight left with his sweetheart in joy and happiness. When the weddings were finished, all of them, great and small, returned to their own countries. (6668)

Let everyone know, high and low, that *The Perilous Graveyard* is finished, since Gawain is safe at court after his travels, and so our romance has come to its end. May God grant us a hundred years of life, in great delight and honour, and may He grant us joy and happiness! (6676)

NOTES

Caradoc

p.6 high table: (6734) despite references to the 'Round' Table, the Arthur of this poem is not 'first among equals', but sits *au mestre dois*, raised above the ordinary knights along with a few chosen favourites.

p.6 something else: (6741) the words *autre chose*, although on the surface quite innocuous, are a frequent euphemism in Old French texts for sexual activities.

p.11 water will never be ... has been seen: (7135) this custom of Arthur's, with minor but significant variations, is mentioned in quite a number of romances, including *Jaufre*, *The Quest of the Holy Grail*, *Daniel of the Blossoming Valley*, *The Vengeance of Raguidel* and *Sir Gawain and the Green Knight*.

p.12 If he can cut off ... presence: (7170) this contest is similar enough to the 'game' proposed by the Green Knight in *Sir Gawain and the Green Knight* that it has been argued that *Caradoc* was the English poet's primary source. The 'beheading game' is found in quite a variety of medieval works, including *Hunbaut* and *The Mule With No Bridle*; the earliest example is in the Irish *Bricriu's Feast*.

p.17 the enchanter's heir: (7523) Eliavrés's first-born son is, of course, Caradoc himself.

p.18 held their land from the King: under normal circumstances, this would mean that Cador is coming to have Arthur confirm him as King of Cornwall; but this would have the effect of making Cador superior in rank to Caradoc, a situation which would cause the poet difficulties in the subsequent plot.

p.18 retinues: (7590) romance authors account for the contrast between the large retinues accompanying ladies in their own time and the relatively free travel of their heroines in different manners. In *The*

Knight of the Cart, Chrétien says that a maiden travelling alone was safer than if she were accompanied by a single knight: another knight who defeated him could do as he pleased with the woman.

p.19 Sir Cador ... over to them!: (7673) Aalardin is not the only rejected romance suitor to threaten his 'beloved' with such brutality. Fellon d'Albarua in *Jaufre* and Gernemant in *The Knight of the Two Swords* do the same, and in Beroul's *Tristan*, King Mark hands his adulterous wife over to a group of lepers.

p.23 strings would break: (7970) since the harp does not play out of tune when Guinier enters, everyone may rest assured that she has not been dishonoured by Aalardin; since the javelin does not strike Aalardin, it would seem that the poet found nothing 'churlish' in his behaviour.

p.31 Fair Good Knight: (8553) this knight is variously known as 'le Biau, le Boen' or 'le Bel, Le Bon' in the manuscripts.

p.47 Loriagort: (9788) in *the Welsh Triads*, Caradoc's horse is called Lluagor ('Host-Splitter'), and in *Culhwch and Olwein* (in *The Mabinogion*), there is a hunt for an extraordinary boar named Twrch Trwyth; this may be the source of these names. The confusion here regarding the separate roles in this matter of Caradoc the father and Caradoc the son – not to mention the question of how they managed to ensure Eliavrés's compliance – suggests the possibility that in an earlier version of the story these animals were the product of Eliavrés's earlier deceptions of Caradoc the father.

p.56 The good man ... compunction: (10492) although the poet does not have a cleric's interest in the precise categorization of sins, he seems to accept the hermit's view (and Caradoc's) that Caradoc has acted sinfully.

p.66 came from: (11237) despite King Caradoc's earlier threats and the poet's insistence that they would be fulfilled (above, lines 9983–92), this is the last we see of the enchanter.

p.70 her nipple: (11518) in the later *Chronicle of Saint-Brieuc*, the holy Azenor similarly entices a snake from her father's arm by anointing her breast with oil and milk. She cuts off her own breast, which the snake has seized, and throws them both into a fire.

p.71 'Briebras': (11580) in *The Welsh Triads*, Caradoc is called

'Cariadawg Vreichvras', or 'Strong-Arm'. French poets seem to have read Welsh 'Breichbras' or Breton 'Brechbras' as a French word meaning 'Short-Arm' or 'Swollen-Arm'.

p.75 neglecting chivalry: (11932) similar warnings that too much attention to a wife leads to a loss of chivalry are common in romances; in Chrétien's *Erec* and *Yvain*, the resulting tensions play a major role in the plot.

p.78 the gold ... efforts into it: (12186) Azenor's breast is also replaced in gold, but by God rather than by a man who had previously tried to rape her. For other examples of this unusual motif, see Gwennolé le Menn, *La Femme au sein d'or* (Saint-Brieuc, 1985).

p.79 if anyone ... my will: (12253) women with secret marks on their bodies are frequently the target of unscrupulous men who learn about them and then use their knowledge as proof of the woman's infidelity. This is in fact what happens to Azenor. Given his past history, Aalardin's knowledge concerning Guinier's breast is rather ominous.

p.80 spilling the wine on himself: (12334) this episode, containing a motif found in independent poems such as Robert Biket's *Lai du Cor* and with analogues in other longer romances such as *The Vengeance of Raguidel* and Heinrich von dem Türlin's *The Crown*, seems rather tacked on. The poet's obsessive concern with Guinier's chastity outweighs any interest in purely literary questions of structural unity.

The Knight with the Sword

p.87 Good Knight: (4) Gawain is frequently given this unofficial title.

p.87 One may ... Chrétien de Troyes: (17–18) these lines are problematic, and may read 'One *may* reasonably reproach ...'; they have formed part of an argument (which has not won great approval) that this poem is *by* Chrétien de Troyes.

p.89 never yet seen one of them return: (180–1) the 'Castle from which No Man Returns Alive' is a common motif in romances; the hero always manages to be the first.

p.90 Gringalet: (226) Gawain's horse is given this name in a wide variety of romances, French, Dutch and English. In Gerard of Amiens's

Escanor, it is said that Gawain won it from Escanor whose uncle had received it as a gift from a fairy.

p.91 she: (323) the editors have emended this line so that it would mean 'which *he* would never bring to a conclusion'.

p.95 his death: (556–7) the first English critic of the poem spoke of the father as 'weary[ing] the patience of his daughter by so many rehearsals of the bridal character': a different paraphrase, such as 'using her as sexual bait', might suggest a more accurate picture.

p.96 from her: (636) the editors' emendation would lead to the translation 'if *she* escaped from *him* in that way'.

p.97 blood: (713) blood-stained beds are adduced as proof of sexual misconduct in other romances; curiously, the blood is always the man's.

p.98 The sword ... here: (760–1) it is never made clear whether the sword has 'chosen' him because he is Gawain or simply because he never acted his intentions out fully.

p.99 his adventure: (860ff.) this second part of the poem has been criticized for being unrelated to the first, but the connection is clear. Now that he has acquired the 'power of the sword', Gawain is about to be given an opportunity to display it.

p.103 his desires: (1102) the editors' emendation would lead to a translation 'if *he* does not fulfil all *her* desire'.

p.104 another thing: (1183) the poet's references to 'performance' and Gawain's use of the words *d'autre chose* may be compared to another 'faithless woman, faithful dogs' episode in *The Vengeance of Raguidel*, in which the author describes how Ydain left Gawain for another man whom she observed urinating in the woods.

p.104 He abandon ... to her: (1191) prior to this point, the poet has been omniscient enough to know what his characters are thinking; his ignorance here is a sham, for he and his audience knew well what would happen to a young lady abandoned in the wilderness.

The Perilous Graveyard

p.109 nones: (18) 'nones' is the ninth hour after sunrise.

p.111 Caradoc Briebras: (138) romance authors rarely cared enough

NOTES 213

about consistency with other writers' work to be concerned with how the presence of Caradoc and Erec, for example, squares with the events of their own romances.

p.112 **catch up with him:** (221) Gawain's concern with table manners may seem extreme, and is perhaps best seen as a necessary prerequisite for the extended chase which follows.

p.112 **knight had taken:** (247) readers of other romances would know without doubt that in these circumstances Kay is bound to fail.

p.117 **when I left:** (605) in a comparable situation in *The Knight of the Two Swords*, Gawain simply tells people who he is; some refuse to believe him, and others attack him because they are relatives of the man who is claiming to have killed him. Both poets want to create an anonymous Gawain, and fit their stories to suit the need.

p.119 **a young lord:** (766) this young lord, or 'lad' as he is often called, plays a major role in Gawain's subsequent progress, but he receives little in return either from Gawain or from the poet.

p.130 **compline:** (1568) compline is the last hour of daylight. The progressive loss of strength as the sun progresses through its course is more often associated with Gawain.

p.130 **a fairy:** (1579) elsewhere Gawain is the son of a perfectly human sister of Arthur's; she is named Morcades in the *Enfances Gauvain*, and our author may have confused her with Morgan la Fée.

p.147 **the rest:** (2804) the author uses the word 'sorplus' here, a frequent euphemism for intercourse.

p.150 **She stays ... brought out:** (*51) similar episodes may be found in the *Dame à la Lycorne*, the prose *Roman de la Violette*, and *Claris and Laris*.

p.155 **tierce:** (*458) tierce is the third hour after sunrise.

p.160 **excess:** (3119) the poet uses 'sorplus' again.

p.161 **a guarantor ... praised:** (3234) a comparable episode occurs in *Hunbaut*.

p.161 **When ... ladies:** (3247) these lines make it all too clear that the episode in which Gawain learns of his own death would have been more effective if it had been delayed until later in the poem.

p.174 so much: (4235) see above, lines 2850–959.

p.176 horses: (4371) see above, line 2730.

p.186 above all other knights: (5102) other young ladies who love Gawain on the basis of his reputation alone are found in *The Knight of the Two Swords, The Vengeance of Raguidel*, and *The First Continuation of the Perceval*.

p.186 He won ... his nose: (5135) this is a direct allusion to the events at the beginning of Chrétien de Troyes's *Perceval*.

p.195 second maiden: (5780) in fact it was the third maiden, since the first two had fainted.

p.195 once I have ... healed: (5842) like Eliavrés and Aalardin in *Caradoc*, and like many other romance characters with supernatural powers, such as Fada de Gibel in *Jaufre*, the Faé Orgueilleux's abilities were limited in his earlier encounter with the hero by the author's greater concern with local effect than with consistency.

p.197 'If you wish ... with me!': (5955) the text really does not make it absolutely clear which of the two knights offers to share the woman and which refuses; the reader's choice is therefore a matter of literary, not textual, interpretation.

p.201 dear friend: (6228) in other romances, generally near the end, battles between close friends, between brothers, and between father and son are similarly stopped when the participants recognize each other. Le Laid Hardi is not noted elsewhere as having any special tie with Gawain, and this scene is therefore less effective than, for example, the duel between Gawain and Caradoc or between Gawain and Yvain in Chrétien's *Yvain*.

p.203 reliquary: (6371) the poet has not told us how the body came to be here, and he seems to have forgotten about the head.

p.203 when I was born: (6399) the mystery of the source and nature of the Faé Orgueilleux's magical powers is only compounded by these brief explanations.

SUGGESTIONS FOR FURTHER READING

For further information about these romances and the critical work that has been done on them, consult *The Arthurian Encyclopedia* (New York, 1986) or *The New Arthurian Encyclopedia* (New York, 1991), both edited by Norris J. Lacy; *Arthurian Bibliography*, edited by Cedric Pickford (Woodbridge, 1981–96); *Arthurian Legend and Literature: An Annotated Bibliography*, edited by Edmund Reiss (New York, 1984); or the *Bibliographical Bulletin of the International Arthurian Society*, published yearly.

Readers of these poems may also be interested in the following texts:
Amadas and Ydoine, translated by Ross G. Arthur (New York, 1993).
Béroul, *The Romance of Tristan*, edited and translated by Norris J. Lacy (New York, 1989).
Chrétien de Troyes, *Arthurian Romances*, translated by D. D. R. Owen (London, 1987).
Christine de Pisan, *The Treasure of the City of Ladies*, translated by Sarah Lawson (Harmondsworth, 1985).
Curial and Guelfa, translated by Pamela Waley (London, 1982).
The Death of King Arthur, translated by James Cable (Harmondsworth, 1971).
Der Stricker, *Daniel of the Blossoming Valley*, translated by Michael Resler (New York, 1990).
Early Irish Myths and Sagas, translated by Jeffrey Gantz (Harmondsworth, 1981).
Fergus of Galloway: Knight of King Arthur, translated by D. D. R. Owen (London, 1991).
Gottfried von Strassburg, *Tristan, with the surviving fragments of the Tristan of Thomas*, translated by A. T. Hatto (Harmondsworth, 1960).
Heinrich von dem Türlin, *The Crown: A Tale of Sir Gawain and King Arthur's Court*, translated by J. W. Thomas (Lincoln, Nebraska and London, 1989).

Heldris de Cornuälle, *The Story of Silence (Le Roman de Silence)*, translated by Regina Psaki (New York, 1991).

Jaufre: An Occitan Arthurian Romance, translated by Ross G. Arthur (New York, 1992).

[Jehan], *The Marvels of Rigomer (Les Mervelles de Rigomer)*, translated by Thomas E. Vesce (New York, 1988).

King Arthur's Death: Alliterative Morte Arthure and Stanzaic Le Morte Arthur, translated by Brian Stone (Harmondsworth, 1988).

Kudrun, translated by Brian O. Murdoch (London, 1987).

Lancelot of the Lake, translated by Corin Corley (Oxford, 1989).

The Mabinogion, translated by Jeffrey Gantz (Harmondsworth, 1976).

Marie de France, *The Lais of Marie de France*, translated by Glyn S. Burgess and Keith Busby (Harmondsworth, 1986).

Martorell, Joanot and Martí Joan de Galba, *Tirant lo Blanc*, translated by David H. Rosenthal (New York, 1984).

Penninc and Pieter Vostaert, *Roman van Walewein*, edited and translated by David F. Johnson (New York, 1992).

The Quest of the Holy Grail, translated by P. M. Matarasso (Harmondsworth, 1969).

Renaut de Bâgé, *The Fair Unknown (le Bel Inconnu)*, edited by Karen Fresco and translated by Colleen P. Donagher (New York, 1992).

The Saga of Tristram and Ísönd, translated by Paul Schach (Lincoln, Nebraska and London, 1973).

Sir Gawain and the Green Knight, translated by Brian Stone (Harmondsworth, 1974).

Ulrich von Zatzikhoven, *Lanzelet*, translated by Kenneth G. T. Webster (New York, 1951).

Wirnt von Grafenberg, *Wigalois: The Knight of Fortune's Wheel*, translated by J. W. Thomas (Lincoln, Nebraska and London, 1977).

Wolfram von Eschenbach, *Parzival*, translated by A. T. Hatto (Harmondsworth, 1980).

MEDIEVAL LITERATURE IN EVERYMAN

A SELECTION

Canterbury Tales
GEOFFREY CHAUCER
EDITED BY A. C. CAWLEY
The complete medieval text with translations £3.99

Arthurian Romances
CHRÉTIEN DE TROYES
TRANSLATED BY D. D. R. OWEN
Classic tales from the father of Arthurian romance £5.99

Everyman and Medieval Miracle Plays
EDITED BY A. C. CAWLEY
A fully representative selection from the major play cycles £3.99

The Vision of Piers Plowman
WILLIAM LANGLAND
EDITED BY A. V. C. SCHMIDT
The only complete edition of the B-version available £4.99

Sir Gawain and the Green Knight, Pearl, Cleanness, Patience
EDITED BY A. C. CAWLEY
AND J. J. ANDERSON
Four major English medieval poems in one volume £3.99

The Piers Plowman Tradition
EDITED BY HELEN BARR
Four medieval poems of political and religious dissent – widely available for the first time £5.99

The Birth of Romance: An Anthology
TRANSLATED BY JUDITH WEISS
The first-ever English translation of these fascinating Anglo-Norman romances £4.99

Of Love and Chivalry: An Anthology of Middle English Romance
EDITED BY JENNIFER FELLOWS
A unique collection of tales of courtly love and heroic deeds £5.99

£3.99

AVAILABILITY

All books are available from your local bookshop or direct from
Littlehampton Book Services Cash Sales, 14 Eldon Way, Lineside Estate, Littlehampton, West Sussex BN17 7HE. PRICES ARE SUBJECT TO CHANGE.

To order any of the books, please enclose a cheque (in £ sterling) made payable to Littlehampton Book Services, or phone your order through with credit card details (Access, Visa or Mastercard) on 0903 721596 (24 hour answering service) stating card number and expiry date. Please add £1.25 for package and postage to the total value of your order.

In the USA, for further information and a complete catalogue call 1-800-526-2778.

SAGAS AND OLD ENGLISH LITERATURE IN EVERYMAN

A SELECTION

Egils saga
TRANSLATED BY
CHRISTINE FELL
A gripping story of Viking exploits in Iceland, Norway and Britain £4.99

Edda
SNORRI STURLUSON
TRANSLATED BY
ANTHONY FAULKES
The first complete English translation £5.99

The Fljotsdale Saga and The Droplaugarsons
TRANSLATED BY
ELEANOR HAWORTH
AND JEAN YOUNG
A brilliant portrayal of life and times in medieval Iceland £3.99

The Anglo-Saxon Chronicle
TRANSLATED BY
G. N. GARMONSWAY
A fascinating record of events in ancient Britain £4.99

Anglo-Saxon Poetry
TRANSLATED BY
S. A. J. BRADLEY
A widely acclaimed collection £6.99

Fergus of Galloway: Knight of King Arthur
GUILLAUME LE CLERC
TRANSLATED BY
D. D. R. OWEN
Essential reading for students of Arthurian romance £3.99

£4.99

AVAILABILITY

All books are available from your local bookshop or direct from
Littlehampton Book Services Cash Sales, 14 Eldon Way, Lineside Estate, Littlehampton, West Sussex BN17 7HE. PRICES ARE SUBJECT TO CHANGE.

To order any of the books, please enclose a cheque (in £ sterling) made payable to Littlehampton Book Services, or phone your order through with credit card details (Access, Visa or Mastercard) on 0903 721596 (24 hour answering service) stating card number and expiry date. Please add £1.25 for package and postage to the total value of your order.

In the USA, for further information and a complete catalogue call 1-800-526-2778.

ANCIENT CLASSICS IN EVERYMAN

A SELECTION

The Republic
PLATO
The most important and enduring of Plato's works **£5.99**

The Education of Cyrus
XENOPHON
A fascinating insight into the culture and politics of ancient Greece **£6.99**

Juvenal's Satires with the Satires of Persius
JUVENAL AND PERSIUS
Unique and acute observations of contemporary Roman society **£5.99**

The Odyssey
HOMER
A classic translation of one of the greatest adventures ever told **£5.99**

History of the Peloponnesian War
THUCYDIDES
The war that brought to an end a golden age of democracy **£5.99**

The Histories
HERODOTUS
The earliest surviving work of Greek prose literature **£7.99**

£5.99

AVAILABILITY

All books are available from your local bookshop or direct from
Littlehampton Book Services Cash Sales, 14 Eldon Way, Lineside Estate, Littlehampton, West Sussex BN17 7HE. PRICES ARE SUBJECT TO CHANGE.

To order any of the books, please enclose a cheque (in £ sterling) made payable to Littlehampton Book Services, or phone your order through with credit card details (Access, Visa or Mastercard) on 0903 721596 (24 hour answering service) stating card number and expiry date. Please add £1.25 for package and postage to the total value of your order.

In the USA, for further information and a complete catalogue call 1-800-526-2778.

POETRY IN EVERYMAN

A SELECTION

Silver Poets of the Sixteenth Century
EDITED BY
DOUGLAS BROOKS-DAVIES
A new edition of this famous Everyman collection £6.99

Complete Poems
JOHN DONNE
The father of metaphysical verse in this highly-acclaimed edition £6.99

Complete English Poems, Of Education, Areopagitica
JOHN MILTON
An excellent introduction to Milton's poetry and prose £6.99

Selected Poems
JOHN DRYDEN
A poet's portrait of Restoration England £4.99

Selected Poems and Prose
PERCY BYSSHE SHELLEY
'The essential Shelley' in one volume £3.50

Women Romantic Poets 1780-1830: An Anthology
Hidden talent from the Romantic era rediscovered £5.99

Poems in Scots and English
ROBERT BURNS
The best of Scotland's greatest lyric poet £4.99

Selected Poems
D. H. LAWRENCE
A new, authoritative selection spanning the whole of Lawrence's literary career £4.99

The Poems
W. B. YEATS
Ireland's greatest lyric poet surveyed in this ground-breaking edition £7.99

EVERYMAN'S BOOK OF EVERGREEN VERSE
EDITED BY
DAVID HERBERT

£5.99

AVAILABILITY

All books are available from your local bookshop or direct from
Littlehampton Book Services Cash Sales, 14 Eldon Way, Lineside Estate, Littlehampton, West Sussex BN17 7HE. PRICES ARE SUBJECT TO CHANGE.

To order any of the books, please enclose a cheque (in £ sterling) made payable to Littlehampton Book Services, or phone your order through with credit card details (Access, Visa or Mastercard) on 0903 721596 (24 hour answering service) stating card number and expiry date. Please add £1.25 for package and postage to the total value of your order.

In the USA, for further information and a complete catalogue call 1-800-526-2778.